The Song of Solomon

Love, Sex and Relationships

By

Jeffrey A. Johnson, Sr.

**With a foreward by
Joel Gregory, Ph.D.**

To Sharon…
　　　　my loving wife,
　　　　　　　my best friend,
　　　　　　　　　　and my own Beloved

With this, my first book, I also want to express my deep love and appreciation to others who, with Sharon, have enriched my life and helped make me who I am today:

　　　　My mother, Mary Coleman
　　　　My father, Alonzo Coleman
　　　　My grandmother, Mary Lester
　　　　My sons: J. Allen, Jordan, Jalon, and Josiah
　　　　The Eastern Star Church family

Table of Contents

FOREWORD

Celebrate Sex:
The Song of Songs as a Celebration
of God's Great Gift

When God created all that exists, He called it "very good" (Gen. 1:31). Part of what He called "very good" was the reality that "they were both naked, the man and his wife, and were not ashamed" (Gen. 2:25). There must be a connection between that last verse of the first chapter and that last verse of the second. It was good that they were not ashamed. That included His great gift of sexual intimacy, the transcendently joyous union of a man and a woman in the bonds of committed marriage. Do not drag God down to the level of tawdry lust. Yet, you can lift up the act of physical intimacy into the presence of God Himself. His initial and most basic act is the act of creation.

That is the very point of the *Song of Songs*. Overly scrupulous commentators have attempted in various ways to tone down or positively obscure the sexual celebration of the book. Yet the celebration of intimacy in the *Song of Songs* cannot be kept in theologizing or allegorizing chains. Over and over the *Song of Songs* breaks out for what it is: a celebration of sexual love as a transcendent human experience.

This book is the longest sustained narrative in the Bible on human sexuality. There may be one explicit mention of God in the book, but even that is questioned. The book devotes itself to the expression of love between a man and a woman. The book breaks the bonds of culture and presents a love that is neither exploitative nor hierarchical. Both the man and the woman want one another. Both are free to express that desire fully. Even though there are attempts to control the woman's sexuality by her brothers (1:6) or by city guards (5:7), she acts in perfect freedom to fulfill her desires.

What is even more remarkable is the absence of the motive of procreation in the motives of the male or the female. The clear teaching is the passionate sexual enjoyment of one another. In later teaching the joys of human sexuality were often downplayed by the non-biblical teaching that the exclusive purpose of sex is procreation. Here in the *Canticle* one finds a woman and a man enjoying one another freely without mention of procreative purpose.

Perhaps this remarkable piece of biblical literature was used in some way related to weddings or marriage ceremonies. It may even be remotely related to what has been delicately called in modern times a "marriage manual." Using metaphorical language, it describes the bodies, sounds, fragrances and sensory appeal of the man and the woman.

Efforts have endlessly been made to turn this literature into an allegory of Christ and the church. This is to miss the point of the author. It is to import a later theology back into an antecedent theology, a mistake warned against by Walter Kaiser, the president of Gordon Conwell Seminary. Here is an untrammeled ode to the joys of sexual love. In that regard, it is of interest that the most famous exegete in Protestant history, John Calvin, did not write a commentary on the *Song of Songs*. Neither did the famous expositor Alexander MacLaren of Manchester preach or write any sermons on the book. Perhaps these iconic interpreters were convinced that the book indeed spoke to matters of intimacy that their cultures prohibited to be discussed in the pulpit or similar venues. The famous British Baptist preacher Charles Spurgeon did preach from the *Song of Songs,* but turned it into an allegory of Christ and the church.

His sermons are delightfully devotional, but do not touch the actual purpose of the book.

C.S. Lewis famously maintained that everything evil is a perversion of something good. Gluttony, for example, is a perversion of the very appropriate desire for food. In Lewis' view, lust and its cousin pornography are the perversions of the very good desire for expression of the sexual instinct. This book is put forth in a biblical celebration of that intimacy. In a world flooded with the perversion of God's gift, Pastor Jeffrey A. Johnson, Sr., sets forth for married men and women a celebration of God's gift.

Joel Gregory, Ph.D.
George W. Truett Theological Seminary
Baylor University

Introduction

⧡

Market Square Arena was once the focal point of sports and entertainment in Indianapolis, Indiana. It was the home for the Indiana Pacers' basketball games. The Indianapolis Ice, Checkers, and Racers all played hockey there over the years. The Indianapolis Twisters used the arena for soccer. The Barnum & Bailey Circus performed there. Concerts, gymnastics, wrestling, NCAA championships—Market Square Arena hosted them all. It was even the site of Elvis Presley's last concert.

But after Indianapolis built Conseco Fieldhouse, the new home for the Indiana Pacers, the city no longer had a need for Market Square Arena because the years had taken their toll on the old structure. Maintaining it would be too expensive, so the city decided to implode Market Square, demolishing it in a way that would make it collapse inward. Explosives were set, and the building came down without hurting anyone or any neighboring structures. It was an implosion that was intentional and strategic.

Prior to that time, our own church had investigated Market Square Arena as a possible worship center, but the twenty-five-year-old arena just had too many structural problems. We could not build a ministry in a place with a faulty structure. It was necessary for Market Square Arena to come down.

There are plans now for a high-rise condominium project to be built on the site of Market Square Arena. A variety of businesses, restaurants, and specialty shops will be located on the lower levels, and above them will be homes in a high-rise tower. There would never have been an opportunity for people to live in high places on that lot had there not first been an implosion. Before the new structure could be built, the old one had to be torn down. Now there will be a new edifice—not just a place for playing games, but a place where people can live their lives.

In this book, as we dig into the Song of Solomon, it won't be enough to take new principles and set them in faulty structures. In our friendships, relationships, and marriages, some of us need to begin by strategically imploding the old structures, tearing down what we have now so we can build better homes in higher places.

It's time to forgive each other for past faults. It's time to say good-bye to the past. It's time to stop playing games, manipulating and scamming, and putting each other down. To build homes in high places, we have to tear down the faulty old infrastructure and start over. Whatever mess you've got now, go ahead and implode that thing. It's time to let go of the old so that you can move forward to receive what God wants for you regarding your friendships, relationships, and marriages.

When I look at what is happening in our society, both at large and in our own community, I feel compelled to share the lessons that we can learn from the Song of Solomon. When we listen to the news, we hear of date rape, sexual harassment, and molestation. We hear of pedophiles, teenage pregnancies, unwanted pregnancies, and babies born out of wedlock. We hear of rising rates of sexually transmitted diseases, abortions and divorce. We hear of a drug called Ecstasy, touted as a sexual stimulant that is often life-threatening. We hear the voices of a world that celebrates fornication and adultery.

In the midst of all of this, we can study the Song of Solomon to learn what God has to say. Truthfully, the problems I just mentioned are not only happening "out in the world," but they are also taking place in the church and in the kingdom of God. Many of us don't just use sex, we *mis*use sex. Undoubtedly, someone reading this book is suffering from damaged self-esteem and a distorted self-image because of a bad relationship. We need to know what God's Word says about friendships, relationships, and marriage so that our relationships can bring honor to God.

According to tradition, the Song of Solomon was written by King Solomon, David's son. At least 3,000 proverbs and 1,005 songs are credited to Solomon, but the song we are studying here is his best, which is why it is entitled "Song of Songs." The Hebrew people didn't say something was "the greatest"; instead, the way they expressed the superlative was through repetition. So, instead of "greatest king", they said, "King of kings," or instead of "greatest Lord," they said, "Lord of lords," as we see in I Timothy 6:15 or Revelation 17:14. So, here, they didn't say, "The Greatest Song"; instead, they said, "The Song of Songs." Of all the songs that Solomon had written, this was his greatest one.

I believe one reason it's so great is because it's a love song—but not the kind of love song we frequently hear today. Most modern love songs are solos, with just one lover singing. Every time I hear a solo love song, I wonder what the *other* person is thinking. King Solomon leaves no doubt in *his* song: this is a duet. Throughout the song, you hear Solomon and a woman singing back and forth to each other. He is called the Lover, and she is identified as the Beloved. This woman he's singing to is a Shulammite, one of African descent.

Many scholars believe that the first four verses of the Song tell about the couple's marriage. Keep in mind, however, that the book isn't written in chronological order. The writer doesn't say, "We met here, and then we did this, and then we did that." It's not a book of history; it's a poem of love. When someone is singing a love song, history and chronology are not that important. All that matters is his love for her and her love for him.

So, sometimes the singers speak as a married couple, and other times they sing as though they are still single. That's what makes the Song applicable to everyone, regardless of marital status. Married people can learn how to relate to their partners, and single people can learn principles that can help them to live a saved, sanctified, and *satisfied* single life. This is a wonderful love song that can help you and me improve our relationships—if we would just go back and implode what we already have, and then start building on God's Word and the foundation of Jesus Christ.

Chapter 1

You Can't Hurry Love

> [1] Solomon's Song of Songs.
> [2] Let him kiss me with the kisses of his mouth—
> for your love is more delightful than wine.
> [3] Pleasing is the fragrance of your perfumes;
> your name is like perfume poured out.
> No wonder the maidens love you!
> [4] Take me away with you—let us hurry!
> Let the king bring me into his chambers.
> We rejoice and delight in you;
> we will praise your love more than wine.
> How right they are to adore you!
> *(Song of Solomon 1:1-4, NIV)*

When some ministers preach and teach on the Song of Solomon, they say that this book is an allegory about God's love for Israel and Jesus' love for the church. In this book we *may* see God's love for Israel, along with Jesus' love for the church. The Song of Solomon is also about human relationships, and there is much we can learn if we read it in that light. It's about passion and tension, sex, marriage, relationships, and love.

Passion and Affection

The text begins with the Shulammite woman singing to Solomon, her husband and lover. She says, "Let him kiss me with the kisses of his mouth." *The Message* translation of the Bible says, "Kiss me—full on the mouth!" This song opens with great passion and affection. Remember that this is the Word of God, and the first thing this woman says is, "I want his lips on my lips." She wants him to embrace her, to make love to her, and to be passionate with her. She speaks with so much desire and tenderness.

This book literally set me free. Like many people, I grew up in a church that often seemed to think something was wrong with having a sexual appetite. Because we wanted lips on our lips, tongues on our tongues, arms around us, and body-to-body contact, the church tried to make us think that something was wrong with us. If we are normal and healthy, we are going to want sex, passion and affection. There is nothing wrong with that. God didn't create us only as physical beings, psychological beings, or emotional beings; he also created us as sexual beings. He gave us sex as a gift. It isn't the *use* of sex that is the problem; it's the *misuse* or *abuse* of it.

Some people have a hard time putting "God" and "sex" in the same sentence. When I preached a sermon series on the Song of Solomon, some people refused to come. They chose to stay home rather than talk about such things as relationships and sex in church. Now, we talk about the subject at home, in movies and videos, on the job, at school, on the playground and in the streets. In church, however, the subject is much too often taboo. But if *God* speaks about it, then *we* can speak about it. In fact, if God's got a word about it, we *ought* to talk about it as well. We need to know what God says about sex. It is *not* something unholy.

If you have a big sexual appetite, there is nothing wrong with you! Some folks say, "When I got saved, the Holy Spirit just took my sexual desire from me." He *didn't* take it away from you! If anything, He increased it! As we get to know God better, He frees us to fully become the people He created us to be, which includes us recognizing that we were created as sexual beings. I became more sexual as I got to know God more because He freed me to fully become the man He created me to be. In other words, the more spiritual I've become, the more sexual I've become.

Some people say that an excessive sex drive is a consequence of Adam and Eve sinning in the Garden of Eden, but this is not what the Bible teaches. Adam and Eve were created as sexual beings in chapter

1, but they didn't sin until Genesis 3. As Genesis 1:27 says, "…male and female he created them." God designed them with the capacity for sexual relations; in fact, the very first commandment God gave to humankind was to have sex! He told Adam and Eve to "be fruitful and multiply," and there is only one way for that to happen.

The problem, then, is not about sex itself or a good, healthy sexual desire because God ordained it and gave it to us for our enjoyment. The issue is how we satisfy that desire. Sex is a legitimate desire, just like hunger. If I either refuse to eat or become gluttonous, I am not satisfying that desire as God intended, so that desire will be controlling my behavior. Likewise, if you satisfy your sexual appetite any way other than within the boundaries of marriage, it becomes something God did not intend: sin. In marriage, sex is holy. As Hebrews 13:4 says, "the bed is undefiled" (KJV). But outside of marriage, sex becomes twisted and messed up, whether it is premarital sex, co-habitation or adultery. Any sex outside the boundaries of marriage is distorted, unholy and often hurtful.

Some will say, "This is the twenty-first century, man. You're kind of outdated and antiquated. That's old school; that stuff don't play no more." The fact is that the Word of God is still true. It was true in the first century, and it's still true in the twenty-first century. Sex is undefiled in marriage, but it is wrong outside of marriage.

Direction

So, here in the Scriptures is a woman full of passion and affection, *and* she is going in the right direction. She is saying, "I don't want just *any*body to kiss me. I don't want *every*body to kiss me. I want the one I love to kiss me." The one she's talking about is her husband—her man. She's saying, "I want it to come from the one I love, and the one who loves me." We should never get to the point where we let our passions move us in the wrong direction. Some of us are more interested in kissing than in *whom* we're kissing. Wrong direction. Some of us are more interested in dating, than in *whom* we're dating. Wrong direction. Some of us are more interested in getting engaged, than *whom* we're engaged to. Some of us are more interested in being married, than *whom* we marry. That's wrong because it's misdirected passion.

I would venture to guess that some of you reading this have already picked the church where you're going to get married, along with the time of day. You already know the colors, the bridesmaids, the maid of honor, the best man, and the groomsmen. You know where the reception is going to be held and what the invitations are going to look like. You have your dress or tuxedo picked out. You've got everything settled, but you're not even dating anyone yet!

Some of us want so much to get married that it doesn't matter *who* we marry. It's fine that you want to be married. That's a natural, normal desire, but to be willing to marry someone who isn't suitable for you is misdirected passion. Your affection is wonderful, but it has to be directed in the right way. Some of us are premature in the selection of our marriage partner, but we just can't hurry love.

Sometimes, we get in such a hurry that our choice doesn't have anything to do with the other person's heart, mind, soul, relationship to God, or involvement in the church. Much too often, the first question is, "What does the person look like?" A friend says, "Hey, I've got someone I want you to meet." You often respond, "What does he (or she) look like?" We too often choose people based on physiology, biology, and sexuality, but we need to realize that if someone is pretty outside but ugly inside, that person is still "pretty ugly."

We know that we should wait to get to know people, but we get in a rush. We long to be kissed, held, and caressed. We're full of God-given passion and affection, but too often we channel it in the wrong direction and end up in a big mess.

Remember Matt Emmons, who was on the USA shooting team in the 2004 Olympics in Athens? He had already won his first gold medal and was doing well in his second event, which was almost over. It appeared that he was going home with another gold medal. All he had to do on his last shot was to get near the bull's-eye. Emmons stood, facing the target in lane two. He needed an 8.0 to win the gold. He lifted his rifle, aimed, and shot. He waited, but nothing registered on the target. He knew it was a good shot, and even the officials were puzzled. They came over quickly and looked at his rifle to see what was wrong. They were about to tell him to shoot again, when suddenly his shot registered after all. He needed an 8.0, and his shot registered at 8.1. Yet, Emmons went home without the gold medal because he was in lane *two*; the target registering the winning points was in lane *three*. He had hit the wrong target! The next day, the headlines read, "Great Shot, But Wrong Target."

Somebody reading this right now is in a situation like Emmons— only in a spiritual sense. You've accepted Jesus Christ as your personal Savior, and you've been filled with the Holy Spirit. You've got your big ol' boom-box Bible, along with a cross around your neck. You are really trying to be right and live right, but then you go out and pick up someone who doesn't know Jesus or isn't walking with the Lord. This is someone you can't be equally yoked with because you're going in two different directions. That person is wrong for you. I'm not saying you didn't make a great shot, but you just hit the wrong target! You were aiming at the gold, but you are going home with nothing.

There is likely also someone reading this book who is the exact opposite of those who are willing to take anybody—just to be married. You instead have totally given up, even on friend-ships, because somebody hurt you or stabbed you in the back. Now you've got your defense mechanism up, and you won't get close to anybody! "I'm done with the dating scene. I'm sick of that. It never goes anywhere. I'm not doing that any more." You may have come out of a bad marriage or a dead-end relationship, so even the idea of friendship turns you off. You figure that with more than half of the married couples getting divorced, there certainly *must* be something wrong with marriage.

It isn't that friendships, relationships, or marriages are wrong. God honors these. He instituted marriage, so there's nothing wrong with it. What's wrong are the *people* who get married. If you pick the wrong person, you're going to have a bad situation, but if you choose the person God wants you to have—somebody you love and somebody who loves you—it will make all the difference.

After he left office, former President William Jefferson Clinton discovered he had a heart condition. The vessels going to his heart were ninety-percent clogged; his heart couldn't pump enough blood because his arteries were almost closed. Upon examination, he was told that his heart was in such bad shape that he would have to undergo bypass surgery to stay alive. Now, this was a former president, so it wasn't just any doctor who was brought in to do the surgery: it was one of the best heart surgeons in the nation. If the right doctor had not been brought in to help bring about the healing, President Clinton could have died from a broken heart.

You may have a broken heart. Whether you're going through a bad relationship, struggling from a failed marriage, or recovering from betrayal in a friendship, your heart has quit functioning properly. Just as the doctors told President Clinton, you *can* be whole again. Not just anybody can come in to handle your heart, however, because you are too important. Something so priceless cannot be placed in the wrong hands, but the right person can come into the situation and help mend your broken heart.

Intoxication

In the second part of verse 1, the Shulammite woman says, "Your love is better than wine." Now, if she's comparing his love with wine, it means she must know something about both. That makes me wonder a bit about her wine consumption, but I don't believe she is like some people who have to get drunk or high before making love. There is something wrong when someone can't be intimate without being intoxicated.

Now the Bible, of course, doesn't always speak about wine in the negative sense. Psalm 104:15 speaks of "wine that gladdens the heart." Ecclesiastes 9:7 says, "Drink your wine with a joyful heart." Ecclesiastes 10:19 says, "Wine makes the heart merry." "Your love is *better* than wine," she said.

If wine makes the heart merry, and real love is *better* than wine, why are some people always so miserable in their relationships? Love can lift the heart and take us from misery to merriment, but only when it is *real* love. In Esther 1:10, we read that wine can even lift the spirit of a king. In I Timothy 5:23, Paul told Timothy to use a little wine for his stomach because there are some healing properties in wine. Yet, the Beloved said, "Your love is *better* than wine."

If wine can help bring healing to the stomach, how much more can love help heal the broken heart?

Love is a wonderful thing. First Peter 4:8 tells us, "Love covers a multitude of sins." Love also covers a multitude of faults. That's why before you marry somebody, you had better make sure you love that person. No matter how wonderful the other person is, in your marriage you're going to see a multitude of faults in him or her. There are going to be a lot of mistakes, as well as a lot of failures. If love is not there, forgiveness will not be there, either. Love keeps forgiving over and over again. That's why the Bible says that "God demonstrates his own love for us in this: While we were still sinners, Christ died for us" (Romans 5:8). While we were yet sinners and still sinning, Christ died, and His love forgives us over and over again.

First Corinthians 13:5 tells us that love does not keep count, keep score, or keep a record of wrongs. Love doesn't say, "Okay, this is the third time, or the eighth time, you did this." It could be the 491st time. ("Okay, you've used up your seventy times seven.") No, love covers a multitude of sins.

The Apostle Paul reminds us, "Christ's love compels us… that those who live should no longer live for themselves but for him…" (2 Corinthians 5:14-15). You don't have to beg us as Christians to serve Jesus because His love compels us to serve. Moreover, that service isn't limited to Christ, but it should be apparent in all of our relationships. My wife knows that I love her—not only because I tell her, and not only because we share the same bed, but because my love compels me to serve her. If the person who says, "I love you" isn't also serving you, that's a sign that the love isn't genuine.

There are several hospitals around the country that have special volunteers who come in just to hold and cuddle newborn babies who are in need of special attention. The medical profession has learned that touch, affection, and caring can actually help a baby to grow stronger and become healthier. Love is powerful.

In fact, you can literally "love the hell out of someone," which is what God did. His love for us "while we were still sinners" (Romans 5:8) transformed us. God "loved the mess out of us." The person you marry, no matter how kind or how Christian, will also have some mess within. If you're not willing to love the mess out of somebody, then don't say "I do." If your partner isn't willing to love the mess out of *you*, then don't marry that person. You need a love that covers a multitude of sins.

Reputation

The woman in our story didn't just talk about being intoxicated with her husband's intimacy, but she had also checked out his reputation. In verse 3, she says, "Pleasing is the fragrance of your perfumes; your name is like perfume poured out. No wonder the maidens love you!" Before she made up her mind to connect with him, she had checked him out. You can't hurry love because it takes time to get to know someone.

When the woman says, "Your name is like perfume," she's talking about the "fragrance" that hangs around each one of us— the effect that we have on the atmosphere when we walk into a room. One person can walk in and provoke inward groans from others because he or she always has a problem, a complaint, or an issue to air. Another person, known for encouraging others, will immediately brighten the atmosphere with his or her entrance. While we're checking out the other person's fragrance, we need to take note of how people respond when *we* enter a room. How is *our* fragrance affecting the atmosphere?

After I was newly married, fried catfish was a favorite dish of mine. When my wife made it, I didn't have to go into the kitchen to know what was cooking. No matter where I was in the house, I could smell the aroma of that fish. In the same way, you know when a brother or a sister is cooking something up, just by what you smell. A person's "fragrance" includes not only character, but also conduct.

The Beloved had said to her Lover, "Your *name* is like perfume...." To the Hebrews, names were indicators of one's nature, character, and destiny. She had checked his name out. She knew his nature, character, reputation, and what other people thought of him. We should never connect with anybody until we have checked out the person's name. If you're going to carry his name, or if she's going to carry your name, you need to know what that name stands for.

My friend, Bishop Derek Triplett, has a teenage daughter, and the young men are starting to call. Apprehensive that she's going to get married one of these days, Bishop Triplett says that before he gives her away, he's going to make it his business to check out that man's name. He's not going to give her away to someone with an untrustworthy name. She carries *his* name for the time being. The Bishop told me, "With *my* name, there's influence. With *my* name, she can get a house. With *my* name, she can get a car. With *my* name, she can get something done!" So, any name she exchanges her father's for had better be as good.

When you are checking someone out, you can't ignore those warning signs. If you sense there is an issue, there almost certainly is one. If you sense there is a problem, undoubtedly there *is* one. Earlier, I mentioned former President Clinton's heart problem. When he found out about the problem, it wasn't during a routine examination. He went to the doctor because there were some warning signs in his body. He had some tightness in his chest, he was short-winded, and he couldn't breathe properly. He realized something wasn't right, so he went to the doctor to have it checked out. The headlines read: "Had Bill Clinton Ignored Warning Signs, It Would Have Killed Him." Do you want to know why our relationships, marriages, and friendships keep dying? It's because we keep ignoring the warning signs.

Consummation

In verse 4, the woman speaks of the king bringing her into his bedroom. Some scholars suggest this verse is a wedding song that speaks of the consummation of their union. They're getting ready to have sex within their marital relationship. In verse 4, the woman says, "Take me away with you—let us hurry!"

You may be thinking, "But I thought you said you can't hurry love." Remember, this relationship didn't start with consummation, but rather with passion, then intoxication, and then checking the reputation. Only *now* is it moving on to the consummation, when the woman wants to hurry. Everything is in order, so now there is no reason to delay.

Unfortunately, many people like to start at the end. They start in bed, and *then* they think about checking the other person out. That's why the bed has become a burden for so many people—it's full of loveless sex. I feel compelled to address a word specifically to the sisters because I want you to understand something. Any brother can have sex with you, but he may not really care about you. A man can sleep with you, have sex with you, get busy with you, and then not think anything about you later. Medical doctors and psychologists alike explain that men are immediately stimulated by sight. If you look good to a man, he may sleep with you, but may not have any feelings for you.

Most women, however, want to have a relationship first. In short, a woman has to care about the man. She has to feel some emotional ties with a man before she will sleep with him. An emotionally needy woman may be so starved for love that she will accept the superficial declarations of love and affection that a man uses simply as a tool to get her into bed. Love doesn't come that easily, however. A lot of women's hearts would not have been broken had they simply taken the time to discern that the brother's talk was only that—just meaningless words. Sex without love turns into a burden.

Do you know what else is a burden in a bed? Love without sex. Sexless love happens when two people in marriage claim to love each other, but they aren't having sex. Now, that's a burden. Do you want to know the main problem I've faced during my twenty-seven years of counseling ministry? One of the major challenges has been how to get single people to stay out of bed, and how to get married people to get into bed. As comedian Chris Rock once quipped: "If you want to get single people to stop having sex, just let them get married." To be in love with someone and married to that person but unable to enjoy a sexual relationship together is a burden that God did not intend for us to experience.

Some married couples have little sex because they overfill their schedules and see each other only they're when exhausted. Still others have had the "stay away from sex until you're married" principle so thoroughly drilled into them that they follow it even *after* they're married.

Sex is not about trying to gratify your own desires. It is a physical expression of love, designed by God to be mutually enjoyed between marital partners. Sex is not a sin, but a way to show deep love and affection to your spouse. It is not designed *solely* for the purpose of producing children in marriage. Yes, God said, "Be fruitful and multiply," but sex is also about recreation. Whatever else you do as a husband and a wife, you ought to have some recreation in bed. It ought to be fun, not something to dread. You shouldn't think, "Oh, no. It's our sex night." If things are right in the marriage and in the bedroom, your response should be like the Shulammite woman's: "Take me away with you—let us hurry!"

Many of us, however, are experiencing loveless sex because we didn't take our time to regroup from the *last* relationship before rushing into another one. Too often, we're busy trying to prove something to the last person who left us. We want to be able to say, "You're going to be sorry you left me." Our hurry to get another man or another woman allows us to boast, "Somebody wants me, even if you don't." Yet, that's not the way it's supposed to be.

I remember once when my wife Sharon and I were ready to take a direct flight home to Indianapolis from a trip to Miami. We were on the plane, settled in, and ready to go. At what should have been our takeoff time, the pilot came over the sound system and said, "We're having mechanical difficulties, so we're not going to be able to take off right now. It's going to take a little time." Then he explained, "Here's how we're going to solve the problem. We're going to shut the plane down completely. When we do that, the plane will reset itself. Then we'll start it back up, and it will be able to take off."

Imagine what might have happened if that pilot had decided, "I'm not going to let anything delay my schedule. I'm not going to waste time shutting down the plane, so I'm going to take off right now. I have my reputation to think of." Now, I need to say a word to some of the single people reading this book. You've been having mechanical difficulties in your relationships—spiritual, ethical, and moral difficulties. You've gone from one bad relationship to another, and then another. The thing to do is not rush into yet another one, but to shut it down! Determine this in your heart: "I'm not dating anybody right now. I don't have to go out with anyone right now.

I'm not accepting any phone numbers; I'm not giving any numbers. I'm going to shut it down—completely!" Then allow the Lord to reset your behavior. Place yourself under the authority of His Word. Pray, and then listen to hear God's voice. Consecrate yourself to the Lord. He will renew you, revive you, reset you, and readjust you. Then, after that, you can start your love life back up. God will bring that right person into your life, and you'll be able to take off. But you just can't hurry love.

Chapter 2

Burn, Baby, Burn

⁵I am black, but comely, O ye daughters of Jerusalem,
as the tents of Kedar, as the curtains of Solomon.
⁶Look not upon me, because I am black,
because the sun hath looked upon me:
my mother's children were angry with me;
they made me the keeper of the vineyards;
but mine own vineyard have I not kept.
(Song of Solomon 1:5-6, KJV)

A heavyweight champion, Joe Louis was one of the best boxers in the history of sports, but he was a Black man who was boxing during a time when racism flourished in America. So his (White) handlers told him, "If you beat a White man… if you knock a White man down, or out in the ring, do not stand over him, looking intimidating. If you knock him down, or knock him out—even if you win the match, don't celebrate over him. Don't lift your hands, don't jump up and down, don't stand over him. Just put your head down, turn around, and walk slowly back to your corner." That's just what Joe Louis, the Brown Bomber, did. He never celebrated his victories over White men.

Muhammad Ali was another Black heavyweight champion who came on the scene soon after Joe Louis. He was also told, "If you defeat a White man or knock him down, don't stand over him. Don't say anything to him. Don't celebrate. Just put your head down and walk slowly back to your corner." But Ali wouldn't have any of that.

29

He didn't care what color his opponent was. If Ali knocked someone down or out, he would stand over his opponent and say, "I'm a bad man! I'm young, I'm fast, I'm pretty. I'm the greatest! I can't be beat!" Ali had already made up his mind: "If I get the victory, I'm going to celebrate."

Likewise, we as believers should be willing to celebrate our spiritual victories. There is always someone telling us not to celebrate. We gain one victory after another, but people try to make us keep our heads down and walk quietly back to our corner. Some of us can't even get our praise on because we're too busy listening to people tell us not to celebrate when something special happens in our lives. Our God is worthy to be praised! We've got to celebrate what God is doing in our lives.

Celebrate Your Identity

You may be wondering what celebrating has to do with Song of Solomon 1:5. Look at how this woman celebrates. She says, "I am Black and beautiful." This is a Shulammite woman, a Black African sister who has checked herself out and said, "I am fine! I really look good!" She begins to celebrate her identity and God's creativity in her life. You need to do that. Even if nobody else thinks you're beautiful, *you* ought to, because your perception of yourself eventually goes a long way in determining what others think. You've got to appreciate your identity in God, as well as your beauty.

This is an issue for many people, especially for women, because of the way physical beauty is touted in magazines, on television, in movies, in beauty pageants, and even in everyday conversation. In his book *What Wives Wish Their Husbands Knew about Women*, Dr. James Dobson of Focus on the Family says that one of the major problems American women have is low self-esteem—self-doubt, or feelings of inferiority. Many individuals' self-concepts come not from what they think about themselves, nor even from what other people think about them, but from what they *think* other people think about them.

Ponder that for a minute. We don't know what people think about us because we can't read their minds. Yet, we project onto other people what we *think* they think about us, and then we begin to think of ourselves in the very same way. What a strange phenomenon! If I think that you think I look good, then I think I look good. If I think that you think I'm intelligent, then I'll think that I'm intelligent. But, if I think that you think I'm ugly and stupid, then I'll think that I'm ugly and stupid. Far too often, we are basing our self-image on our imagination—what we *imagine* to be true in another person's mind. It's that faulty thinking that accounts for why so many of us have low self-esteem.

In recent years, many women have taken a lot of flak for choosing to stay home to care for their families instead of being part of the workforce. This is especially true for educated women who have sacrificed their own professional careers because they wanted to be the ones who nurture and influence their own children. Instead of being able to enjoy their victories as Ali did, however, they are listening to other voices that tell them they are pandering to paternalism by staying at home. Those voices tell them they are setting a bad example for their daughters, who will believe that they have no other options in life than to be a "housewife." Their chosen profession, or *calling*, to be a homemaker is not respected in many circles today. This causes some women to think less about themselves, simply because others don't recognize or value their successes.

Some women try to affirm themselves through men. A woman sees a man she likes, and thinks, "If I can get this man to click with me, then I'm fine, too. Right now, people think I'm not worth much, but if they see me with him, they'll know better." She feels that she has to have this particular man. If she has her arms around somebody important and significant, then *she will feel* important and significant.

Men may also deal with their self-esteem issues through sexual attraction. Consider the phenomenon of the "trophy wife," the beautiful, young bride who makes her husband feel fine when he is seen with her. Such men try to impress others by exhibiting their wives. King Xerxes, who later made Esther his queen, was like that. Remember his first wife, Vashti? Esther 1:10 and 11 tells us: "On the seventh day, when King Xerxes was in high spirits from wine, he commanded the seven eunuchs who served him…to bring before him Queen Vashti, wearing her royal crown, in order to display her beauty to the people and nobles, for she was lovely to look at." He wanted to show off his wife, and when she refused to cooperate, he became so angry that he took away her title and banished her from his presence.

Most men, however, don't get their self-esteem from a woman. That's why a man can be in a bad relationship with a woman and still not have his self-esteem affected one bit. Even if a woman doesn't like him, he still thinks he is somebody. Most men get their sense of self-worth from their jobs, rather than through a woman or a relationship. A man may subconsciously think, "If I just make a lot of money, I can feel good about myself." Or the rewards may even be non-material: "It doesn't matter if my wife doesn't celebrate me; just look what my patients are saying about me." They may even get a boost in their self-confidence when their business partner says, "Man, what you did was awesome." Drawing from his performance in the workplace, his education, or intelligence, a man can still feel quite successful and good about himself, even when his relationships are crumbling around him.

Most women are different. A woman can have a Ph.D. or an M.D., own her own business, and make a six-figure income, but if things aren't right with the man she loves, she may still be thinking, "Something must be wrong with me." Sisters, you need a higher source for your self-worth! You need to affirm yourself on the basis of what God thinks of you, instead of focusing on a man you may or may not get. Focus on God, because you already have Him.

Genesis 1:27 tells us that God created "them" in His own image—Eve as well as Adam. Sister, *you* are created in the very image of God. The fact that *God* has made you ought to be enough reason to celebrate. As Psalm 100 says, "It is he [God] that hath made us, not we ourselves" (KJV). Psalm 139 tells us that while we were in our mothers' wombs, God shaped and formed us. In Jeremiah 1:5, the Lord says, "Before I formed you in the womb I knew you, before you were born I set you apart...." You were created by God Himself and set apart for a particular purpose even before you were born. The fingerprints of God are all over you. Your life has meaning and destiny, but it is not based on any man!

Remember, too, that woman was the last recorded creation of God. He created the heavens, the earth, the trees, the grass, the sun, the moon, the stars, the beasts of the field, the fish in the sea, the birds of the air, and even man. The last thing that He made was woman, but that doesn't mean she was an afterthought. God didn't say, "Well, everything is done, and everything is all right. But, wait a minute: Adam doesn't look too happy here. I'm going to have to figure out what to do with him. Oh, I know; let me throw a woman into this package." No, you were already in the mind of God. I believe God saved His best for last!

When God created Eve, Adam did not say, "You're too big." "You're too tall." "You're too skinny." "You're too Black." "You're too White." "You're too brown." "You're too light." "You're too dark." No, he accepted her the way that God made her, saying, "You are bone of my bone, and flesh of my flesh." Adam knew that you don't mess with a masterpiece! You don't change the smile on the *Mona Lisa*. You don't add more stars to Van Gogh's *Starry Night*. You don't mess with Michelangelo's *Pietà*. Likewise, you don't mess with a woman whom God has created. You just don't touch a masterpiece! Sisters, you're worth something, and some of you don't even know it!

When God made you, He was the first one to bless you and meet with you (Genesis 1:28), the first one to give you something (Genesis 1:29), and the first one to compliment you: "It is very good!" (Genesis 1:31). Now, if God was the first one who blessed you, talked to you, gave you a gift, and complimented you, why are you chasing after some man, trying to get from him what you've already got from God? You need to understand instead how much God values you.

Appreciate Your Beauty

The Beloved in this story also recognizes her beauty as a black woman. She says: "I'm Black and beautiful" (NRSV). I love that. Some versions say, "I'm black but comely" or "...*yet* lovely." In the original Hebrew, the translation is not necessarily: "I am black, *but* beautiful." As the New Revised Standard Version translates it, she is not saying, "I am beautiful in spite of my blackness"; instead, she is saying, "I am beautiful because of my blackness. I am conscious of my beauty, and my beauty lies in my blackness." This is difficult to grasp for some of us African Americans because we grew up in a racist nation which tried to convince us that anything black or dark has something wrong with it. Just think about the negative "black" terminology that has been passed down throughout the generations: "black sheep of the family," "blackmail," "black-out," "black-ball," "black market," "black Monday," "dark horse," and "black hole." Even in the grocery store, *devil's* food cake is dark, and *angel* food cake is white.

Well, I'm agreeing right along with the Shulammite woman: I'm black *and* beautiful. Black is *not* always negative or wrong. Africans of all countries have contributed to culture, science, religion, and civilization. The color black not only can attract all rays of color and light, but absorb cosmic radiation as well. The very capstones of the ancient Egyptian (African!) pyramids were often black. Black clothing is considered the dressiest. "Black-tie" indicates a highly formal occasion, and the "little black dress" is a proven staple in a woman's wardrobe. A black suit can make a person look distinguished, refined, and even authoritative. Judges wear black robes; priests and nuns wear black gowns and hats. College graduates wear black caps and gowns. The highest level of expertise in the martial arts is a "black belt." Chauffeur-driven limousines are often black as well, and being "in the black" means being out of debt. Black is about power and influence. We need to appreciate our blackness.

Now, even as I deal with this color issue, someone is going to feel offended that I am bringing this up at all. Let me help you understand something. Just because I feel positive about being Black doesn't mean I feel negative toward those who are White, or any other color, for that matter. I love *everybody*. Our inherent value is not determined by our color. Because we are all created in the image of God, we are all beautiful.

Going back to our text, we see the same sister who proclaimed, "I'm black and beautiful" saying in verse 6, "Do not gaze at me because I am dark." "Don't stare at me because I'm black" is what she's saying to the other women in the community. In one verse, has she gone from celebrating her blackness to being concerned about what others think of it? Look more closely at what she says: "I've been exposed to the sun, and it's darkened me." In other words, God made her black and beautiful, but that natural beauty has not been protected. *The Message* translation explains it: "My brothers ridiculed me and sent me to work in the fields. They made me care for the face of the earth, but I had no time to care for my own face."

During this particular time period, women had very little say about their lives. Men were considered authority figures, whether they were fathers, husbands, or even brothers. Subsequently, women were subject to most of the men in their lives. This Shulammite woman's brothers became angry with her, but we don't know the reason why. They made her take care of their vineyards and, in doing so, the woman had to neglect her own. Let's see what we can learn from her experience.

The Shulammite woman was in a nonreciprocal relationship with her mother's sons. She wasn't married yet to a loving husband. She did not love a particular man, and there was no man in love with her. Her relationship with her brothers was not even one based on mutual care and respect. Instead of watching out for their sister's welfare, they took advantage of her. Rather than letting her take care of her own fields and her own face, they made her take care of *their* fields and watch out for *their* interests, even while her own face was burned by the sun. The men in her life were just using her.

Even now, centuries later in a very different society, there are women who are neglecting their own vineyards and their own faces to care for uncaring and selfish brothers. The woman is doing all the giving, while the brothers are doing all the taking. Their interests are flourishing and productive, but hers are languishing. The woman thinks, "I'm busy supporting them, but they aren't doing anything to help me out. I'm trying so hard to keep them encouraged, but they never say anything to encourage me. I was so busy trying to help them finish school that I had to drop out myself. I was helping them pay their rent to the point that I couldn't even pay my own. I helped them get cars, but my own car was repossessed. I was trying so hard to help them with their children that I neglected my own."

Sisters, stay out of nonreciprocal relationships with men. If they care about you, they won't just expect you to help them in *their* fields; they will help you in *yours*, too. Do not let a brother keep you from holding yourself together, especially in the spiritual realm. Many a woman has let a brother come between her and God. Before she met him, she was at church every time the door opened, filled with the Spirit, singing, praising God, living a holy life, involved in a ministry and blessing other people. Then she met this man, and now she's paying so much attention to him that her spiritual life is falling apart. Dr. Theron Williams, my good friend and pastor of Mt. Carmel Baptist Church in Indianapolis, has a favorite sermon called, "Kidnapped from Church," in which he talks about ungodly, worldly men who come into our churches just to date our women. As soon as one of those men gets the woman he's after, we don't see either of them anymore. A lot of sisters let men come between them and their relationship with God.

Nonreciprocal relationships affect us psychologically and emotionally as well. Don't let a brother get so much into your head that you can't think clearly. You may be ready right now to drop out of school because you're trying to make it work with him. In order to focus more time on him and his stuff, you're going to give up on education and not even finish your degree, even though you're not married to this person yet. The relationship is not reciprocal, but your feelings are so tied up with him that you are willing to sacrifice everything to try to get this man who doesn't even care about you. Stop and think about what you are doing.

Obsession with a nonreciprocal relationship can even cause you to give up on life. You may be depressed all the time, even having suicidal thoughts, because things aren't working out with your man. You've allowed him to get into your heart and mind to the point that you don't feel you can live without him, even though he's making your life miserable. Well, believe me, if you let go of him, you *will* get over him. It may hurt terribly right now, but the pain *will* eventually go away. Stop considering a permanent solution for a temporary problem.

You may instead have given up in less drastic ways because of a relationship you have with this kind of man. God blessed you with natural beauty, but you didn't accept the responsibility to keep yourself fit. Instead, you let yourself go. Your man wasn't attentive to you and stopped complimenting you. He didn't seem to care whether you looked good or not. You couldn't see yourself as attractive through his eyes, so you began to think that you were *not* attractive. Your man now makes you feel as though you aren't good enough for him, so you think you're simply no good. You've begun to think that it doesn't matter how you treat yourself, so you've stopped exercising and watching what you eat. You may even have begun eating and drinking things that you know are bad for you. He doesn't care about you, so you decided not to care about yourself. Instead of treating yourself as a person created in the image of God as His daughter, you have allowed this one man's bad attitude to cause you to forget who you are, but you've got to remember that you must take care of your own stuff.

The woman in our text needs to go back to verse 5, and remind herself that she was fine before these guys came into her life. Once she understands what she has with God, she will be able to handle those kind of men. *You* need to be like she was in verse 5. You were fine before they got here, you're fine while you're with them, and if they leave, you are still fine! Your identity is not dependent upon them, and they can't take your beauty from you.

Vulnerability

How did this woman become so vulnerable in this situation? How did she get burned so badly? I think she became vulnerable because of the absence of her father. I've read the whole book of the Song of Solomon more than once, in more than one translation, and I've never seen any mention of her father. Her mother is mentioned more than once, as well as the other women in the community. Her mother's sons, her brothers, and other men in her life are mentioned, but we don't hear anything about her father. For whatever reason, her father is absent. When a father is absent, you don't know what kind of man is going to roll into his daughter's life.

I wish I could get across to you men reading this book how important it is for you to have a right relationship with your daughters, as well as your sons. If you have a daughter, you need to be involved in her life. The relationship she has with you will color every other relationship she has with men. Read Norman Wright's *Always Daddy's Little Girl*. It will help you to understand how your daughter will be affected by her relationship with you—whether you are in the home or not, attentive or not, a good father or a bad one. You can't opt out without scarring her life forever. How your daughter relates to other men throughout her entire life will depend largely upon how you have related to her.

I have four wonderful sons, but no daughters. If I did, I would follow the example of one of my best friends. He has an only daughter and is a wonderful father to her. They spend a lot of time together, and periodically he takes her on a "date." It doesn't matter where they go; the important thing is that they are together and he is spending time with her, talking with her, and encouraging her. A few months ago, he bought her a ring, just to symbolize their father-daughter relationship. Another time, he gave her a little pendant with a family picture in it. He is setting an example for her, showing her how she should expect to be treated by a man. If she's getting attention, love, and gifts from her father, she isn't going to be stalking some brother to get the same things from him. Nor is she going to stick around in a nonreciprocal relationship and let some man take and take from her until she has lost her beauty, her dignity, her well-being, and her self-respect. When a woman has a right relationship with her father, she knows how to relate to a brother.

Now, if your father *wasn't* there, and you keep picking the wrong men, you may be tempted to blame your father all of your life. You may want to resign yourself to nothing but bad relationships. But remember, even if your earthly father was never there for you, your heavenly Father has always been there. If you get your relationship right with your heavenly Father, you don't have to rely on an earthly brother for self-esteem.

But there is another reason for the Shulammite woman's vulnerability: her sense of fear. This is not a rational fear of a particular person or situation, but an inner anxiety that is always with her, springing up from her own sense of inferiority and unworthiness. Her very concept of self was messed up. We don't know what happened between verses 5 and 6. In verse 5 she had it together, but in verse 6 she didn't feel good about who she was. A woman who doesn't feel good about herself is a magnet that attracts thugs and dogs in this life. They know what you think of yourself; they can just tell. They know you are fine, but they also know that you don't realize that you're fine. When you have a messed-up self-concept, you wind up in messed-up relationships. On the other hand, when you value who you are, you don't let other people *de*value you. When you appreciate who you are, you don't let other people *de*preciate you. When you understand your worth, you don't let other people treat you as worth*less*.

When we don't feel good about our self-image, it gets in the way of our relationships with God, ourselves, and other people. In Psalm 139, David said, "I will praise him, because I am fearfully and wonderfully made." He knew that God had watched over every aspect of his development, even while he was in the womb. God had given attention to every detail. Because he was fearfully and wonderfully made, David had a right relationship with God, and he praised God for it. Some people won't praise God because they don't understand how special they are. When you understand that He made you, then you recognize how much you are worth. When you have it right with God, you can get it right with yourself.

God commands us to love our neighbors as ourselves. How can I love my neighbor as myself, though, if I don't love myself? If you don't love yourself, you will never be able to truly love anyone else. Likewise, if you are in a relationship with someone who does not love himself or herself, that person will never love you the way that you expect, want, and need to be loved. It's very important to understand that.

Twenty-first Century

We have even less of an excuse than the Shulammite woman for putting up with poor treatment. She lived in a male-dominated society. In her day, women were treated like property. They weren't supposed to think, make decisions, or have expectations for themselves. But this is the twenty-first century. Sister, you can stop making a fool of yourself and walk out of that field anytime you want to. You don't have to be subject to your "mother's sons." The Shulammite's brothers were uncaring, cruel, and sadistic. They may have enjoyed seeing her getting burned by the sun, knowing that she had few opportunities for escape. But if you, in this twenty-first century, have a sadistic brother who enjoys watching you burn or seems happy when you're hurting, why are you still in his field? Why don't you get out of there and go take care of your own fields? If you're getting burned by one brother after another, what you need to do is let them go, because until you get away from these wrong brothers, you'll never hook up with the right brother. You may be thinking, "But, I love him so much. And, I need him so much. And, I've had him in my life for so long. Besides, who else would want me?"

We can learn a lesson from Aron Ralston. In 2003, he was rock climbing by himself in Utah's Blue John Canyon when a huge boulder was dislodged. He fell, and the boulder landed on his right hand. Even though he tried everything he could to free himself, the 800-pound boulder wouldn't budge. He lay there for five days with just one bottle of water and a small meal he had packed for his lunch that day. He felt himself becoming weak and knew that the likelihood of his rescue was slim. That area of the canyon was very narrow—only about three feet wide in some places. There was no way that a rescue team, either by helicopter or by land, would be able to see him.

After considering his situation, he realized that he had only one alternative to simply allowing himself to lie there and die. If he was going to survive, he had to free himself from his hand that was constrained by this boulder. Although he couldn't move the boulder, he reasoned that he could cut off his arm with his pocketknife to save his life. Of course, the idea seemed preposterous at first, but the longer he lay there and the weaker he became, the more he allowed himself to begin thinking the unthinkable. By the sixth day, he made the decision to do it. By twisting his body, he was able to break the bones in his forearm, which allowed him to use his pocketknife to cut through the soft tissue and free himself. Wrapping a tourniquet around his arm, he made his way down the canyon and found people who helped him get to the rescuers to fly him to a hospital by helicopter, so he survived to tell his story.

Of course, when it happened, people everywhere were asking themselves if they would cut off their arm in order to live. Many people declared, "I could never have cut off my own arm. I would have just had to die right there. I couldn't have done it." But Aron made the decision because he wasn't willing to stay in bondage. He chose to lose something of significance, rather than to die and lose everything. He knew that if he didn't cut away a part of himself—even though it brought pain and trauma—he was going to die in bondage.

I know that some of you single people are facing gut-wrenching decisions. I know it's hard. I know how important that man or woman is to you, but you have to see your attachment to that person for what it is—bondage. Through the power of the Holy Spirit, you need to cut yourself free so that you can move on. How are you going to find the right person when you are bound to the wrong person? You can't. You have to set yourself free. Aron Ralston said that as he cut through the nerves in his arm, it felt like being burned with molten lava. In order to save his life, however, he decided that he had to let it burn. At these crucial times, you need to take drastic action to free yourself and save your life. In other words, you've just got to let it burn.

By the time we get to verse 7, our Shulammite woman has met a brother who is different; this one truly loves her. No longer bound by her mother's sons, she is free to pursue this new relationship. She has met a brother who appreciates her for who she is. In verse 8, he starts talking, but the King James Version—"O thou fairest among women"—doesn't do the original Hebrew justice. What he really said is: "You are the finest sister I have ever seen!" He is able to see in her what she cannot even see in herself. Remember in verse 6 that she had said, "Don't stare at me; something is wrong with me." But when he saw her, he didn't see her the way she saw herself; he saw her the way God saw her. Sister, that's what you need; you need someone who's able to see in you the beauty you can't even see in yourself. You need a man who can appreciate you, even during those times you can't appreciate yourself. You need a man who will love you the way that God loves you. Keep in mind, though, that what is happening now with the Shulammite woman and this man would never have happened had she not become free from those other men who were holding her in bondage. She had to become free to be loved.

Finally, you have to make a decision about how you will look at yourself and how you will let others look at you. Bishop Joseph Walker demonstrated with a hundred-dollar bill: "If I hold that bill up to the light, I can see the small line and the hidden face in it that proves it is authentic—that it is worth $100. Now suppose I take that bill and wad it up into a ball, spit on it, throw it on the ground, stomp on it, kick it to the curb, and then turn around and walk away from it. Eventually, somebody will come by and notice that bill lying there. It's dirty and crumpled, but it looks like money. He will pick it up and say, 'It's a hundred-dollar bill! I just found a hundred-dollar bill!' Then he'll unfold it, clean it up, and put it somewhere safe because he recognizes the value of what he has just found."

Sister, I don't care how the last man dogged you, mistreated you, or kicked you to the curb. There's another brother coming along who will recognize your value and know how to treat you as you deserve to be treated.

Chapter 3

Show Me How to Love You

⁷ Tell me, you whom I love, where you graze your flock
and where you rest your sheep at midday.
Why should I be like a veiled woman
beside the flocks of your friends?
⁸ If you do not know, most beautiful of women,
follow the tracks of the sheep
and graze your young goats
by the tents of the shepherds.
⁹ I liken you, my darling, to a mare
harnessed to one of the chariots of Pharaoh.
¹⁰ Your cheeks are beautiful with earrings,
your neck with strings of jewels.
¹¹ We will make you earrings of gold,
studded with silver.
¹² While the king was at his table,
my perfume spread its fragrance.
¹³ My lover is to me a sachet of myrrh
resting between my breasts.
¹⁴ My lover is to me a cluster of henna blossoms
from the vineyards of En Gedi.
¹⁵ How beautiful you are, my darling!
Oh, how beautiful!
Your eyes are doves.
¹⁶ How handsome you are, my lover!
Oh, how charming!
And our bed is verdant.
(Song of Songs 1:7-16, NIV)

My wife and I are taking horseback riding lessons at Fort Harrison State Park. At the time of the first lesson, I'd been on horses before but didn't really know how to handle them. So when the instructors told me what to do, I listened closely. They told me how to get on the horse, how to hold my feet, how to use my hands, and how to sit. That first lesson was mostly about the right way to use my hands—how to work the reins and how to guide the horse's head because of what the bit in the mouth did.

We started riding and the instructor stopped me every now and then to teach me a little bit more. We were about thirty minutes into the ride when he stopped me, gave me some additional instructions, and then waited for me to follow through with what he had just told me. So, I'm sitting there, trying to get this big ol' horse to move, but she won't go anywhere. Now you've seen all those old cowboy movies, just like I have. You know how the cowboys make their horses move. Well, I'm doing all that stuff—kicking her, moving the reins, and making those clicking noises with my mouth. I'm doing all that, but she's not going anywhere. Finally, the instructor asked, "Do you know why she will not respond to you?" "Why not?" I asked. "Because she knows you don't know what you're doing." Many women are not responding to their men for the same reason. "Show Me How to Love You" is a sentence every brother ought to practice saying to the woman he loves.

Sister, you need to be willing to help your brother out. Your man may love you and want to make you happy, but he may not know what he's doing when it comes to making a love connection. You may think, "He can't love me for real because if he did, he wouldn't do this; he wouldn't have said that; he would have gone there; he would have done that. He doesn't do these things that I need for him to do, so I'm convinced he doesn't love me." It could be that he just doesn't know *how* to love you. That knowledge doesn't automatically come with the wedding ring. It isn't an innate understanding that he's born with. You're going to have to show him. You're going to have to teach your man how to love you the way you want to be loved.

Communication

Now, brothers, you can find a few pointers in the Song of Solomon, chapter 1. If you love your woman, one thing you ought to be doing is talking with her. You may be thinking right now, "That's why I don't read books like this. You're not saying anything. My marriage is hurting, and I'm so desperate that I picked up this book hoping it might help. But instead of saying anything new or special, all you're telling me is that I need to talk to her. I feel like throwing this book across the room." Hang on, brother. Hear me out. This may sound like no big thing to you, but it's one of the biggest to women. Conversation is one of her main needs.

In fact, a woman reading this may be thinking, "It's just talking. How come he can't do that? Is it too much for me to want to communicate with my husband? It's so simple, but he just won't do it." In most cases, sisters, it isn't that your husband doesn't *want* to please you; it's simply that talking isn't always that easy for a brother.

I cut out headlines for sermon illustrations all the time, and one that I recently found says, "Men Walk, Women Talk." When we go through issues in our lives and are facing trials or stress, men and women respond differently. Men like to get off by themselves and deal with it on their own. When a woman is in a stressful situation, however, she almost always wants to talk with the one she loves.

Listen to the Shulammite woman in verse 7. She goes up to the man she loves, and asks, "Where are you going to be at noon?" He responds, "I'm going to be down at the tent of the shepherd, watering my flock and taking care of my sheep." Now, this blows my mind, because she's asking a grown man where he's going to be, and, brothers, he answers her! Come on, now. The last time your woman asked you where you were going, how did you respond? Chances are, your answer wasn't as matter-of-fact or as patient as the Lover's response.

If you have any doubt that women find conversation easier than men, a visit to our church's childcare center would be enlightening. Even with children, the differences are quite apparent. The little girls are together in one area of the room talking about what they like and don't like, and how they *feel* about different things. On the other hand, the boys are huddled in another part of the room, making growling sounds like airplane engines, and maneuvering their little cars around on the floor yelling, "Beep! Beep! Beep! Beep!" Even scientific studies show that men process speech on the left side of the brain, while women use areas on both the right and left sides of the brain. We are definitely wired differently.

Often, when a husband gets home from work, his wife greets him with, "Hi, honey, how was your day?" The worst part is—she really wants an answer! She honestly wants to know how his day went. She doesn't want to hear, "Fine," or "It was okay"; instead, she wants *details*. It's not always easy for a man to talk on that level. Sometimes he's already through talking for the day. My good friend Freddie Haynes, pastor of Friendship West Baptist Church in Dallas, quoted this statistic in a sermon at our church: "Men use about 12,000 words a day in conversation; women use 25,000 words a day—*minimum*."

Minimum! A woman's minimum is more than twice a man's maximum! It's worse if the man has a full-time job and his wife doesn't. He may have talked to more people—answering the phone, going to meetings, talking with clients, attending board meetings, and conversing with coworkers. In short, he's been talking all day. So he gets home with his quota used up, only to discover that his wife still has 15,000 or more words to go! But he's finished! Let me tell you, brother, this is when the principle of sacrifice for love is put to the test. When you love her, you talk with her.

We need sisters, though, who will be patient with us because we aren't made like them. What's natural for them isn't natural for us. But, brother, you've got to understand your woman and the need for her to talk with you. You know Ephesians 5:25: "Husbands, love your wives, just as Christ loved the church and gave himself up for her." How can you say that you're willing to give yourself up for your wife if you're not even willing to *talk* with her? You'd give up your life, but you won't even have a conversation with her?

By holding a conversation, I mean being fully in touch with what's going on. Too often, when we men are talking, we're working on solutions. When my wife is talking, she's not trying to solve any problems; often, she just wants to talk. It's about emotional and relational issues. She wants me to empathize with her, hearing her out and then discussing it. But sometimes while she's talking—every time she pauses—I'm giving a solution. She'll say, "This happened in the kids' school today...," and I offer a solution, another way of looking at the situation. Then she goes back over the details, reiterating what she just told me, and pauses again. I'm thinking, "Babe, I just gave you the solution for that. We don't need to talk about that anymore." But she doesn't want a *solution*; she just wants the experience of talking it over with me. To her, the purpose of the conversation isn't coming up with an answer; instead, it is the conversation itself.

Another aspect of communicating that we men have to watch is our tone of voice and body language, which are indeed part of the conversation. Your words may say one thing, but if your tone of voice is saying something else, your wife will pick up on that. Or, you may say with your mouth, "I'm listening," but the newspaper in front of your face tells her you aren't.

Look again at what the Shulammite woman says to her Lover in verse 7. She asks him, "Where are you going to graze your flock, and where will you rest your sheep at noon?" She's asking him, "Where can I find you?" Is that a female thing or what! Why do women always have to know where their husbands are going to be at a certain time? What blows my mind about this man, however, is that he tells her where he's going to be! Like it or not, we all have to be accountable. Without accountability, we will be tempted to misuse our freedom. The man in this text is allowing his wife to hold him accountable. He tells her, "This is where I'm going to be," and that's exactly where he was. Some men have no problem telling their wives they will be at such-and-such a place, but they really never intend on going there.

When it comes to accountability, too many men like to quote Ephesians 5:22: "Wives, submit to your husbands as to the Lord." Every man who goes to church knows that verse. What we often ignore is the verse immediately before it: "Submit to one another out of reverence for Christ." There's a time when she submits to you, but there are also times that you submit to her. Just as there will be times when you hold her accountable, so there will also be times when she holds *you* accountable.

That's what marriage is all about. If you want to keep all the freedoms of being single, don't get married. Also, remember that if you're married, you don't have those freedoms anymore. From the moment I got married, my body has belonged to my wife, and my wife's body has belonged to me, according to 1 Corinthians 7:4. We hold each other accountable and submit, one to another. The only person who doesn't have to give an account to anybody is God. Since you're not God, you need to start submitting to one another; otherwise, you'll soon be misusing your freedom.

But, sisters, notice that the Beloved asked, "Where are you going to be at noon?" She wasn't asking him about every hour of the day—not 24/7, so she wasn't stalking her man. Some sisters have their men on leashes. They expect regular check-ins like these: "I'm in the grocery store. I just bought the bread. I'm out of the store now. I'm getting in my car. I'm driving down the street. I'm one block from home. I'm pulling in the driveway. I'm walking up the steps. I'm on the porch. My hand is on the door. See you in a second." If you feel that you have to stalk a man like that, he's not really your man. Remember, accountability is about communicating with the one you love, not holding him or her in bondage.

Honesty is a major factor in all of this communication. *This* man was where he said he was going to be. I love that. He could be honest with his woman. That's another need every wife has—openness and honesty. Men, you can't get close to the woman you love if you lie to her. You just can't do it. You can have physical contact, even sex, but you cannot be intimate with her. Openness and honesty are essential to intimacy.

In the book of Genesis when God brought Adam and Eve together, Adam said she was "bone of my bone, flesh of my flesh." Then the verse says, "And, they were both naked and not ashamed." This was a husband and wife who were open and honest with each other. They could reveal the most intimate, private areas of their lives to the other without shame. Now, that's a wonderful relationship. That's the kind of relationship all of us ought to be working toward.

Sisters, if that's what you want, you have to wait and *let* it happen; you can't force it. You have to create an environment where openness and honesty can flourish. No brother is going to be open and honest if he gets his head chopped off every time he says something. Adam and Eve started out with open and honest communication with each other because they were in an environment in which that could happen. Neither of them made the other feel ashamed or afraid to reveal their intimate areas of life.

Instead of fostering an environment of intimacy, some women create an environment of inquisition. She *says* she loves him, she trusts him, she believes in him, but then she asks a question like, "Are you ever tempted by other women?" Now, what's a brother going to do here? If he says "no," he's lying, because even Jesus was tempted in all points just as we are. He isn't at some level higher than Jesus. But if he's honest and says "yes," this woman is going to say, "I knew it! I saw it!" No, what's needed here is the cultivation of an environment where openness and honesty can emerge without fear of any repercussions.

Occupation

Now, let me really start meddling. Men, if you really love your woman, one of the ways you can express that love is through gaining productive employment. The Shulammite woman knew that her Lover was going to be tending to his job that day; she knew he was going to be grazing his flock and tending his sheep. In essence, she was saying, "I know you're going to be working, but where are you going to be during your lunch break?" Her man had a job; he was working. Man, if you love a woman, you've got to be working somewhere. If you can't hold down a job, how do you expect to maintain a relationship? A man who has a problem keeping a job is a man who has a problem keeping a relationship. No sister wants a man who won't work for the sake of their life together. It is especially true with this sister. Remember, the last relationship she had was with her mother's sons, and she got burned working in their fields *for them*. She's tired of being in a relationship where she does all the work. A man shouldn't be surprised if a woman says, "I've been burned before. I've got to make sure you are holding down a job."

Notice, though, the balance between his work and his relationship with her. She knows he's going to be grazing his sheep, but he lets her know where she can find him. He isn't pushing her out by making her feel that his work is more important than she is. He's letting her know that he's going to be at work, and if she needs to find him, she'll know how to do that. Also, she isn't asking him not to go to work, or trying to make him feel that if he is performing the duties of his vocation that he is neglecting her. She isn't making him choose between her and his job; she just wants the assurance that even while he is at work, there is still a place for her in his thoughts. Likewise, husbands and wives in our society must make sure that they both put their jobs in perspective.

Now, here's a word for my single sisters. You may hear some woman complaining that her husband doesn't work, won't go to church, lives off of others, and spends no time at the Good Shepherd's tent. It's most likely, however, that he's just doing the same thing he did before they got married. She probably had the unrealistic idea that she could change him so that he would be different after they got married. Remember when Eve connected with Adam? He already had a relationship with God and walked with Him in the cool of the day. Also, he already had a job taking care of the garden before they got married. A marriage license isn't going to force anybody to get a job, go to church, develop a relationship with God, or become more thoughtful toward others. Sisters, keep your eyes open. Don't go into marriage blindly.

Notice, too, that in our text from Song of Solomon, it wasn't just the man who was working. The man tells his Beloved to follow the tracks of the sheep "and graze your young goats by the tents of the shepherds." He had a flock of sheep, but she had a herd of goats. They are both working. She doesn't just want him for what he has: she's got stuff of her own. Too many sisters are waiting in their predicament for some brother to come up on a white horse and pull them out of poverty, but they'll probably be waiting forever. A man wants the same thing you want in a marriage partner. He wants somebody who's got something, or is on her way to becoming something. You have to bring something to the table, too. In fact, the more you bring to the table, the better your options. If you've got your own degree, your own house, your own car, your own money, and your own ability to think, it's going to take a stronger brother to satisfy you. You won't have to settle for less.

Also, the man in our text isn't emotionally hurt because his woman has a job and her own flock of animals and doesn't need for him to provide for her. He respects her, and his words indicate that he isn't expecting her to neglect her obligations to her job in order to have a connection with him. In fact, he helps her by telling her where she can graze her goats. The text says specifically, "young goats," which are also called "kids." Even though you may not have any goats, you may have some kids, or you will likely have some in the future. When you are considering spending the rest of your life with a particular man, you need to be sure that he will help you to care for the children. It doesn't matter how good he looks, how much money he makes, or how much he says he loves you. If you have children, and he isn't willing to accept them along with you, he isn't the right man for you. If he truly loves you, he will love your children because they are part of you.

Think about the story of Mary and Joseph. The Holy Spirit overshadows Mary, and she becomes pregnant with the baby Jesus. Joseph was ready to annul their engagement. But then an angel came with a message from God telling him not to be afraid to marry this woman because she was pregnant with the One who was to become the Savior of the world. Why would any man give up a woman who has Jesus in her? The only reason we even know today about Joseph is because of his connection with Mary. How can a man walk away from a woman who has the favor of God? What I love about Joseph is that even though Jesus wasn't his biological son, he treated Jesus as his own. In essence, he said to Mary, "I love you and you're my wife, so everything that is a part of you becomes a part of me."

If I can be somewhat crude for a minute, let me share an incident that happened here in Indianapolis. On the west side of town, a woman was arrested because she and her children were living in a small house with 21 dogs—and it smelled like it! You can only imagine how nasty the place was. The police arrested the woman for child neglect because she was raising her children in an environment where she was exposing them to too many dirty dogs. In a different sense, some women are guilty of bringing one man after another into their house, and they end up making a mess and having a negative impact on their children.

Appreciation

Now, let me show you another positive aspect of the Lover's behavior toward his wife: he knew how to show his appreciation for her. When she asked him where he'd be at noontime, she wanted to meet him for lunch. Look at how he responds to her: "If you do not know, most beautiful of women...." She's asking him where he's going for lunch, and her husband can't resist talking about how beautiful she is. Of all the women around, she is the only one to whom he is attracted. She is more beautiful to him than any of them. Verse 9 says, "I liken you, my darling, to a mare harnessed to one of the chariots of Pharaoh." He's talking about her value. In verses 10 and 11, he continues, "Your cheeks are beautiful with earrings, your neck with strings of jewels. We will make you earrings of gold, studded with silver." In verse 15, he goes all out: "How beautiful you are, my darling! Oh, how beautiful! Your eyes are doves." He knows when he compliments her that it shows his appreciation for her. He says to her, "I accept you; I approve of you; I value you."

Brother, your woman wants compliments, and she wants them from you. Oh, it's not that she isn't getting any compliments. In her workplace, at church, and in other settings, other men are telling her, "Your husband is so lucky. I hope he appreciates what he has." But even in the midst of all that, the person whom she *really* wants compliments from is you—the man she loves. This is very important to her because it shows your acceptance and your approval of her.

Notice the order in which the Lover pays compliments to his Beloved. He starts with her cheeks, her neck, and her eyes. In other words, he starts at the top and works his way down. As you'll see later on, he's eventually going to go down, but he starts at the top. Too many brothers start at the bottom, and think about the top later. As the popular pastor Freddie Haynes says to women, "Some of you let brothers treat you like a Church's Chicken drive-thru. They come up and order two legs, two breasts, and two thighs, and you give it to them." This Lover starts with the head, because the rest of the parts don't matter if there's something wrong with her head—with the way she thinks.

Affection

The Lover doesn't stop, however, with showing his wife appreciation; he also showers her with affection. Watch how the woman is speaking in verse 12: "While the King was at his table, my perfume spread its fragrance. My lover is to me a sachet of myrrh resting between my breasts. My lover is to me a cluster of henna blossoms from the vineyards of En Gedi." The encounter is becoming affectionate now, and notice that it is the woman who is bringing the affection. The Lover has been talking with her, conversing with her, and expressing appreciation to her. Now *she* turns the conversation to affection. In the King James Version, she says in verse 13 that her lover will lie all night between her breasts. That's a sexual reference, and *she* brought it up. He had talked with her, expressing appreciation for her, and now *she* initiates the sexual encounter. He didn't even have to ask for anything! She just wanted to give it to him.

I have already noted the importance of talking, listening, understanding, and communicating to meet a woman's needs. What some men don't understand is that the Lover was *talking* with his Beloved in verse 8, and then he was *touching* her in verse 13. Why are you trying to touch her in verse 13, if you didn't talk to her in verse 8? You've got to prepare the environment with affection before you get to the event of sex. Because men and women are wired so differently, our needs are also different. Women desire much affection; that's why they want the compliments, the flowers, the cards, the calls, and the attention. They want to be held, caressed, and touched. Here's the major difference: brothers just want some sex. I'm sorry to say it, but that's it. For men, sex is the number one need.

Sharon and I have been married for twenty years. Early on, I knew somewhat that women desired affection, but I couldn't really grasp it because, while I liked affection too, I am a man. We men can skip affection and go right to the sex and not miss a beat. Men want sex, but women want affection, which are two different needs entirely. When I was a young married man of twenty-four, I couldn't grasp that concept. Then I read a statement in a book that really got my attention. I don't even remember the title or author of the book, but I do remember the point it made: women desire affection as much as men desire sex. I thought, "If Sharon wants affection as much as I want sex...." Then I realized I had to help to create the environment for sex by meeting her need for affection. Hear me, husbands. Making love doesn't start when you get in bed at night; it starts when you get out of bed in the morning. You have to work all day to create the environment in which the needs of you both are satisfied.

That's why the Shulammite woman is talking about perfume, fragrance, a sachet of myrrh, and a cluster of henna blossoms. She is responding to the ambience of the environment. When you create the right environment by showing affection, your wife will have no problem giving you sex. That's why this woman said, "My man is going to lie between my breasts all night." Brothers, when was the last time you and your wife had sex all night? That's what she's saying, and, best of all, he did not initiate it!

You can bring that scenario into your life today. The husband sets the tone by praising his wife and expressing appreciation for her early in the morning as they are getting ready for work. He goes out to care for his flock, or whatever it is he does for a living. She goes off to care for her own flock, or whatever it is she does for a living. She meets him for lunch, where he continues expressing his affection for her. Then she says, "How about taking off work early? I've got something for you tonight. I want you to lie between my breasts all night." (Sisters, don't try this at home unless you really mean it. Once you promise your husband that kind of sex, he won't be able to concentrate on his work for the rest of the day!)

Men, do you wonder why your wife never initiates sex? It's probably because you haven't created the right environment. You've got to show her how much you love her—the way *she* wants to be shown, not the way *you* want to be shown. You've got to communicate how you appreciate her. When you do these things, you are dealing with the totality of your woman. Don't try to touch her physically until you've touched her emotionally and spiritually first. You have to show that you recognize her as a whole human being.

D. Z. Cofield, pastor of Houston's Good Hope Missionary Baptist Church, spoke at our church's men's retreat a few years ago. He asked that audience of three or four hundred men: "Why is it that your woman—your wife—keeps talking about how great the pastor is? 'Pastor this, Pastor that. Pastor, Pastor, oh, you should have seen the pastor…. Oh, you should have heard him today.' Why does your woman keep talking about the pastor?" It's not that the pastor has touched your woman physically, he explained, but every week he's touching her spiritually, intellectually, emotionally, and mentally. Then you rush home, and just want to touch her physically, even though she barely has time to say your name. You haven't learned how to create the right environment.

On the other hand, wives, your husband *needs* sex. Even as he is meeting your needs, you have to meet his. Do you know when the frustration for the man comes in? It happens when a wife keeps trying to do to her husband what she wants her husband to do to her. The wife sends her husband flowers and cards, writes him poetry, and calls him on the phone to say, "I love you. I miss you. I can't wait to see you tonight." All of that's good. I'm not saying to stop that, but his needs still have not been met. Then he rushes home, and all you get from him is bang, boom, three minutes, and he's finished! Why? Because that's what he wants you to do to him! He has spent years trying to do to you what he wants you to do to him, and you've spent years trying to do to him what you want him to do to you. Now you're both frustrated, and neither of you is doing anything to meet the other's needs.

There are married couples who haven't touched each other in years because they got frustrated. "I was trying hard and got no response; nothing happened," you say. You didn't get a response because you didn't know what you were doing, and now you're mad at each other.

Even as some brother is reading this, he is asking, "Why should I show her any affection? Why should I bother with cards, letters, poetry, and all that kind of stuff? She's not even giving me any sex!" His wife, who probably gave him this book to read, is thinking, "I'm not giving him any sex, not until he starts treating me right." It's a vicious cycle, and there's only one way to break it. At least one of you has to start meeting the other person's needs. People go where their needs are met. If the husband starts meeting his wife's needs with affection, she will soon be saying, "You are like a sweet fragrance in my life; come and make love to me all night." When the wife starts meeting her husband's needs with sex, he'll have an easier time communicating with her, complimenting her, and taking care of her the way it's supposed to be done. Too many of us are content to stay frustrated because we're too selfish to give before we get. As a result, we never get a chance to be what God wants us to be as individuals or as a married couple.

Protection

Next, men, if you love your wife, you've got to show her that you love her in terms of security and protection. In Song of Solomon 1:16, we read: "How handsome you are, my lover! Oh, how charming! And our bed is verdant [green]. The beams of our house are cedars; our rafters are firs." Look at how these things are connected: "How handsome you are, my lover...our bed is green...the beams of our house are cedars...our rafters are firs." This is a woman who feels secure and safe because her husband is treating her lovingly. She has a strong house with a roof over her head, which gives her the feeling of security. Within this kind of environment, she can be free with her man. The reason a lot of women do not respond sexually, even in marriage, is that they don't feel secure in their marriage. Without this sense of security, they are hesitant and reserved, so they're never able to give themselves freely.

Look at the significance of what the woman is saying here. In verse 4 she said, "Let's go to *your* house. Let's go to *your* bed." Now, she is saying, "This is *our* house. This is *our* bed. These are *our* rafters." It was no longer *his* home, but *their* home. Her husband had created a home for her, so she had a place with him where she belonged. She felt secure in the home they had together.

This is a very practical point. Having a house of her own helps a woman feel secure. Moving from a rented apartment into a house of her own can make a world of difference in how a wife feels about herself, her husband, and her marriage. Owning a home adds stability. A house isn't just another place to live; it's more important than that. With it comes community, neighborhood, church, school, and all that. The wife feels that she's got her own home, rather than living in somebody else's place. Some men may say, "Well, I just bought her a car!" A car is cool, but it depreciates over time. Who would feel secure in something that's mobile and depreciates? A house, on the other hand, is stable and appreciates over the years.

Do you remember the Houston Oilers—now the Tennessee Titans? For the first year the team moved to Tennessee, they played in Memphis but couldn't get a following at all that year. They couldn't sell season tickets or get the support of the crowds. Hardly anybody would go see them. Do you know why people wouldn't go see the former Houston team in Memphis? Because the people in Memphis knew that the team wasn't staying there. They were just waiting for their new stadium to be built in Nashville. The people of Memphis didn't see the Titans as *their* team. Their attitude was, "Why should we support you when you're not going to stay here?" It became so embarrassing that the next season the owner moved their games to Vanderbilt Stadium. The numbers increased to the point that *now* you can hardly even get a ticket to see the Titans. That's because they have their own stadium now—their own house. Now they've got support, they're getting victories, and they've got an MVP on their team.

Likewise, brother, if you get your finances together, save your money, and get out of that apartment, your wife will believe that you see this as a permanent relationship. You don't need a mansion—just find a little place, anywhere that you and your wife can say, "This is our house." You'll find your wife turning into a MVP, and you're going to win a lot of victories together.

Also, men, as well as putting a physical roof over their heads, we also have to learn how to "cover" our wives spiritually. Remember, the Shulammite woman's brothers had left her out in the field where the sun burned her. Her Lover didn't do that; instead, he said, "I've got a house. I've got a covering for you." Spiritually speaking, we are to serve as a covering for our wives and children, an umbrella of protection over them.

I remember seeing a little boy named Jacob on the "Today Show." He and his brother had been playing with two other boys on thin ice.

The ice broke, and all four fell into the water. Jacob and his brother were rescued, but the other two drowned. During the interview, a reporter kept trying to learn from Jacob how he made it out while the other two didn't, but Jacob didn't know how to explain it to the woman. He kept saying, "We swam to the shore, and they pulled us out." This conversation unfolded:

"But why didn't your friends make it to shore?" the reported probed.

"I don't think they made it because the water was just really cold," Jacob replied.

"But wasn't the water cold to you, too?"

"Yeah, it was cold, but I had my coat on."

Jacob made it through the same icy waters that took the lives of others only because he had his coat on: he was covered. Men, we need to provide a covering for our wives and children. God has delegated authority to us so we can serve as a coat of protection for our families. We should be praying for them, nurturing them with the Word of God, and providing spiritual leadership and guidance. Even by doing that, we recognize that the only reason any of us are saved today is because we're covered with the blood of Jesus Christ. We have a relationship with God through His Son.

Chapter 4

When Somebody Loves You Back

> [12] While the king was at his table,
> my perfume spread its fragrance.
> [13] My lover is to me a sachet of myrrh
> resting between my breasts.
> [14] My lover is to me a cluster of henna blossoms
> from the vineyards of En Gedi.
> [15] How beautiful you are, my darling!
> Oh, how beautiful!
> Your eyes are doves.
> [16] How handsome you are, my lover!
> Oh, how charming!
> And our bed is verdant.
> [17] The beams of our house are cedars;
> our rafters are firs.
> *(Song of Songs 1:12-17, NIV)*

Last week I was trying to assemble an outline in time for a Bible study. Our church has three locations throughout the city of Indianapolis. I was studying at our northeast campus, but my administrative assistant was at our central location. Usually, in that situation, we send the outline drafts back and forth by fax. This time, I was faxing things to her, but I wasn't getting any faxes in return. So I called my assistant.

"Lisa, you need to get the outline back to me."

She said, "Pastor, I already faxed it."

"Lisa, I'm standing in front of the fax machine. Nothing has come through."

"I'll fax it again."

Five minutes later, she called back. "Pastor, did you get it?"

"No. I'm standing in front of the fax machine, but it didn't come through."

"Okay, I'll fax it again."

This went on for about thirty minutes. Finally, I gave up and said, "We may just have to do without outlines today." I went back to my office. A few minutes later, someone knocked on my door.

"Pastor, I just put some paper in the fax machine, and all these faxes started coming out."

I had worked hard on that outline, putting a lot of energy and effort into getting it right. I really wanted it to please and satisfy the people who would receive it. After faxing Lisa everything she needed, I stood there waiting at the fax machine with great expectations, but none of that mattered because I forgot one of the most important components in the process.

You may be in a relationship that's failing to meet your expectations for the same reason. You've been working really hard and putting forth a lot of energy because you've really desired to please and satisfy your spouse. Yet when it comes time to receive something back, you stand there waiting, but you haven't been getting anything. I'm going to suggest to you that maybe you have forgotten one of the most important components. Despite all the things you've done, there is still a key element you've left out.

In the first three chapters of this book, we've focused largely on all the things a man ought to do for a woman: the conversation, the touching, the talking, and the caressing. We emphasized the importance of dealing with the totality of a woman's being—not just her body, but her mind, emotions, and will. But this can't be a one-way process: it only works *when somebody loves you back*. So in this chapter, I want to focus in on what the wives ought to be doing for their husbands.

Sisters, if you really love your husband, you have to understand that his needs are different from yours. You need to learn how to demonstrate your love in a way that will be meaningful to him. You don't want to give all your energy and effort to doing things for him that you want him to do for you, if that's not really what he wants. Because what you need is so different from what he needs, you'll end up confused and upset, thinking about all you've done for him and wondering why you're getting nothing in return. We've already mentioned that a man's greatest need is sex, but what else does a man need?

Respect

The woman in this text knows. After evaluating the needs of her man, she is doing what is necessary to meet them in a spirit of self-sacrifice. She gives him what he needs, even if she doesn't feel like doing it, because that's what love is all about. Look at what she says in verse 12: "While the *king* is sitting at his table...." Don't miss this. She recognizes his station and his status in the home.

You may be thinking, "Well, she's talking about King Solomon." I'm not so sure. Some theologians say that her Lover is a lowly shepherd, and King Solomon, the playboy that he is, tries to come between the woman and the shepherd. Verses 7 and 8 certainly make the Lover sound like a shepherd. He's leading, resting, and feeding his sheep, and going by the shepherd's tent. Sounds like a shepherd, doesn't it?

Take a look back at verse 4: "The king is in his bed chambers." He's a king in verse 4, a shepherd in verses 7 and 8, and a king again in verse 12. Is he a shepherd, or is he a king? This is getting confusing. One thing I notice, however, is that whenever she refers to him as a king, he is always at home. No matter what this man is elsewhere, when he comes home, he's a king. That's because his wife understands that her man doesn't need the same things she does, so she wants to give him what he needs. What he needs is her respect, reverence and honor for him.

A good wife can say to her husband, "No matter what you are in the community, when you get home, you're the king. You may be a lawyer, a doctor, a janitor, or a teacher, but when you get home, you are the king." Sister, if you are ever going to get what you want out of your relationship, you need to realize that in spite of everything you're trying, you're "leaving the fax paper out." You've got to give your man the respect and the honor he needs.

Your man has an ego. You can argue with that ego, try to diminish that ego, or even attempt to remove that ego. But when you're finished trying all that, he's still going to have an ego, and you aren't going to change that. So, instead of trying to change him, why don't you learn to use his ego in a way that benefits what the two of you have together? "Lover, I'll allow you to exercise your authority. You're the king here. I'll give you the royal treatment at home by treating you with honor and respect."

Let me point out something in Ephesians 5:25, which says, "Husbands, love your wives." Do you know why this verse tells the husband to do that? Because the wife needs love. She needs to know that she is the most important thing in the world to her husband and has his full attention. As well as physical caressing and holding, she needs him to touch her mind, emotions, and inner being. In other words, she needs him to love her. Remember, the first words out of the mouth of the Beloved back in verse 2 were, "Let him kiss me with the kisses of his mouth." That kissing is important to her.

You won't hear a brother talking about just wanting to be kissed. He may want that, but it isn't his most important need. So there you are—kissing him all day, every day, wondering, "How come I'm getting no response?" It's because the Bible never told you specifically to love your husband. It's *natural* and *good* for you to love your husband, but by just loving him, you are trying to do what the Bible told him to do for you—not what it told you to do for him. Ephesians 5:22 says, "Wives, submit to your husbands as to the Lord."

Ephesians 5:33 puts it all together: "Each one of you [husbands] must also love his wife as he loves himself, and the wife must respect her husband." Your husband needs respect, reverence, and honor. He needs to understand that he is the king of his castle when he comes home. If you aren't meeting his needs at home, he'll just go elsewhere to get those needs met. He goes where he's getting respect and honor...even if it's simply hanging out with his buddies.

There is some brother right now who has a nice, big house, but he hates to go home. Do you know why? Because he's not getting any honor or respect there. So, he's paying the mortgage on a great big ol' *house*, but it's an ugly *home* because his family doesn't give him any respect. Sister, you need to be your man's greatest cheerleader. Do you know what sports fans do at a home game? Here in Indianapolis, at a home game for the Indiana Pacers, they wear the team's colors of blue and gold, and hold up signs of support that say, "We are for you." Even before the game starts, they begin cheering, just because the Pacers are in the house.

Then the fans begin to call out the players' names. When a favorite player like now-retired Reggie Miller comes out on the court, they begin shouting his name repeatedly: "Reggie, Reggie, Reggie." Those fans are saying, "We have come to support you and offer you the home court advantage." Now, if we do that for our favorite teams, why can't we do it at home? Your man needs to see some signs in the house that he's got your support, and he must hear you calling his name as well. He needs to know you are on his side, giving him the respect he needs. He needs the home court advantage.

The Shulammite woman says, "I don't care what they call you at work. I don't care what they call you in the community. I don't care what they call you in the media. When you come into *this* house, you are the king."

Also, this woman is the queen. She said earlier, "This is *our* house. This is *our* bed. These are *our* rafters." Because she's the queen, she doesn't have a problem treating her husband like a king. So if some sister starts offering you advice beginning with the words, "If I were you...," tell her, "You probably wish you were me, but you're not!" Treat your man like a king. Remember, you reap what you sow. If you sow royal treatment for the king, you'll reap royal treatment as the queen.

But, sister, you don't give a brother the royal treatment until he's made you his queen—his wife. Just moving in with him doesn't count. You can be all over his house, cleaning up his messes, cooking his dinner, washing his clothes, sleeping with him all night, and wondering, "When are we getting married?" But he's not even thinking about marriage. Why should he? He's already got everything he wants because you're already doing everything.

Don't treat him like a king until he legally and spiritually makes you his queen.

Environment

Now notice what follows: "...while the king was at his table." She says, "My perfume spread its fragrance." The King James Version uses the word *spikenard*. Remember when Mary washed and anointed the feet of Jesus after she broke open that alabaster box? That was spikenard, an expensive perfume. So the Beloved is saying, "I love this man. He's the king of my house. I'm going to give him respect, *and* I know how to stimulate my man." Watch how she's stimulating him—with the smell of spikenard, perfume, and cologne. Sister, don't you know that a lot of men are stimulated by smell? Using pleasant aromas, you can create an inviting environment that stimulates a man. As we continue through the Song of Solomon, you will see that when you're in love, all of your senses come into play. (The Lover has already used his hearing. Now he's using his sense of smell, and in a minute he's going to use his sight. He has already used his sense of touch, and in a couple more chapters he's going to use his sense of taste.) When you're in love, you will use all of your senses. The problem comes when you try to get love without any stimulation of the senses whatsoever.

Notice also that the *stimul*ation follows *relax*ation. She said, "My man, the king, is sitting at the table." In Solomon's time, people didn't sit up straight in chairs while they were eating. They reclined on the floor, on cushions, or at low tables. The Beloved is saying, "My man is relaxing. When he's been stressed, strained, and struggling, he doesn't go out on the town for his relaxation. He comes home. I'm letting him relax right here, at *our* house." This is where men really want to relax; they want to feel at home in their own homes.

A man wants to find peace and rest at *his* house, but often he doesn't. There was once a commercial that was frequently played during football games—I don't even remember what the product was. After a football referee makes a controversial call, the coach gets up in the referee's face and explodes, "How can you do that? You can't see!" The coach goes on and on like that while the referee just stands there. The announcer says, "How can he stand there and do nothing? Where do you train for such a verbal beating?" Then the scene changes to the referee's house, where he's dressed in casual clothes, sitting silently at the table while his wife is in his face, yelling at him, "You don't love me! When was the last time you told me you loved me?! Why don't you take the trash out?" A man's house shouldn't be the place where he goes to learn how to take a beating. It should rather be a safe haven where he comes to get refreshed from the beatings he's had to take elsewhere.

Proverbs 19:13 says, "...a quarrelsome wife is like a constant dripping." Proverbs 25:24 adds, "Better to live on a corner of the roof than share a house with a quarrelsome wife." Let me paraphrase that for you: "It is better to eat soup on the top of the roof than to eat filet mignon in a house with a wife who's nagging." No man wants to live with a whiner or a woman who criticizes him whenever he sits down. The Beloved knows better than that. She knows her man isn't lazy; he's been working today, according to verse 7. Also, it isn't that he never does any work around the house, but she doesn't expect him to be doing it *every moment* he's at home. She gives him time to rest and relax because she knows he needs that.

It was while he was relaxing that his Beloved said, "I'm going to stimulate him now with some fragrance." This brother has the stinky job of herding a flock of sheep, which can get awfully smelly! But when he comes home, he smells the pleasant aroma of his woman's perfume wafting throughout the whole house. She's been in the shower with the scented bath gel, soap, and bath oil. When she gets out of the shower, she doesn't wipe away any scent with a towel; she just drip-dries. Then she puts some spikenard behind her ears, on her neck, and especially on her wrists—where the pulse is beating—the place she knows her man will be stimulated. So when he gets home, the atmosphere of his environment has already been permeated by this sweet fragrance.

Remember also, sister, that when the Bible talks about something physical, it often has a deeper spiritual meaning as well. It's not just the perfume's aroma that pervades the atmosphere, but also the woman's attitude. She has a sweet demeanor, and that's what the brother walks into when he comes home. He looks forward to coming home to such a sweet-smelling fragrance.

This woman not only stimulates her man with smell, but by sight. Men are very visual. If you doubt that, notice that the first thing out of the Lover's mouth is a compliment about his Beloved's appearance. In verse 8, he tells her that she is "the most beautiful of women." Then in verse 15, he says, "How beautiful you are, my darling! Oh, how beautiful!" Today, he might say, "You are fine, my love; you are really fine." So if you want to stimulate your man, you need to look good to him. I'm not talking about any phony, beauty-pageant sort of look. Just learn how to keep yourself healthy and do those things that accentuate the natural beauty God has given you.

It amazed me when I heard that pornography is a $10-billion-a-year business in the United States. Think of how many men have to be involved to develop a $10 billion industry. Men don't buy *Playboy* just for the stories. They don't read the annual *Sports Illustrated* swimsuit issue to keep up on the latest styles. Don't misunderstand me. I do not condone in any way the exploitation of women's bodies to feed lust or to make money; I'm mentioning these things only because I am trying to make the point that men are visual beings. To meet a husband's needs, his wife has to give him something to see. Notice how the Lover compliments his Beloved in verse 10: "Your cheeks are beautiful with earrings, your neck with strings of jewels." In verse 15, he speaks of her eyes, and later on, he compliments her hair, lips, and other parts of her body. The man is stimulated by what he sees in his wife.

Now, some women are afraid to get their hair done, put on pretty outfits, or wear jewelry because they think it's a sin against God. They read in 1 Peter 3:3 (KJV): "Whose adorning let it not be that outward adorning of plaiting the hair, and of wearing of gold, or of putting on of apparel." But look closely at that verse for a minute. If that verse literally means "never get your hair done," it would also mean "never put on any apparel," that is, "never wear *any* clothes." Do you really think that's what it says?

I understand that whatever is not of faith is sin. If you don't understand your freedom in Christ and feel that you are sinning if you get a new hairstyle, then that is a sin to you because you can't do it in faith. But even if you lack the sufficient faith and sense of Christian freedom to get your hair professionally done without feeling guilty, surely you'll agree that there isn't any sin in combing it! Make *some* effort to look attractive; your man is worth it. Don't get mad at me. I'm just trying to help you put some paper in your fax machine.

While we're on the subject of hairstyles and jewelry, we might also talk about make-up. Again, some women think that wearing make-up is a sin. One preacher—not me—was asked, "Is it a sin for a woman to wear make-up?" He replied, "It's a sin for some women *not* to wear it." But there is another side to this issue as well. Some brothers don't like to see their women wearing any make-up at all. This isn't a religious issue with them; they just prefer "natural beauty." Like Song of Solomon 1:5, they want to see their wives looking dark and lovely, with nothing artificial to change that look. If your man is like this, but wearing make-up makes *you* feel good, you're going to have to work out a compromise in the spirit of love.

But even if both you and your husband agree about styling your hair and putting on make-up, you may not know how to do it properly. Few people are born with that innate ability, so go to a professional to either do it for you or show you how to do it so that you will look your best.

A woman reading this may be thinking, "I like to look good, but I want to look good for *me*." There's nothing wrong with that; in fact, it's important for boosting your self-esteem, which we've already discussed. But if you're married, you need to look good for your man as well. He wants something to see. Just as you want him to talk to you and touch you to meet your emotional needs, you also need to satisfy his visual needs.

A man wants his wife to remind him of the woman he married. Some sisters, however, get things backwards. When they go to church, parties, concerts, and plays, they look fine. But when they're at home, they aren't giving their man anything to see. When they were dating, he couldn't catch her with her hair up in rollers, but since they got married, he can't catch her out of rollers at home. Remember, your husband is visual; you've got to give him something to see.

So what's the Shulammite woman wearing when *her* husband gets home? Her hair and face are together. But what does she have on? In particular, what did she have on that night? She said in verse 13 (KJV), "...he shall lie all night betwixt my breasts." She knows he's stimulated by sight, and they're going to do it all night. What is she wearing? Let me ask you, sister, what do *you* wear to bed at night? I hear some of you saying, "Well, I just wear this warm-up suit because I like to be comfortable when I go to sleep." Yes, there is a place for comfort when you sleep. But if both of you aren't going to sleep right away, you'd better put on something more stimulating than a fifteen-year-old pair of warm-up pants and a mismatched top.

Even now, some sister is arguing with me in her mind, "Well, my husband needs to accept me for who I am. He shouldn't care if I do dress like this." You weren't saying that when you were dating him. You stumbled around on your high heels with your cute little outfit on, and fixed yourself up when you thought there just might be a possibility of seeing him at church, at work, or wherever you happened to meet. You spared no time, effort, or expense to get him to notice you. Now, here you are, covered from head to toe in an old warm-up suit, complaining, "He doesn't have any desire for me." Yes, he does, but he just can't get past that outfit.

Some woman is thinking, "Well, I'm glad I'm not married to a man who needs all that visual stuff. My man isn't like that." Yes, he is. That's why he keeps shopping for you at Victoria's Secret or Frederick's of Hollywood, but you just keep putting that stuff deeper and deeper in your dresser drawer. Take the hint: stimulation.

Getting back to our story, look at verses 13 and 14: "A bundle of myrrh is my well-beloved unto me; he shall lie all night betwixt my breasts. My beloved is unto me as a cluster of camphire in the vineyards of En Gedi" (KJV). He's a bundle of myrrh—a cluster of camphire. Myrrh comes from a plant that was used for making perfume. Camphire were wildflowers, probably henna, a colorful plant from which dye is made. The Lover is a bundle, or a cluster, of fragrant, colorful wildflowers.

Now, these are *wild*flowers. They show up naturally in the desert, just popping up here and there. But even though he has the fragrant and colorful attributes of the *wild*flowers, he isn't scattered throughout the desert. He is together—a cluster, a bundle, a bouquet of wildflowers. His Beloved is saying, "I don't mind you being wild, just don't be wild everywhere, with everybody. I want you to be wild with me. I'm not tripping off your energy, wildness, or excitement, but I need you to pull it together so that we can have a relationship of substance. You can't be wild everywhere, popping up in different places, and still be lying between *my* breasts. But you can be as wild as you want to be with me." Husband and wife, here is a benefit of marriage—you can be as wild as you want to be, and still be in the will of God.

Now, a note to you brothers before you start demanding your right to be wild and free. You may think, "I'm a wild man, and I'm married, so I get to do what I want in the bedroom." Yes, you and your wife have the freedom in Christ to express your wildness to each other any way you want. But you've got to be careful with your wife. There *are* people who have not yet learned to appreciate their Christian freedom. Some women are taught that there are things you don't do sexually, even with their husbands. They don't understand that "the bed is undefiled in marriage," as it says in Hebrews 13:4. In other words, a married couple can do whatever they want.

When I was growing up, my church talked about sex almost as though it were a sin, even for married people. Others have grown up in churches—or families—where no one ever said anything at all about sex. Also, many women have been burned in earlier relationships. Your wife may even have been physically or emotionally abused, and it's hard for her to get past something like that. So, while you're trying to be a cluster of wildflowers, she may be unwilling to be wild because of her past. You've got to be patient, prayerful, and most of all, *loving*. You've got to stay in the Word. Many good Christian books are available about sexual activity in marriage, along with insightful Christian counselors who can help couples deal with the past if it is keeping the present from being all that it could be.

I remember a newspaper story about a woman whose house had caught on fire. When the fire department arrived, the fire had already burned itself out. As they conducted their investigation, however, they found that even though there were no flames, the fire was still smoldering, and there were still some hot spots. The woman had been burned. The firefighters not only had to bring her out to safety, but they had to go through the house and put out all the hot spots, too. Man, if your wife was burned by someone in her past—or maybe even by you—even though you don't see the flames, there may still be something smoldering. You have to take your time and put out the hot spots.

What I love about the woman in our text is that even though she has been burned by her brothers in the past, she's not going to let that get in the way of the relationship she has with her husband in the present. She says to him, "I don't have a problem with you being wild; just be wild with me." To her, he is a cluster, or a bundle: something of substance. She's got a man who brings substance to the relationship; that's why she doesn't mind him lying with her all night.

Sister, you have to be careful about hooking up with someone who treats you as if you are insignificant because you are offering a man something of substance—your body. In this kind of relationship, when your man wants something from you, he speaks of "ours," but when you want something from him, it's "his." When he wants something, he talks like you're married, but when you ask for something, he reminds you, "No, we're single." If the man you're interested in is shallow, he doesn't deserve any substance from you. "Shallow" is words; "substance" is a wedding. "Shallow" is a ring on the phone; "substance" is a ring on your finger.

Think about Adam and Eve. Before Eve even came along, Adam gave up a rib for her. He gave up something of significance, making a major sacrifice. To the Hebrew people, a bone could represent the soul. Adam gave part of his soul to the relationship. Something of such great significance deserves something of significance in return. But if a man brings anything less than that, wanting all of you but unwilling to unite to you in marriage, he doesn't deserve a thing from you. When you give a man your body, you're not just giving him your flesh and blood, you are giving him your mind, your emotions, your heart, your will, and your spirituality—your everything. If you're giving everything and he's just coming to take it, there's something really wrong with that. Look at what Jesus says in Matthew 7:6: "Do not give dogs what is sacred; do not throw your pearls to pigs. If you do, they may trample them under their feet, and then turn and tear you to pieces." Jesus is warning you not to give that which is holy to dogs. If you do, they won't appreciate it. They will trample it like nothing under their feet and will tear you to pieces in the process.

Sex

One last thing: this woman understands that if her husband is doing so much to meet her needs, then she has to give him what he needs. That's why she says, "My man will lie between my breasts all night." As I've already mentioned, the number one need of nearly every husband is sex—not flowers on the job, not a card, not a picture—sex. These other things are cool, but they don't meet his main need. Of course, there are exceptions, but the number one need for most men is sex.

Remember, too, the very first commandment God gave to men and women. Was it "Husbands, love your wives"? "Wives, respect your husbands"? Or maybe, "Honor your father and mother"? How about, "Give praise in all things"? Nope. It wasn't even, "Keep the garden, till the ground, and cultivate the land." No, the first commandment God gave us was, "Be fruitful and multiply." Sex is the only way to accomplish that. God knew the need of the man He had created, as well as the bond that making love would establish between a man and a woman. God designed humankind not only with the capacity to have sex, but also with the desire for the intimacy that sexual intercourse can bring.

The Beloved was eager to be with her Lover, to spend the night with him, and to have sex with him. That's why she says, "My man is going to lie between my breasts all night." All night? How do you have a love that lasts through the night? There are times in the Bible when night simply deals with the time of day, but there are other times when night represents darkness and difficulty. We all need the kind of love that lasts through the dark times—through the difficulties of life. No matter how happy you might be at the moment, at some point you and your spouse will face such times. Can your love deal with that? Can your love—physical and spiritual—last through the dark times?

In the English language, we've got only one word for love. In contrast, the ancient Greeks used various words to express different types of love: *eros* for sensual, sexual love; *philia* for the emotional, friendship type of love (that's why Philadelphia is called the "City of Brotherly Love"); and *agape* for pure, unselfish, volitional love. A good marriage has all three, especially agape love. Today, if you ask people how they know they're in love, they often say, "Well, it's a feeling that I've never had before." That's not love, but infatuation or passion. Anyone who's been married any length of time can tell you that this kind of feeling comes and goes. Agape love, on the other hand, is not sensual or emotional. It is an act of the will, or a choice that we make.

I love my wife Sharon because I *choose*, or decide, to love her. It isn't about how I feel. As in all marriages, there are times I don't feel love for her, but I still *will* it. It's unconditional, as well as an act of the will. If you want to make it through the difficulty or darkness, it will take an act of your will. That's how God loved us. He didn't wait until we became better people: "...while we were yet sinners, Christ died for us" (Romans 5:8). So if you are waiting for your spouse to change to deserve your love, remember that you didn't deserve God's love either. It was while we were still jacked-up, messed-up sinners that God loved us and did what He needed to do to set us free. That kind of love, agape, will last through the longest night.

Going further into our text, the Beloved says in verse 16 (KJV): "Our bed is green." The New Living Translation says, "The soft grass is our bed." In other words, "Our bed is alive. Our bed is not brown, dried up, or dead." They have a bed with some motion in it. Sister, if you want to satisfy your man, your bed has to be alive: you cannot lie dead and motionless in your bed! Yes, the verse says, "He will lie between my breasts all night," but that doesn't mean they are going to be lying motionless in one spot all those hours. Have you ever tried to sleep in one spot all night? It's almost impossible. You may argue, "No, I always sleep in one spot. I never move. I just stay in one spot." I would ask then, "With somebody on top of you?" If that's the case, some part of your body is going to go dead, or your arm is going to fall asleep, but something is going to happen.

The Shulammite woman knows that if her husband is going to lie between her breasts all night, she can't stay in the same spot. She's going to have to make adjustments by changing her position so that their night of passion will last. Some marriages don't work because spouses are not willing to make adjustments. You've got to be willing to change in order to keep your bed, and your marriage, alive. Some comedian has said, "For some, marriage has become like watching cable TV with one channel; it's the same thing night after night." Don't let your marriage be like that. You have 114 channels to choose from; don't get stuck on just one.

A lot of women don't understand that if they aren't satisfied and fulfilled, their husbands won't be, either. You may think, "You're not talking about my husband. He's so selfish that he doesn't care anything about me." He cares a lot about you; that's why he married you. He may just be feeling cheated, because he can't get the sex he's supposed to be able to receive from his wife. He stood at the altar and told you before God and all the witnesses that he would forsake all others, and keep himself only unto you, so long as you both shall live. What he didn't know then was that sex was going to be rationed out to him. He didn't know that while he was giving everything he had, his lifetime partner was going to be lying there, motionless. He is not satisfied until *you* are satisfied.

For some women, it isn't their theology that keeps them from enjoying sex. It isn't that they don't know what to do or understand what their husbands need. Some women don't enjoy sex because they don't appreciate their own bodies. They have never gotten to know their own bodies because they don't like them for one reason or another. You've got to love the body that God has given to you, so you've got to have some movement.

I used to love watching Michael Jordan play basketball. If I knew the Bulls had a game, I wouldn't even call a meeting for that day because Jordan was on. Even when he got traded to the Wizards, I would still rush home to see what Jordan was going to do. He had a lot of different moves and was always surprising people. Some of us would leave work early because the Bulls were playing, and Jordan was going to do his thing that night. We would wait with great anticipation and expectation because Jordan was playing. Do you know why we loved Jordan so much? Why we would pay extra money to go to Conseco to see him play? Why we would even buy a ticket and fly or drive up to Chicago just to see him play? Why we were making investments and sacrifices just to watch him play? It's because Jordan had more than one move; he didn't just do the same thing over and over. Sometimes he would pull a reverse, sometimes a dunk, sometimes a three-pointer, or sometimes an assist. At other times, he would play defense, sometimes he'd make a steal, or sometimes he'd get a rebound. Even late in his career, he never did the same thing over and over. He would pull out an old move every now and then, just to let us know that he still could do it if he wanted to.

Here's what I'm trying to tell you, sisters. If you want your man to come home early from work and start making more investments in your relationship, or if you want him to cancel some meetings and rush home with great anticipation, then you've got to have more than one move. You've got to be able to do more than one thing. You've got to have a bed that is alive.

When your bed is green and alive, it is like a pasture where a sheep can find everything it needs. This woman is saying to her husband, "Whatever you need, you can find it in this bed." She's saying, "You don't have to run all over town. It's in this bed. Whatever you need to satisfy you, whatever you need to fulfill you, whatever it's going to take, you don't have to go anywhere else—everything you need is right here."

Sister, can you tell your husband that? Will you say this to him? "Our bed can meet your needs. I'm willing to sacrifice some time to read some books and experiment together. I'm willing to move out of my comfort zone. I'm open to new teachings and willing to experience new things. I'm willing to listen to what you have to say. Also, I'm willing to go out of my way to make this bed green for us, because I don't want you even tempted by another bed. Everything that you need you can get right here."

The Bible says that marriage is an illustration of Christ and His bride, the Church. Jesus is our Shepherd who provides everything we need. He leads us beside still waters, and He makes us to lie down in green pasture. Everything we need—salvation, deliverance, eternal life, and forgiveness of sin—we can find in Jesus Christ. Our first and foremost commitment is always to God, and we should always put that relationship first. But when our relationship with God through his Son Jesus Christ is good, then we have the love of God in us. Thus, we can do whatever is necessary to meet the needs of the person God has given us.

Chapter 5

Made in the Shade

¹I am the rose of Sharon, and the lily of the valleys.
²As the lily among thorns, so is my love among the daughters.
³As the apple tree among the trees of the wood, so is my
     beloved among the sons.
I sat down under his shadow with great delight, and his fruit
     was sweet to my taste.
⁴He brought me to the banqueting house, and his banner over
     me was love.
⁵Stay me with flagons, comfort me with apples: for I am sick
     of love.
⁶His left hand is under my head, and his right hand doth
     embrace me.
⁷I charge you, O ye daughters of Jerusalem, by the roes, and
     by the hinds of the field,
that ye stir not up, nor awake my love, till he please.
         (Song of Solomon 2:1-7, KJV)

Let's begin our study of chapter 2 with verse 3: "As the apple tree among the trees of the wood, so is my beloved among the sons. I sat down under his shadow with great delight, and his fruit was sweet to my taste." Song of Solomon 2 can help women respond to the question, "Do you have it made in the shade?"

Chapter 2 opens with words from the Shulammite woman, who is loved by King Solomon. They have a wonderful marital relationship at this point. Look at what the woman thinks about herself: "I am the rose of Sharon, and the lily of the valleys." This denotes self-acceptance and self-appreciation on her part. If you don't appreciate yourself, nobody else is going to appreciate you, either. If you don't love yourself, nobody else is going to love you. If you can't live with yourself, then how do you expect anybody else to live with you?

Self-Appreciation

The Shulammite woman shows self-acceptance and self-appreciation even before anybody else speaks to her. She is saying, "This is what I think about myself. I am the rose of Sharon." When she mentions the rose of Sharon, I believe she's referring to maturity—a requirement for a good marriage. She does not say, "I am the bud of Sharon." She says, "I've already blossomed; I'm the rose of Sharon." Too often young people want to get married before they've blossomed; while they're still budding, they insist they are ready. Subsequently, they enter marriage prematurely, and their budding immaturity damages their relationships, even if they are basically right for each other. Anyone thinking about marriage needs to ask himself or herself: "Is this the right time? Have I matured enough to make a lifetime commitment?" I believe that marrying prematurely is the reason so many marriages end within four years. Immaturity makes it difficult to keep the marriage alive. Patiently waiting for the right time to marry allows the individuals and the relationship to grow to maturity, which will make the marriage strong from the very start.

My fourth son, K. J., was born two months early with premature lung disease. Because the lungs are the last organs to develop, his hadn't had time to finish growing. He came out of the womb breathing on his own, but then his lungs collapsed. The medical staff put K. J. in an incubator and fed him through a feeding tube in his nose that went down into his stomach. They had to use needles and all sorts of artificial means to sustain his life because he got here prematurely. Had he stayed in the womb a little longer, such artificial means would not have been necessary to keep him going.

Likewise, this is what happens to many relationships. Instead of waiting for them to develop naturally over time, the couple rushes into marriage, and then they have to keep looking for artificial things outside of themselves to keep the relationship alive.

I'm going to show you why maturity is so important. The woman in Song of Solomon calls herself the rose of Sharon. Sharon was a real geographic place located between Mount Carmel and Joppa in Israel in a very fertile plains area. The pasture land was so abundant that David often grazed his herds there. Grasses, plants, and wild-flowers grew abundantly in the uncultivated areas. The Beloved is saying that she is one of the predominant flowers in a smooth place, but she also declares, "I'm the lily of the valleys." There will be mountains or high places on either side, but the valley itself is a low place. This woman recognizes that she is mature enough to remain beautiful in the low places of life.

After establishing who *she* is, the Shulammite compares her man to a tree in the forest. A forest is a dense, wooded area. Look at the different types of terrain she refers to in her speech: a smooth plain, valleys between mountains, pastoral areas where cattle can graze and wildflowers can grow, and now a dense forest. Her observations about herself, her Lover, and their relationship included allusions to varying terrain because relationships aren't lived out constantly on a level plateau.

Sometimes relationships are up, and sometimes they're down. Sometimes you're traveling on smooth roads; at other times you're struggling through rough terrain. Sometimes you can see a long distance away; other times you can't see the trees for the forest. Relationships have to be able to survive throughout many different circumstances. Unless you're mature enough to understand this, you may fall into the naïve trap of believing that you are different from everybody else. You may think that because you love each other, you will always travel together on smooth ground.

It takes maturity to understand that in our relationships, some-times we're healthy, and sometimes we're sick; sometimes we've got some stuff, sometimes we've got no stuff, but no matter what happens, we've got to stick together. Look again at the "lily of the valleys" image, a sign of purity and beauty. The Beloved is saying, "No matter how down the situation gets, I'm going to remain pure. No matter how deep a valley our relationship might have to go through, no matter how difficult the terrain is to travel, I'm going to be a lily. My thoughts will be pure and my disposition beautiful.

Even if my situation gets ugly, I don't have to." Many of us are purified during our mountaintop experiences, but we become perverted when we encounter the valleys. Your situation, however, does not have to determine your disposition.

Notice that this woman does not say, "I am the Lily of the Valley." Even though we speak of Christ being the Rose of Sharon and the Lily of the Valley, the Beloved says she is the lily of the *valleys*. Most people have to go through more than one valley in the course of their lives. There's more than one thing that can get you down, no matter how holy or mature you may be. Your family, friends, children, marriage, job, or money (or lack thereof) can get you down. But the Beloved says, "My situation may get ugly, but no matter how down it is, I'm not going to let my disposition get ugly. I am the lily of the valleys."

Spousal Appreciation

Now watch what her husband tells us: "She's absolutely right. Not only is she like a lily in the valleys, but she is a lily even among thorns." Besides showing self-acceptance and an appreciation for herself, she is also receiving spousal appreciation. Her husband says, "I see even more in you than you see in yourself. You see yourself as the lily of the valleys, but when I compare you to other women, you are like a lily among thorns."

One of my friends, who is a pastor of a great church in the Midwest, likes to tell his congregation, "You are not your spouse's first choice for a mate. He or she was thinking about somebody else, wanting somebody else, before getting you." He continues, "Now you know that's true because *you* wanted somebody else before you chose the person you got, too. Your spouse wasn't your first choice, either."

So, in our text, the Lover is saying, "I have had experiences with other women in the past. I have gotten to know other women. But when I compare you to the others, they become like thorns in comparison to you. There is nothing about them that attracts me as I am attracted to you. I do not see in anyone else what I see in you." He is letting her know he appreciates her for who she is, and she replies, "I see *you* as an apple tree in the woods." They are expressing their appreciation for each other. They are praising each other, pointing out the good they see in each other.

Look, also, at what specifically they say about each other. He says to her, "You are a lily." She says to him, "You are an apple tree." Think about that. They both recognize how they are different from each other. Yet, he is not trying to make her into what he is, and she is not trying to make him into what she is. They appreciate their differences and value each other for the unique ways God made them. We need to learn from that. Why? Because too many of us try to usurp God's authority and recreate other people into our own images. We take people from what they already are, and then we try to make them into what we want them to be. Nevertheless, God didn't create us in each other's images, but in *His* image. Moreover, He made us different from each other for good reasons.

In his book, *Before You Say "I Do,"* Norman Wright points out that it is our differences which first attract us to other people. We appreciate and value aspects of others that we don't see in ourselves: their gifts, their ways of thinking, and their ways of doing things. After the marriage, however, once we're living with these differences constantly, such things can go from attractions to irritations. Instead of being fascinated because a spouse is so different from us, we become angry because he or she is so different.

Yet, mature lovers appreciate the value of differences. My wife and I have a healthy relationship. We've been married for twenty years, we have four sons, and we support each other in everything we do. But Sharon and I are as different as night and day. She likes to stay in bed late; I get up at five o'clock in the morning. She is a very patient person; I'm very impatient. She likes to plan for events months in advance; I'm very impulsive and can do anything on the spur of the moment. She likes to sit at home and even do nothing; I like being out and going places. We are so very different, but we try to appreciate each other's differences and not make each other change. Also, we know the value of our differences. For instance, Sharon likes to save money; I like to spend money. If God hadn't put us together, she would be sitting on a stack of money, and I'd be broke with a bunch of junk. God put us together to balance each other out.

It took Sharon and me a while to learn this lesson and stop trying to change each other. When you try to change somebody, you're trying to make them into someone God never intended them to be. If you succeed, you may think it's an improvement, but it's really imprisonment. Sharon *likes* to sit at home and do nothing. If I dragged her everywhere and demanded that she be the life of every party, and she cooperated with me just so I would leave her alone, I would have her in bondage. On the other hand, if she tried to force me to stay home night after night, that would be imprisonment for me. We have to accept *and appreciate* spousal differences; that's the reason God put us together in the first place. He wants the two to become one.

Moving on in our text, the woman says, "You are like an apple tree in the woods." Incidentally, what is called an apple tree in translation is more likely a citron or apricot tree. I don't go into a forest often, but I've never seen a fruit tree like that in the middle of the woods. Fruit trees are normally found in cultivated orchards, not in the forest. What she's talking about here is her Lover's distinctiveness in his location. You may be in a location where other trees are barren, but in spite of that, you are producing. You're not using your location or condition as an excuse for lack of production. Even when other trees around you are fruitless, somehow you have figured out a way to produce fruit, which is truly an amazing occurrence. It's one thing to produce fruit in an orchard where you've been strategically planted to get the proper amount of sunlight and water, cultivated, pruned, and cared for. But if you are producing citrus fruit in the woods, where no other tree is doing it, *that* is a miraculous feat.

It's easy to be a Christian at church where everyone works together to produce fruit. But can you be a Christian in an environment in which there are no other Christians? Can you continue to be productive and fruitful while working at the same job, attending the same school, or living in the same neighborhood as others who are not producing? That's what this Shulammite woman is saying about her husband.

Too many of us are more like water than fruit trees in the forest. Ezekiel 21:7 (KJV) talks about people so fearful that their knees are "weak as water." Do you know what that means? Water alone can't hold anything up. It doesn't even have a shape of its own; instead, it takes on the shape of its environment. If you have an oval sink in your bathroom, the water you run into it becomes oval. If you have a square sink in your kitchen, the water in it becomes square. When you run water into a rectangular bathtub, the water takes on that shape. If you spill water on the floor, the water just spreads out and lies flat.

Some of us are as weak as water. When we go to church, we act churchly. When we're with hellish people, we're hellish. If our friends are drinking or smoking weed, so are we. If others talk about sex as casual recreation, we do too. Weak as water, we let our environment determine what we look like and how we act. We need some strong believers who can produce fruit even in a barren environment.

After likening her lover to a fruit tree in the forest, the Beloved says, "I sat down under his shadow." She's sitting in the shade of his protection. Notice that she is hooking up with a tree, not a bush. To come under a bush, she would have to lower herself down. Under a tree, she can stand up straight, strong, and tall. Remember chapter 1, when this woman's brothers exposed her to the elements until she got burned? Now, she has found a brother who will protect her from being burned. She feels comfortable and safe, allowing him to cover her.

Just as the sun is the source of light and life for a tree, so also is the Son of God the source of power for life for each human being. You are probably familiar with 1 John 5:12: "He who has the Son has life; he who does not have the Son of God does not have life." If your man is not standing in the Son, he cannot protect you, because he has no light himself. Now, I love my wife. When she comes under me and gets in my shadow for protection, I intend to keep her from being burned, but the only way I can do that is by keeping a right relationship with the Son. The moment I fall into ungodliness, sin, unrighteousness, fornication, or adultery, I expose my woman to harm. I cannot say, "I'm grown up. I can do what I want to do; it's nobody's business but my own." It *is* somebody's business! Because my wife is in my shadow, I'm going to leave her exposed if I fall into sin. Not only is my wife in my shadow, but my kids are, too, along with all the folks in my congregation. So I've got to keep standing and maintain a right relationship with the Son!

You may think you have it made in the shade because of the neighborhood you live in, the nice house you've got, the school you graduated from, the money you make, or the position you hold. If you do have it made in the shade, however, it's really because the generations before us stood in the Son. Our parents, grandparents, and ancestors stood in the Son. They stood for what was right and holy, also standing against racism, sexism, and social injustice. Just as others provided shade for us, should we not provide shade for the generation following behind us? Men, you need to stand strong in the Son by getting in a right relationship with Him, so that your woman, your children, and others can find protection under your shadow.

Look at the way this woman said, "I'm going to sit in his shadow. I'm coming under my tree. I'm going to sit in the shade of my husband." He didn't have to tell her, "The Bible says you've got to submit to me." No, all he had to do was stand in the Son, and she *wanted* to come to him for comfort and protection. If a man keeps falling into messes and getting away from the source of light and life, why should he expect any woman to seek refuge in his shadow? He doesn't even have a shadow or a place of protection to offer anyone. If he has nothing to offer his woman, he shouldn't be upset with her because she doesn't want to come under him.

Shade of Protection

Now look at verse 3 again: "I sat down under his shadow with great delight, and his fruit was sweet to my taste." She wanted more than just the shade of his protection. What she also desired was to taste his fruit—to make love. We've already observed that when people are in love, they use all of their senses to express it. But watch how she personalizes this: "His fruit is sweet to *my* taste." She isn't tasting the fruit of any other man, and her man's fruit doesn't have to satisfy the taste of any other woman. Taste is distinctive; it's individual and personal. There are people who like the sweetness of juice made from oranges, while others prefer the refreshing taste

84

of freshly squeezed lemonade. Don't tell yourself that your spouse would enjoy sex more if you could be like somebody else; just be the person God has made you to be. If He created you to be a grapefruit tree, don't try to be an apple tree. Be who you are.

Also, make sure you have a taste for your own spouse's fruit. Remember, the Shulammite woman didn't go to one tree for shade and another for fruit: she got satisfaction from the fruit of the tree she was under. Some people go to one tree for protection, but another tree for provisions; to one tree for conversation, but another tree for affection. They are trying to find multiple trees to meet single needs, rather than finding a single tree to meet multiple needs. It's dangerous to eat from the wrong tree: just ask Adam and Eve! God told them they could eat from every tree in the garden except one. He didn't give them everything, but He gave them everything that they needed. In spite of that, they wanted the one thing God said they couldn't have. They thought they were missing out on something—that God was keeping something from them—and they knew their needs better than He did. We're no smarter than they were if we focus only on the things we can't have, convince ourselves that we're missing out on something, believe that we know our needs better than God does, and insist on taking what He hasn't given us. You will find everything you need in the spouse God gave you—in that one tree.

Now, I want to point something out to the brothers reading this. Look again at the woman's words: "I sat down under his shadow with great delight, and his fruit was sweet to my taste." The fruit became sweet to her taste *after* she delighted in sitting in his shade. Her first delight was in having a man standing in the Son, under whose shadow she could find comfort and protection. Some brothers think they are so great in bed that getting their women into bed should be their primary focus. No! Her delight is not in the bed; her delight is rather what you do *before* you get her in the bed! The Beloved did not become delighted with her Lover because she enjoyed their lovemaking. She enjoyed their lovemaking because she was delighted with him. What you do outside the bed is going to determine what happens when you get into bed. Brother, if you want to be delighted in the bed, try to delight your woman outside of the bed.

Place of Celebration

Now look what happens in verse 4, after she tastes of his fruit and finds it sweet. She says, "He brought me to the banqueting house, and his banner over me was love." Another translation for the banqueting house is the "wine house." Either of them would have been a public place of celebration. They first tasted each other's fruit in private by sharing an intimate moment in which they demonstrated their love to each other. But after that, her husband took her to the banqueting house to hang out in public. Some couples keep everything about their relationship a secret. No one even knows they are together. Everything between them is private. Why doesn't he tell other people they are together? Why don't his coworkers even know he's married? Why are things always private and never public? Something's wrong with that. A brother ought to celebrate with his woman in public.

This man takes his wife to a place of celebration, and then he lifts up a banner over her. He hoists a flag, so to speak. A banner usually displays words of celebration: "Happy Anniversary!" "Congratulations!" "Welcome!" A flag is a sign of allegiance—a symbol of commitment and loyalty. The Lover is saying, "I am committed to this woman. My allegiance, my devotion, and my faithfulness is to her. I want everybody to know that." His banner read, "I love her." He made sure that everybody knew it. We need to display public signs to show others what we have in private.

When I make love to my wife in private, it's because I want *her* to know that I love her. But in public, I show love to her because I want *other* people to know I love her. My banner, the symbol I use to let the world know I belong to her, is the wedding ring I've been wearing for twenty years. It's a pretty big ring that is easy for others to see. I wear this ring for two reasons. The first is that I want it publicly known that I am off the market. Any sister who notices me will also notice my ring and know that I'm not available. I want everybody to know that I'm already taken; I'm already committed; I'm in my marriage relationship for life.

The second reason I wear the ring is to remind *myself* that I'm married. If some woman doesn't see my ring, realize what it means to me, or simply disregards it, *I* still see it and know what it means, and honor what it stands for. It's a symbol...a sign...a flag. It's a banner that says to one person and to her alone, "I love you."

Right after our couple has gone to the banqueting house where the Lover has made it publicly known that he is committed to his Beloved, they end up back in the bed! She says to him in verse 5, "Stay me with flagons [or raisins], comfort me with apples: for I am sick of love", that is, lovesick. She's overwhelmed by his expression of love to her: "When you walked into that banquet house—that public place for celebration—and threw up a sign to let all those sisters and brothers know that you are mine, that did something to me. I'm lovesick. I'm so overwhelmed that I'm weak. Give me some raisins to strengthen me; give me some fruit to sustain me. I am faint with love." Now, she's not telling him to go out to the market and buy her some raisins and apples. She's talking about *his* fruit again. She wants him to make love to her.

In the next verse, she says, "His left hand is under my head, and his right hand doth embrace me." Even if you doubt that all the symbolic terms found in this chapter are sexual references, *this* should be clear. He put his hand under her head, placed the other arm around her, and began to embrace her. The only way he could have his hand under her head would be if she was lying on her back. If she were standing up, he could put his hand *behind* her head, but not *under* her head. So they are lying in bed, and he is beginning to make love to her. He is beginning to offer her more of his fruit.

Someone might ask, "Didn't she just eat in verse 3?" Folks, there are things you have to keep doing in every other verse if you want to sustain love! I put gas in my car last week, but if I'm going to keep it rolling, I've got to put in more this week. I took a bath this afternoon, but that's not going to keep me clean for the rest of the month. I ate today at 1:30, but I'll need more food by the evening. Likewise, to sustain a marriage, you have to keep showing affection, engaging in conversation, expressing the passion, and sharing the fruit.

Sleep in Satisfaction

If you are still having trouble believing that the fruit here is symbolic of sex, check out verse 7. Look what happens after the man has embraced his woman and shared his fruit with her again. He is asleep! Many a sister gets disturbed when, after sex, her husband goes to sleep. She's tempted to wake him up and yell at him, "You're sleeping! How can you say you love me and then just fall asleep? Wake up and answer me!" Sister, for a man, falling asleep after sex is a sign of deep satisfaction. It's normal. His sleep indicates that you just satisfied him. Every time you finish having sex, if he gets up and starts working out, working on his car, or mowing the grass, he's not really satisfied. He'd rather that you put him to sleep.

Now, while her husband is sleeping, the woman goes to the daughters of Jerusalem, and says in verse 7, "I charge you, O ye daughters of Jerusalem… that ye stir not up, nor awake my love, till he please." She's telling them not to disturb their marriage—that her husband is satisfied in their relationship, resting in their love. Women are attracted to affection. The more affectionate a man is to his woman, the more attractive he becomes to her. The man in this passage was so attentive to his wife that other women took notice. They saw the way he carried on conversations with her, the way he provided her with protection and comfort, the way he celebrated her in public, and the way he expressed his affection to her. It wasn't just his wife who found all of this attractive.

Notice also that this woman knows what's going on and determines that she isn't going to have other women messing with her man. Her husband is so in love with his wife that he doesn't even realize how other women are attracted to him. But *she* does, and quickly warns the others not to disturb their marriage—to leave her man alone. These women aren't prostitutes—they're good, godly women; the daughters of Jerusalem; the daughters of the Holy City; the women who have relationships with God. Actually, the prostitutes and immoral women may pose the least danger to a Christian marriage because they aren't looking for "religious" men—the ones who are standing in the Son. But Christian women—the ones you'd least suspect of having designs on your man—may find him extremely attractive. So, like the Shulammite woman, you may need to set them straight and let them know that your man is already taken.

If you're one of the "daughters of Jerusalem," you need to realize that anytime you try to get a man who doesn't belong to you, you are just putting yourself in a situation to be hurt. A woman in North Carolina recently sued a fertility clinic for over $400,000 because they had inseminated her with "bad sperm." When she went to the clinic to be inseminated, they gave her sperm that was two days old, left over from a procedure they had done with another woman. When they put that old sperm in her, she got sick, had complications, and ended up suing them. She got sick and was hurt because she got some sperm from a man who was never intended for her. Whenever you try to get something from a man who isn't yours, you're going to get hurt.

I wish every woman could understand that God has somebody for you—a man who will love you the way you're supposed to be loved. You don't have to go after anyone else's man. But the single women reading this may say, "I don't have a tree right now. I don't have an apple tree or a citron tree. I don't have shade, comfort, or provision. How am I going to stay covered? How am I going to stay protected?" Well, the Apostle Peter tells us about another tree, a tree out on Calvary's hill, where Jesus died for you and me. Instead of spending all your life trying to find some man who can be the right tree for you, why don't you go to *that* tree? The Person who died there offers salvation, regeneration, forgiveness, love, comfort, joy, and peace. He offers a second chance. Everyone can find protection and comfort under that tree, and you will find yourself made in the shade.

Chapter 6

Reconcilable Irreconcilable Differences

⁸ Listen! My lover!
Look! Here he comes,
leaping across the mountains,
bounding over the hills.
⁹ My lover is like a gazelle or a young stag.
Look! There he stands behind our wall,
gazing through the windows,
peering through the lattice.
¹⁰ My lover spoke and said to me,
"Arise, my darling,
my beautiful one, and come with me.
¹¹ See! The winter is past;
the rains are over and gone.
¹² Flowers appear on the earth;
the season of singing has come,
the cooing of doves
is heard in our land.
¹³ The fig tree forms its early fruit;
the blossoming vines spread their fragrance.
Arise, come, my darling;
my beautiful one, come with me."
¹⁴ My dove in the clefts of the rock,
in the hiding places on the mountainside,
show me your face,
let me hear your voice;
for your voice is sweet,

and your face is lovely.
¹⁵ Catch for us the foxes,
the little foxes that ruin
the vineyards,
our vineyards that are in bloom.
¹⁶ My lover is mine and I am his;
he browses among the lilies.
¹⁷ Until the day breaks
and the shadows flee, turn,
my lover, and be like a gazelle
or like a young stag
on the rugged hills.
                    (Song of Songs 2:8-17, NIV)

In Pennsylvania, a couple had the first argument of their married life during their wedding reception. This was supposed to be the happiest day of their lives and a beautiful start to their marriage. They had stood at the altar and made vows to each other… "to have and to hold from this day forward, for better or for worse, for richer or for poorer, in sickness and in health, to love and to cherish as long as they both shall live." But during the reception—right after making those beautiful promises to each other—they began to argue about something. By the time they got home, it had escalated and gotten way out of hand. Apparently believing there was no way they could resolve this issue, the man pulled out a gun, shot his bride dead, and then shot and killed himself. He destroyed everything that they had because he didn't think that their differences could be resolved.

Hopefully, you would never consider picking up a gun to kill your spouse, but there are other ways to destroy a marriage. Before we talk about that, though, I'd like to remind you of the good news: God was in Christ, reconciling the world unto Himself. By example, He taught us that He is a God of reconciliation. So, no matter how bad it looks, or no matter how dead it looks, our God can heal your marriage. Our God can raise your marriage from the dead. Moreover, God can help your marriage not just to survive, but to thrive.

One of society's biggest problems today is the breakdown of the family, which I believe expresses itself in the issues and problems we see in our community and throughout our nation. So many of the challenges we see in our society—children in trouble, drug and alcohol abuse, sexual promiscuity, violence, and murder—come as a result of the breakdown of the family. The family is the glue that holds society together. If the glue itself does not stick, what do we expect to become of our society?

Statistics say that more than fifty percent—more than half—of marriages in America end in divorce, usually within the first four years. We don't really even give our marriages enough time to work through the inevitable issues that surface when two individuals become one. Divorce is a major problem for our society, and it has even entered our churches as well. People offer up excuses such as these: "I had to get a divorce because my partner was unfaithful. I had to get a divorce because my spouse wasn't making any contribution to the home. I had to get a divorce because of abandonment. I had to get a divorce because I just couldn't take it any longer." It's just one excuse after another.

Malachi 2:16 tells us that God hates divorce, so we know that divorce is not of God. God's plan is for every husband and wife to stay together until they're parted by death. But I'm not bringing this up to make those of you who have gone through a divorce to feel guilty. Guilt is designed to bring you to repentance. So, if you've gotten a divorce at some point in your life, and you've repented of that, God has forgiven you. God's not declaring you guilty anymore, so you shouldn't feel guilty either. What I'm trying to do is make sure that you don't go that same route again, so you'll avoid making the same mistake twice. Divorce is not of God.

One common reason given today for divorce is irreconcilable differences. The couple believes that whatever they're going through or whatever differences are between them cannot be reconciled. I don't understand how a believer can call *anything* irreconcilable when the Bible talks so much about reconciliation. With everything we did to offend God, all the sin we've committed, all the ungodliness we've been involved in, and as much as we've fallen short of the glory of God, He was still able to reconcile us to Himself. What makes you think He doesn't have the power to reconcile us to each other? No matter how bad it may look in our lives, we serve a God who majors in reconciliation.

Wall of Tension

In our passage, let's continue to look at what is happening between Solomon and the Shulammite woman. Scholars debate whether they are married or single here, but I want to look at this in terms of marriage. I want us to understand how important the family is, along with how important it is for a husband and wife to stay together. Your staying together will bless not only the two of you, but also your family, your church, and your community.

As we take up the story of the Lover and his Beloved in these verses from chapter 2, we see that a wall has been erected between this man and woman. Some kind of barrier, or tension, has come between them. They still love and care for each other, but the barrier between them keeps them from connecting with each other. This is the same couple who showed all that passion, compassion, affection, and conversation—"Where are you going to be?" "Follow me down to the shepherd's tent." This is the same couple whose bed was alive and who found delight in being together, both privately and publicly. But now a wall has been built between them. It doesn't matter how good everything is going in your marriage. Every now and then something's going to raise a barrier in your relationship. It doesn't matter how sweet things are now; every now and then something sour is going to happen. There are times in all relationships when tension comes and walls rise up between you and the one you love.

Verse 8 starts off with the Shulammite woman talking about how her Lover is "leaping across the mountains, bounding over the hills," so some readers may think everything must be okay. Anyone who is behaving like that must be all right. Yet, not everyone leaps and jumps for joy. Think about where he is doing this: he's going through the mountains and the hills. In the Bible, mountains and hills are often used to describe times of difficulty and hardship.

Look at the mountains other people of God had to face. It was on Mount Moriah that God asked Abraham to sacrifice his beloved son Isaac. Think of the pain and the horror he went through in making that decision. I can't even imagine how his heart must have been breaking as he walked with his young son up that mountain.

Moses had his trial on Mount Horeb (also known as Mount Sinai). We may look at his mountaintop experience and only remember that this was where God gave him the Ten Commandments. But we can't forget that this was also the place where Moses spent forty days and nights fasting, without even a morsel of bread or a sip of water. It was also here that he saw God's wrath kindled against His people because they were down at the foot of the mountain committing adultery against God with a golden calf. Think of how Moses must have felt descending this mountain, knowing he would have to face a rebellious and stubborn people who had so lost sight of God that, with their own hands, they created an idol to take His place.

It was on Mount Carmel that Elijah had to face the fact that he was the only prophet who had remained faithful to God, even when all of Israel had turned aside to listen to the prophets of Baal. We probably recall the miracle that took place on Mount Carmel, as God responded to Elijah's prayer by sending fire to burn up the sacrifice and even the water around it, while the 450 prophets of Baal called in vain on their god to send fire. But we need to remember how Elijah felt that day as he stood there—one man speaking the truth in the midst of a sinful people.

Then there was Jesus' mountain: Mount Calvary. I don't have to remind you of what happened there or convince you of the suffering He endured on *His* mountain as He hung on a cross with nails in His hands and spikes in His feet, forsaken by His friends, enduring agony and death for your sins and mine. Mountains depict hardship.

Here in the Song of Solomon, the Lover is leaping and jumping through the mountains, but these are mountains of hardship. Mountains and hills are high. You can experience hardships in high places. Some people think that if they can just get to a certain level of education, this next promotion, or a certain height, there will be no more hardships in their lives. But it doesn't matter how high you go in life; you are still going to have to deal with some difficult circumstance.

The hardship the man in our text experiences is coming from the woman he loves. Can you imagine? You get to the heights you always wanted to achieve; you get the degree you always wanted; you're making the money you always wanted to make; you've got the house you always wanted to live in; you've got the respect of the community that you wanted people to give you. But in spite of all that you now have, you still have hardship. Worse yet, your hardship is not coming from those *outside* your house; it is coming from the person you live with *in* your house.

We can learn a lesson from the way this man handled his hardship. He became like a gazelle or a young stag by learning how to leap and bound across the mountains of difficulty he was facing. You have to learn how to do that—leap and jump, even in the midst of the worst difficulties. The Bible says in Habakkuk 3:19: "The Sovereign Lord is my strength; he makes my feet like the feet of a deer, he enables me to go on the heights." Out of all of the animals he could have likened our feet to, Habakkuk chose the deer. Deer have neither paws nor claws; they have hooves that are strong and solid enough to handle different terrain. If predators chase after deer, they can run up into the mountains, climb to the heights, and maneuver over terrain too difficult for their enemies.

Deer can use their feet not only to run, but to jump, so they can get over obstacles in their way. Likewise, God will give you feet like a deer so you can leap and jump over the difficulties in your life. You may have a lot that you need to get over. Someone has wronged you, and you need to get over it. Someone has said something that offended you, and you need to get over it. Someone has lied to you, and you need to get over it. Someone has hurt you deeply, and you need to get over it. None of that should have ever happened. That person should never have treated you like that, but get over it. Having feet like a deer helps you to get over rough situations.

The man, however, isn't shown jumping over the wall between him and his Beloved. Even though they could see each other through the wall, they still could not reach each other. The woman says in verse 9: "…Look! There he stands behind our wall, gazing through the windows, peering through the lattice." She didn't say he was standing behind *his* wall or *her* wall. She said, "My man is standing behind *our* wall." Both of them contributed to the construction of this wall. That's important to notice, because a lot of us keep thinking, "This isn't *my* wall that's between us. This wall would not be here if my spouse hadn't said that, or done that, or behaved like that. If my spouse hadn't lied like that… or been unfaithful to me… or blown our money… or hurt me so badly… we wouldn't have this wall between us. It's not *my* wall." But the woman in our text says, "No, this isn't just *his* wall; it's *our* wall. I've helped to construct this wall, too."

When I have counseled couples, I usually would start by asking both of them, "What's going on in the relationship?" The wife would say, "Well, he did this. And, he did that. He went here. And, he said that. He shouldn't have done that. He stayed out too late. He cussed. He…." "Okay," I would interrupt, and then I would turn to the husband. He would begin, "She did this. She said that. She shouldn't have done what she did. She never…."

Then I would ask them individually, "What have *you* done to bring on the demise of this relationship? What is your contribution to the destruction of this marriage?" Suddenly, there would be dead silence. People can go on and on describing the other person's faults and failures, but rarely can think of anything they did themselves to damage the relationship. Invariably, both people have contributed to building the wall that stands between them, but strangely, each person is reluctant to admit any fault.

Notice, however, that even though there is a wall described in our text, that same wall has windows in it. The woman's Lover was standing on the other side of the wall, looking through the windows. Anytime you see windows, you know there are opportunities. You may be standing on one side of a wall, looking at your husband or wife—that person who means so much to you—on the other side. You say, "I see my husband, but I can't reach him"; "I see my wife, but I can't feel her"; or, "I see my spouse, but I just can't understand that person anymore." You may think, "…therefore, it's over. The wall is between us. It's insurmountable. My spouse is on one side, and I'm on the other. It's over; we're not together anymore." But wait! Don't forget about those windows of opportunity!

Did you ever notice that there was only one window—and only one door—in Noah's ark? In Genesis 6:16 (KJV), God instructed Noah to put in one door, and put one window up high in the ark: "A window shalt thou make to the ark, and in a cubit shalt thou finish it above; and the door of the ark shalt thou set in the side thereof; with lower, second, and third stories shalt thou make it." I knew what the door was for: everyone who was to be saved, animal or human, had to come through the one door of the ark. This was symbolic of Jesus, who said, in John 10:7, 9 (KJV): "Verily, verily, I say unto you, I am the door of the sheep....I am the door: by me if any man enter in, he shall be saved, and shall go in and out, and find pasture."

At first, I didn't know what the window was for. The window was there because, if you're going to be floating in a storm for forty days and forty nights, every now and then you're going to want to look out. God understood that and gave them a window, but He had Noah put it up high above them. This meant that anytime they looked out, they had to look up. They couldn't focus on how bad their circumstances were; instead, they had to keep looking up to heaven. Their window looked out on their future possibilities, not on their present difficulties. That's the same kind of window we should keep open in our relationships.

What was the wall between the Song of Solomon couple? The text doesn't tell us, and I'm glad it doesn't. If it had said this was a wall of infidelity, you would say, "Well, that doesn't have anything to do with me." If the text said, "It's a wall of deception," you would say, "Well, we haven't been lying to each other." If the text described a wall that arose because of spending differences, you might say, "Well, we've got plenty of money; that doesn't relate to us." Because the text doesn't tell us what the wall actually was, we can call it "whatever is coming between you and that other person in your life." The same goes for the window of opportunity. Whatever it looked like for them, you can look through the same window of opportunity when you address your own relationship issue.

Wall of Protection

Why do we build these walls between ourselves and others? I think we often erect them for our own protection. If someone hurt us once, we don't want to let that person do it again, so we put up a wall to keep him or her from getting to us. What's crazy about the situation in our text is that the woman recognizes the wall between them. She knows it is separating them, but she is still calling him her lover! He's not just any lover; she repeatedly calls him, "*my lover.*" Even though she still wants to be identified with him, she isn't talking about getting rid of the wall. She desires to continue with the relationship, but without the risk of pain. She wants to go through the rest of life without being hurt.

She can forget about that, and so can you. Every action that brings high returns—such as love—requires a high risk. Once, when the disciples had been fishing all night without any success, Jesus told them to go out into the deep water and cast their nets. It didn't make any sense to Peter because they had already *been* working hard all night and hadn't caught anything. Yet, he took the risk of listening to Jesus and went back into the deep water, and they filled two boats so full of fish that they could barely get them back to shore. When you're willing to take the risk, you have the possibility of a higher return.

Someone reading this, however, may have decided that it just isn't worth the risk. But, let me tell you something. After twenty years of marriage, I've learned that whenever you've got high risk, there will also be high returns that go along with it. Thank God for healthy relationships and healthy marriages. If fifty percent of marriages are falling apart, guess what? The other fifty percent of couples are staying together. Fifty percent may not be going anywhere, but the other fifty percent have it going on. If I myself had not taken the high risk of entering and maintaining a relationship, I would not have such a wonderful marriage, and I would not have my four sons: J. Allen, Jordan, Jalon, and K. J. Thank God, I took the high risk, because I'm really enjoying the high returns!

"But," you say, "you don't understand what he did to me." "You don't know what she said, and how she acted." "I've never felt pain like that before." So, now you've put up this wall of protection, which really is just a wall of division. What you were using to try to protect yourself has now become the issue of the division in your home. You thought the wall was going to be for your protection, but it has just turned into a barrier of isolation. You're all by yourself, because the moment you shut your spouse out, you shut yourself in. It has become not a wall of protection, but a wall of dejection.

Take another look at the woman in our text. She's down and depressed. Her man said to her twice, "Arise, my darling, my beautiful one, and come with me.... Arise, come, my darling; my beautiful one, come with me." She had to be down, or he wouldn't be telling her to get up. If she had been in the same joyful frame of mind as she was earlier, he would never have had to ask twice. Before then, *she* was the one initiating their togetherness, eager to be with her Lover. Now, he's asking her twice, and she's still not responding. She has locked him out — and herself in.

Notice that *he* isn't locked in. He's out leaping and jumping. While you're still at home, alone, your spouse may be out leaping and jumping. I know there is no hurt like family hurt! There is no pain like heart pain! If you love and care for somebody who has hurt you, there is no other pain like that. But, I tell you, if that other person is out skipping and jumping, you'd better get off your couch, quit drowning your sorrow in soap operas and chocolate, and start leaping and jumping yourself!

Wall of Division

For the Beloved, a barrier of protection had become a division. She and her husband are together, but they're not *really* together. They are in the same vicinity, but he's behind the wall. She can see him, even though he's looking through the lattice. They are in the same community, but there is no unity. He's in the vicinity, yet there is no affinity. He's close, but there's no close*ness*. You know what I mean. They are together, but they're not *together*. They are in the same home, but not of the same heart. It isn't like it used to be.

Years ago, I told my wife that I didn't want to be in a marriage where I was just trying to survive. There are enough other places where I have to just survive: my job, the community, and the world itself. I'm not going to stay in a survival mode when I go back to my own home. I want to *thrive* in my marriage, not just survive. I want to look forward to going home. I want to be excited. I'm through at work, but I'm getting ready to go home! I don't want to be together with my wife, but not be *together*. It's not enough just to be in the same house; I want to be of the same heart and the same mind with her.

We all know or know of people who have shocked everyone by getting divorced after twenty-five or thirty years of marriage. After twenty years or so, everyone thinks the couple must have a model marriage. They must know the secret of a happily married life, or how else could they have kept going so long? What we didn't know was that they had divorced each other a long time ago…just not officially. Years earlier, they psychologically, emotionally, and then sexually divorced each other. No one goes to bed happy, and suddenly gets up in the middle of the night to say, "I'm getting out of here. I'll have my attorney call you."

No, for anyone who appears to have done that, the psychological divorce had happened much earlier. Emotionally, the person had already given up on the marriage. The sex life of the marriage died much earlier. They were already divorced, but they just hadn't made the divorce public or legal—perhaps for the sake of the children, to get their financial situation straight first, because they were concerned about what people would think, or because they just kept putting off the hassle and drama that they knew a legal divorce would entail. For many years, however, they had been living with their walls of protection, which only amounted to ones of division, isolation, and rejection.

Disposition

Our text talks about the different dispositions, or the different attitudes, this couple had. Both of them went through the same situation, because it is *their* wall—not his wall, or her wall, but their wall. But even though their situation was the same, their approaches were different. She says, "Oh, he's looking through the window in our wall. He's trying to get back with me." Yet, she's not eager to let it happen. She wants to be identified with him, but she doesn't respond when he asks her to arise and go with him.

Notice what he tells her: "The winter is past; the rains are over and gone. Flowers appear on the earth; the season of singing has come, the cooing of doves is heard in our land. The fig tree forms its early fruit; the blossoming vines spread their fragrance." He's saying that the winter is past or done. It's over, and the rains are gone.

He's saying to her, "I know we have this wall, but I still love you. The winter has passed. It's spring now. Come out with me." If you enter into a marriage thinking it's always going to be sunshine and roses, romantic strolls on warm sandy beaches, and summer breezes blowing, your thinking is immature. It isn't always going to be like that. There are going to be different seasons in your relationship.

Our couple's relationship had been through a season of cold, rain, and barrenness, but now the season has changed: it isn't winter any longer. It's spring now. But if the winter is over, why is *she* still cold? That's because they had gone through the same situation, but they had different dispositions. The Lover had been the first to warm up to the new season.

Your marriage may currently be in a winter season. But no matter how cold it is right now, no matter how chilling it is, no matter how callous it is right now, the season is going to change. Just stay right there, because spring is on the way. You will experience new life in your relationship, new growth, and some new experiences. If you hang on, the warmth of summer will come, followed by the beauty of autumn, because seasons change. Unfortunately, what happens too often with us when we go through the winter season—when things are cold, nothing seems to be growing, there's a gray sky, and ice and snow make it difficult to get around—we are ready then to give up. We're ready to walk out. But the answer isn't walking out; the answer is waiting for the season to change. Right now, you may feel like Job, trapped in a seemingly endless onslaught of pain. But in the midst of his suffering, Job said, "...all the days of my appointed time will I wait, till my change come" (Job 14:14 KJV).

If, however, you're the one who still feels cold while your lover has gone on to experience new growth, you're probably wondering, "How can I be sure that the season has changed? How can I be sure he's not going to do the same thing he's already done? How can I be sure it's not going to be the same deception, the same lie—the same thing that happened in the past? When he comes back, talking about how the times have changed and how everything is going to be different now, how can I believe him?" First, you need to use those five senses we've talked about before. If it's spring, shouldn't it feel a little bit warmer? If it's spring, shouldn't you see the grass turning green again? If it's spring, shouldn't you hear the birds singing, be able to taste the ripening fruit, and smell the tree blossoms and the flowers? If the change is authentic, you ought to feel something, see something, hear something, taste something, and smell something different. If a man says he's changed but is still calling you dumb or stupid, or abusing, disrespecting, and dishonoring you, why in the world would you want to stay in that situation? If there is change, there can be reconciliation, but there can be no reconciliation without repentance.

Right now, you and your husband may have separated so that you could remove some of the pressure between you while you take time to sort things out, figure out what went wrong, and determine how you can work things out between you. Your goal should be that of reconciliation. Sometimes I have had couples in that situation come and tell me, "We've been separated, but we're going to try to get back together," or "We got divorced, but now we want to get married again, to try to make it work." My first question to these couples is always: "What has changed?" If nothing has changed, why do they think things will be different when they come back together? Doing the same things that separated them in the first place won't lead to different results the second time.

Reconciliation is wonderful: that's what we want to see happen. But in order for reconciliation to occur, there's got to be some repentance. Both parties have to repent for their contribution to the wall they constructed. Remember that repentance isn't just saying, "I'm sorry." Repentance rather implies going in a different direction, or doing things differently from the way they were done before. If one or both individuals isn't willing to repent, then more misery, another change, or another divorce, is inevitable. Reconciliation comes because of repentance.

In our text, it looks as if everything has changed, except the woman. It's only the man who is talking about everything being changed. Just because winter has passed for him, however, doesn't mean that it's passed for her. The problem in many relationships is that we always want the other person to feel like we do. If it's still winter for me, and I'm cold and chilly, I expect you to be cold and chilly too. But if I've moved on from winter to springtime, then everything seems different to me, and it's frustrating to find that you're still cold. Relationships are rarely synchronized perfectly. Our man here needs to be patient with his wife—it took him time to get through his winter, and he has to give her time to get through hers—but she has some responsibility too. She has to stop living in the past. We know that she's living in that past because winter is over, but she's still in it.

Do you know how elephants are trained? The trainers start when the elephant is a baby by putting a huge steel stake in the ground. Then, they connect the elephant's foot to a chain. The baby wants to go somewhere and tries to go, but he can only go as far as the chain will let him. The stake always keeps the elephant within its boundaries. Now when you go to the circus, you see that same baby elephant all grown up; he isn't a baby anymore. But if you notice, you'll see that he isn't being held in place by a huge chain and a stake. There is just a little bitty peg and a narrow rope around his foot, keeping the elephant in place. Obviously, he's physically strong enough to break free, so why does he stay confined? It's because of his memories of the past. Physically, he can break free, but mentally, he is thinking, "I can't get loose. I can't be free. As long as this thing is around my foot, I'm captive." Spiritually, you are able to break free from the hurt and the pain from your past, but psychologically you still have yet to overcome it. You need to stop being chained to your past, and accept the truth that God has set you free. You need to let go and move on.

Recently, I was boarding a plane, when one passenger raced up at the last second. As he approached the gate, an attendant stopped him: "You can't get on the plane with that bag. It won't fit in the overhead rack." "I've got to get on the flight," he protested. "Do I have to go back and check this?" "No," she responded, "I can check it for you right here." "Okay, I don't have a problem with that." He handed her the bag. "I need to get a destination tag for your bag so the handlers know where it's going.... Oh, I see that you already have one." "No," he said, "that's not for Indianapolis. That's for the place I just came from."

Had he neglected to mention that, or had he refused to let her take off the old tag and put on a new one, the baggage handlers would have sent his bag back to where it had come from. Likewise, you may need to get new destination tags and let the old ones go. You've got to rip up the memories of the past so that they don't keep you from moving on to your future. Your history may be all jacked up, but your destiny is in the hands of God. God is able to take you from where you've been to where you need to be.

Restoration *can* happen. There's no such thing in the kingdom of God as irreconcilable differences. God can even bring the dead back to life again. Ask Jairus' daughter, ask the widow's son, ask Lazarus, ask Jesus Himself. But if you want your marriage relationship to experience reconciliation, you've got to have some resolve of your own. Resolve in your mind that you aren't leaving or going away from the person you love. In the text, the woman sees her man. He's behind their wall because they've still got issues between them. Something is separating them, but he's still there. He's still at the house, trying to talk with her. Do you know why my wife and I have made it for twenty years? It's because twenty years ago we made a promise to each other that whatever happened, neither of us would leave. No matter how bad it gets, neither of us is getting out.

The natural response to trouble is to run away. Some of us can't keep a job because we're too quick to say, "I don't have to take that!" Also, some of us aren't raising our own kids because we ran into an issue, so we ran out on them. Some of us don't have any friends because every time there is a problem, we say, "I don't want to deal with that—or them." This is the reason why some of us are in our fourth or fifth marriages right now. But in our text the brother says, "Listen, I don't care what went down. I'm standing right here. I know we've got a wall between us right now, but I'm still here. I know we hurt each other, but I haven't gone anywhere. I know it looks bad now, but I'm still here, willing to communicate with you."

Distractions

Walls don't usually come ready-made, appearing suddenly and fully formed. They are built one small stone at a time, or one brick at a time. If we are ever going to be reconciled to each other, we have to watch out for "little" distractions that can so easily trip us up. When the enemy attacks our families, sometimes he uses small but deadly weapons. Look at verse 15: "Catch for us the foxes, the little foxes that ruin the vineyards, our vineyards that are in bloom." We've got to catch the little foxes because they come in and ruin the growing, productive, fruitful areas of our lives. Little things often lead to big things.

Think about a huge forest fire. It didn't start out big, but rather began with one little spark. If the little spark had been put out in the beginning, the big fire would not have destroyed acres and acres of trees and property. Likewise, we're vigilant in looking for big sins in our lives: adultery, infidelity, and the mismanagement of money. We're ready to deal with the big things, but we ignore the little things that come in and destroy our relationships, marriages, and families—things such as apathy, taking someone for granted, ingratitude, inattention, or a lack of caring. It's the little things, too, that can keep a relationship strong. For instance, it's good to say "good morning" to the one you live with. How about saying "good-night"? Every now and then, ask them how they are doing: "Is everything okay? How was your day?" Send some flowers or a card once in a while. Call sometime during the day. Say, "I love you." Let's face it: it's the little things that are messing us up!

Reconciliation

The Lover continues to try to get back together with his woman. Look at the text again: she is in the cleft of the rock. Throughout the Bible, the Lord is referred to as our Rock. First Corinthians 10:4 makes it very clear: "...for they drank from the spiritual rock that accompanied them, and that rock was Christ." The woman is in the cleft of the Rock, hiding in God. If you ever want to have reconciliation in order to start over, you're going to have to begin by abiding in the Lord. The woman may have known about the clefts of the Rock if she knew about Moses.

In Exodus 33, we find Moses needing some encouragement from God because he is feeling overwhelmed by the responsibility of leading the people of Israel. He is especially afraid that God's presence might not stay with them, and they would be all alone amidst their enemies. In essence, Moses says, "God, we are supposed to be friends. Let me see Your face, and that will be all the encouragement I need to lead these people." God answered, "Moses, I love you, but you can't see Me face-to-face. No man can see My face and live. What I can do, Moses, is put you in the cleft of the rock. I'm going to pass by, but I'll shade your eyes till I pass by. Then, I'll let you look at the trail of My glory."

Just as Moses is protected in the cleft of the Rock, so also is the Shulammite woman finding her assurance and foundation in that same Rock. But remember, her Lover is leaping and bounding over the mountains. He's saying, "I want you to come out and go with me." She's saying, "No, you've got to come down, and get in with me." They love each other, but they can't work this thing out. Do you know why they can't work it out? Because both of them are right, and both of them are wrong. Anybody who's been in a relationship for longer than twenty-four hours knows exactly what I'm talking about.

He's right that it's good to be on the mountaintops and in the hills; elevation is a good thing. He's saying, "Listen, baby; just come on out of there, and come up here with me. You can hear the birds better, the grass grows taller, there is more fruit growing here, and even the flowers smell better." Today, he might say, "Baby, come on out! Up here they've got four-car garages, custom homes, and tailor-made suits. Up here everybody has two or three vehicles. Baby, you need to be elevated."

Some of us think that as long as we're secure in Jesus, we don't need anything else. Yes, we do. We need a house, a car, money, a job, somebody to love us, and friends. Do you think that when we're broke, lonely, and sad, that we are automatically blessed? Do you believe that a long face is a sign of holiness? If a long face is a sign of anything holy, then a donkey's got more religion than all of us! There's nothing holy about being broke, lonely, or sad. We need some of those physical and material things, as well as other people, in our lives. Remember, Jesus said in Mark 10:29 and 30 (KJV): "...Verily I say unto you, there is no man that hath left house, or brethren, or sisters, or father, or mother, or wife, or children, or lands, for my sake, and the gospel's, but he shall receive an hundred-fold now in this time, houses, and brethren, and sisters, and mothers, and children, and lands, with persecutions; and in the world to come eternal life." Why would Jesus talk about giving us houses and lands and putting people in our lives if this were not a good thing?

At the same time, the woman is also right, because you need the foundation of the Rock so that you can hide yourself in the cleft. She's saying, "I'm not worried about being elevated. You need to get yourself situated here on this Rock with me. You need the foundation!" He argues, "No, you need the elevation!" They're both right, and they're both wrong! It's not either/or, it's both/and! Some people are so earthly-minded that they are of no heavenly good, while others are so heavenly-minded that they are of no earthly good.

You may feel at this point in your life that your marriage is over, finished, and done. You may have already given up on the relationship, lamenting, "Our situation is different. It isn't reconcilable. We tried everything we could. There is no hope for us. It's over."

But let me tell you about a seventeen-year-old girl named Laura Hatch. In 2004, in Redmond, Washington, near Seattle, Laura disappeared while driving home from a party. After eight days, the authorities gave up the search. One of the police officers said, "I've been with the police department over twenty-four years, and I've never heard of anybody going without water and food for over eight days and remaining alive." Even her family had lost hope. Her mother said, "We had already let her go in our hearts. We believed that our daughter was dead."

What no one knew is that Laura had been in a car accident. Her car had slid two hundred feet down a ravine. Of course, as it tumbled down that long distance, the car crashed and crumbled, and Laura was thrown into the back seat where she lay motionless for eight days with a blood clot in her brain.

After eight days, everyone gave up looking. The authorities thought she had probably run away from home, while the family thought she was dead. But there was one woman, someone who had been praying for Laura and her family, who had a dream that night. She said God showed her a wooded area and an intersection that she was familiar with.

The next day, the woman and her daughter drove to the intersection. They got out of the car and looked around, but they couldn't see anything. The woman felt so strongly that her dream was from God that she climbed down into the ravine bordering the road. About one hundred feet down, she came to an embankment and had to climb over it, but she kept going. Finally, from a distance, she could barely see the wreckage of a car.

When she reached it, she found Laura, injured and dehydrated, but able to talk. A rescue team got her out and rushed her to the hospital, where she was able to make a complete recovery. One of the many miracles of this story is the fact that the blood clot she had did not spread in her brain. A doctor explained that one of the things they do when there is a blood clot in the brain is use medication to dehydrate the person so the clot doesn't expand. Laura's natural dehydration—eight days without food or water—had worked better than any chemical medication. The thing that should have killed her was exactly what God used to heal her.

In your marriages, many of you have been through experiences so devastating that they would have destroyed many people. Yet God has a way of taking what could destroy you and using it instead to heal you. Your relationship can still be saved. Ask God to show you the state of your marriage from His perspective. From where you're standing, you may not see any way out of the problems, but God can reveal to you what needs to be done. Then you've got to step out in faith. You might have to get down on your knees to get over that barrier, but you've got to resolve not to let anything keep you and your spouse apart: "I'm not going to let anything come between my woman and me! Whatever it is, I've got to climb over it! I've got to get over it! I've got to tear it up!" That's what Jesus did. There was a veil in the temple that separated us from God's presence, but when Jesus died on the cross, the curtain was torn from top to bottom, because He was saying, "I'm not letting anything come between My bride and Me!"

Chapter 7

Twisted: Looking for Love in All the Wrong Places

¹ All night long on my bed
I looked for the one my heart loves;
I looked for him but did not find him.
² I will get up now and go about the city,
through its streets and squares;
I will search for the one my heart loves.
So I looked for him but did not find him.
³ The watchmen found me
as they made their rounds in the city.
"Have you seen the one my heart loves?"
⁴ Scarcely had I passed them
when I found the one my heart loves.
I held him and would not let him go
till I had brought him to my mother's house,
to the room of the one who conceived me.
⁵ Daughters of Jerusalem, I charge you
by the gazelles and by the does of the field:
Do not arouse or awaken love
until it so desires.
        (Song of Songs 3:1-5, NIV)

There are gas stations that make you pay before pumping fuel into your tank. With every other kind of shopping, I get the product, then pay for it. But there are certain gas stations that I try to avoid because they insist I go inside, pay for a set amount of gas, then go back out and pump it. If there's any change due, I have to go in and out a second time. It's really a hassle.

One day, however, I had almost no fuel at all. My light had been on for some time. I had already been traveling around for a while, so by now I had to be riding on fumes. I had to stop at one of those pay-first gas stations. I went in, paid, and then came back out to pump my gas, only to discover that the pump was not working. I stuck the nozzle into my gas tank and pressed the handle, but nothing happened. I flipped the switch again; then I pushed the button again. I pressed the handle again, but no gasoline was coming out. Already upset that I had to go into the station once, now I had to go back in again to tell them that the pump was not working.

Here is what the attendant asked me: "Did you flip the switch? Did you push the button?" "Yeah, I did all that." ("I, at least, went to the third grade," I was thinking.) "I know how to do that. It's still not working." So he said, "Let me do some things in here." He did some things, and I went back out. The pump was still not working.

This time he came out to where I was and noticed something that I didn't. He observed that the reason there was no flow from the pump to my car was because the hose had been twisted. Even though the tank had the gasoline and I had pushed all the right buttons, I was not getting the proper flow because the hose was twisted.

Some relationships are like that. We're doing all the right things and pushing all the right buttons, but the relationship just doesn't flow. It isn't that we're expecting the impossible. Perhaps, however, we possess a mentality or disposition that is so twisted that we cannot get things to flow.

Let's pick up our Song of Solomon text at chapter 3:1: "All night long on my bed, I looked for the one my heart loves; I looked for him, but did not find him." Most scholars believe that in chapter 3, the Lover and the Shulammite woman were single and still working on their relationship. At this point, they have some division or separation between them. By the end of chapter 2, they were still apart. He wanted their relationship to go to another level, but she was in the cleft of a rock, saying, "Until the day breaks and the shadows flee, turn, my lover, and be like a gazelle or like a young stag on the rugged hills." The King James Version is more specific: "Until the day break, and the shadows flee away, turn, my beloved, and be thou like a roe or a young hart upon the mountains of Bether." Because she wants him to be like a deer on a far-off mountain, she is trying to put distance between them. Bether means separation. There is something not right between them.

Chapter 3 opens some time later, with them still apart. She says in verse 1, "All night long on my bed I looked for the one my heart loves; I looked for him but did not find him." At this point, the woman was twisted in her thinking, but not because she was searching for love. There is nothing wrong with wanting someone special in your life, and wanting to be special in someone else's life. There is nothing wrong with desiring to hold somebody and desiring somebody to hold you. Some people have gotten so holy, however, that they try to act as though they don't need a relationship: "I don't want anybody because I'm so filled with the Holy Spirit and the anointing of God that I just don't need anybody. It's just me and Jesus." You know, some people are just too holy for me. When the Lord saved me, he did not take away my sex drive. He saved my soul, but he didn't dehumanize me! Sex is a natural desire. Again, the issue with sex is not the *use* of it, but rather the *abuse* of it.

There *are* some people whom God calls to remain single for life, but that is the exception, not the rule. Most of us, every now and then, are thinking about having somebody in our lives. Most of us have nights like the woman in our text: "*All night long,* this is what's been on my mind." In fact, the original Hebrew actually says, "*Night after night....*" "Night after night on my bed, I've been thinking about the one I love." If you don't have anyone in your life right now, you may have one night, or even a few nights, go by without wanting someone. But let enough nights go by of getting no calls, no letters, no cards, and no dates.... I don't know who said, "Absence makes the heart grow fonder," but I'll bet there's a statute of limitations on that. Let enough nights go by and absence isn't growing fonder; it's just growing frustrated. It may be even harder when you've had someone once, and that person is no longer there.

Looking for Love in the Bed

The Shulammite woman says, "Succeeding nights have past, and I want my love. I've been looking for my love." Now, here's where I think this woman's thinking is twisted—not that she's looking, because there's nothing wrong with that. I think she's twisted in her mentality due to *where* she is looking for her love. When you get really lonely after unsuccessfully trying as a single person to find someone to be the significant other in your life, where do you end up finding that love? She says, "Night by night on my bed I've been looking." You've been looking *in your bed* for love? I'm suggesting that your bed is not a good place to be when you're trying to find true love. You can find a lot of stuff on your back while lying in your bed, but love just isn't one of them.

You have got to understand the difference between lust and love. Just because a man or woman jumps in your bed doesn't mean that person loves you. Sex is not an initiation into love, but rather it is supposed to be the consummation of love. It's twisted to say, "Okay, I'm looking for love, so I'm going to start this relationship off in bed." The bed is not where it should start; the bed is where your love should lead you after you are married.

We've got this whole concept twisted when we talk about love because the word can mean a variety of things: "I love my car. I love my house. I love my friends. I love my wife. I love football." The Greeks didn't have this problem because they used different words to distinguish the various kinds of love: *agape* for unselfish, unconditional love; *philia* for friendship (brotherly or sisterly love); and *eros* for sexual, sensual love. When you're married, you need all three types of love activated in your relationship. I know, for example, that I need to love my wife unconditionally as an act of my will; nothing she does or says should make me stop loving her. I also need to love my wife as a best friend—someone I can talk with about anything. Moreover, I need to love my wife erotically, expressing my love for her in sexual and sensual ways. But—and this is important—I have to love her *in that order*. Many people start off in bed, hoping that the relationship will develop into friendship and then into unconditional love. This kind of relationship is all backwards; in fact, it's twisted.

To do relationships right, you must start by loving *everyone* unconditionally—as God loves them and us. If you have God's love, when that special person does come along, you won't insist that he or she "prove" their love for you is real. The Bible tells us there are boundaries in the sexual relationship. The bed is undefiled inside marriage. You can have as much sex as you want in marriage; outside of marriage, it is ungodly and wrong and ends with someone being hurt. God has given us boundaries in order to protect us and provide for us. Too often we think when God puts restrictions on our sexual activity that "God is trying to prevent me from having a good time." We must remember that God is the one who created sex! He gave us sex for celebration, release, and recreation. He's not trying to prevent you from having fun; He's trying to protect you *while* you are having a good time.

I'll never forget something that happened in our church one Wednesday after a noon Bible study on the Song of Solomon. A petite young woman, probably no more than twenty-two, came up to me and said, "Pastor, I need you to pray for me." "Okay, I'll pray for you. What is the issue?" I asked. "I just heard from one of my ex-boyfriends. We had unprotected sex while we were together, and he called this morning to tell me he's been diagnosed with HIV. I'm going to the doctor for a test after I leave here." I prayed for her and anointed her with oil. She called the next day, thrilled: "Pastor, the test has come back negative!"

I praised God for protecting her, but I also realized that if she had followed His instructions from the beginning, she wouldn't have had the worry in the first place. When God tells us, "Don't have sex till you get married," we often accuse Him of trying to prevent us from having a good time. Actually, He wants to protect us from messes like that by preparing us for mates who will "keep themselves only unto us" and keeping us from being exposed to the kinds of diseases you get from people who live life for pleasure. It's not about prevention: it's about protection.

Proverbs 14:12 says, "There is a way that seems right to a man, but in the end it leads to death." In case we don't get it the first time, the words are repeated in Proverbs 16:25: "There is a way that seems right to a man, but in the end it leads to death." By looking for love in bed, you can kill your self-esteem, develop guilt feelings, destroy a relationship, contract some sexually transmitted disease or get an unwanted pregnancy. You can get into all kinds of messed up, ungodly relationships by looking for love in bed. That is not the place to find love.

But let's read on in our text. Watch what the Shulammite woman does. She says in verse 2, "I will get up now..." I love that. The King James Version says, "I will arise." She's saying, "I'm not going to take this lying down anymore. I'm going to get off of my back, and get on my feet!" In a few more verses, she's going to find her love, but she doesn't find him until she gets on her feet. She takes a stand. Notice the type of man she's looking for—one like Solomon who can provide her with a royal relationship. She's looking for a man like we described earlier—one who hangs out with the sheep, knows something about the shepherd, and spends time at the shepherd's tent. She's looking for a man who has a relationship with God. That kind of man is looking for a woman who spends time on her feet, not on her back! Men who only want to see you on your back in bed will never offer you a royal relationship. When a brother is in a right relationship with God, he wants to see his woman take a stand. He wants to see her on her feet! That's what motivated the Shulammite woman to cultivate her relationship with her Lover.

A pastor friend of mine just bought a new BMW 600 convertible. That thing is sweet! It's a beautiful vehicle. On one occasion, he invited three of us to preach, and go out together afterwards. Even though we all loved his car, it's only a two-seater, and there were four of us. So we took another car, and our host asked someone else to drive the convertible home. As he handed over the keys, he said, "I've got to remind you that the only way to start my car is with your foot on the brake." With this model, you can't jump in, turn the key in the ignition, and get it to go when you want. The only way to get this car started is with your foot on the brake.

When my friend was explaining that, the Holy Spirit spoke to me about applying this process to relationships. You can't let just anyone jump into your life, stick a key in, and do whatever they want to do. You've got to start off with your foot on the brake. You've got to put a brake on that fornication and those casual sexual affairs!

But look back at the woman in our text. Even though she's on her feet, she's still twisted. What difference does it make if she gets on her feet, but then goes to the wrong place? Look at verse 2: "I will get up now and go about the city, through its streets and squares; I will search for the one my heart loves. So I looked for him but did not find him." Remember, she was the one who sent her man to the mountain of Bether after telling him, "This isn't working for me. We've got a wall separating us. Just leave me alone." But night after night, she began to think about what she had done. Realizing now what she has lost, this woman stood up, an act which took her to a whole new level. If there's ever going to be reconciliation at any level, somebody's got to rise above the issues. This woman says, "I'm not going to take this lying down. What happened between my man and me was not right; it should not have happened. If I'm ever going to make it right, I've got to rise above it."

Before you decide that your situation is beyond reconciliation, remember how bad your situation used to be with God before you were saved. In Ephesians 2:14, the Apostle Paul talks about a "dividing wall of hostility" that was between us and God. Isaiah 59:2 says, "But your iniquities have separated you from your God; your sins have hidden his face from you, so that he will not hear," and Romans 6:23 says, "…the wages of sin is death." But Jesus, in John 12:32, said, "But I, when I am lifted up from the earth, will draw all men to myself." The third day after Jesus died on the cross, God raised Him from the dead. Because He was lifted up from the earth, above what you and I were facing, He was able to reconcile us back to God. Now, if we are Christians, we're supposed to be Christlike. If Jesus rose above our sins and failures to get us back into a relationship with Him, then why can't we also rise above the sins and failures of others so that we can be reconciled with them?

Looking for Love in the Streets

The woman in our text finally got up in verse 2. But look where she's searching for her lover. The New International Version says,

117

"through the streets and squares." But I like the way the King James Version portrays it: "in the streets and in the broad ways." She's out in the broad ways looking for love. Now, that's twisted, because I remember what Jesus said in Matthew 7:13 and 14 about the broad way: "Enter ye in at the strait gate: for wide is the gate, and broad is the way, that leadeth to destruction, and many there be which go in thereat: Because strait is the gate, and narrow is the way, which leadeth unto life, and few there be that find it" (KJV). Yes, you will find lots of people in the broad way, but that isn't where Christians ought to be looking for their lovers because the broad way leads to destruction. Christians ought to look for their lovers in the narrow way—in the church, among other believers.

Some sisters especially find that frustrating because there are more men on the broad way—out in the world—than in most churches. So some, like the Shulammite woman, start looking for potential husbands in the broad way where they have more options. But, sisters, you've got to think about where such relationships will ultimately end up. They may look good at the beginning, but God, who sees the final destination, says they lead to destruction.

When I first read verse 2, I didn't see this. I thought this woman was just determined to find her beloved—willing to go anywhere, even out to the streets, to find the man with whom she could have a relationship. It takes determination to get on your feet—to get up and start doing what you need to do to enter into a good, healthy relationship. At first I thought that's what she was exhibiting, but then I looked more closely and realized that her actions seem more like desperation than determination. For one thing, this woman gets up out of bed and wanders out into the night looking for a man. Is that determination or desperation? In verse 3, she's walking out in the streets, talking to the night watchmen about her lover. Is that normal behavior? Is it determination or desperation?

Here's how you can tell when you're desperate. When you're desperate, you hang out in places you wouldn't normally be, with people you wouldn't normally be with, doing things you wouldn't normally do. Think about it. Where have you been hanging out, who have you been hanging with, and what time are you getting in? This woman used to run with the daughters of Jerusalem; now she's hanging out with strange men in the middle of the night. She was determined in chapter 1—running with the sheep and working with the flock. She was determined in the first part of chapter 2—like a rose in the plains of Sharon and a lily in the valleys. She was determined at the end of chapter 2—safe in the cleft of the Rock. But in chapter 3 her determination has given way to desperation. At three o'clock in the morning, she's hanging around men she doesn't even know, looking for someone she sent away.

Someone will probably take issue with me about what I am saying here. You're thinking like this woman and saying, "I wouldn't be here in the street if my man weren't lost. I would be at home and asleep by now. But because he's lost, that's why I'm out here." But I wonder who is really lost here. The woman talks about looking for her man as though he is lost, but in verse 3, she says, "The watchman *found me* as they made their rounds in the city." Why does it say the watchmen found *her*? Is it possible to get lost looking for love?

Once, she had her stuff together when she was in the cleft of the Rock—in Christ. But now things have gotten twisted, and she's gotten lost trying to find somebody else. I'm not convinced that her man was even lost! She may have *thought* he was lost because she had told him to get lost, but just because somebody tells you to get lost doesn't mean you have to. Just because somebody says, "You're going to be nothing without me," doesn't mean you've got to be nothing! Just because somebody says, "Nobody else is going to love you" doesn't make it so. This woman thought that because she had told him to get lost, he did that; instead, he was still leaping and jumping through the mountains.

The Shulammite woman isn't looking in the mountains for her Lover, however. She mistakenly thought that everybody who's lost is out in the streets. Yet, there are a lot of lost folk who don't hang out in the streets; it is possible to be lost right at home. Not everyone who is lost is in the streets doing drugs or alcohol, or sleeping around with lots of people. There are lost people who come to church every week, but they're still lost. If you don't know Jesus as your personal Savior and believe that God raised Him from the dead, you can carry a Bible, wear a cross around your neck, and have a "What Would Jesus Do" bracelet on your wrist, but you're still lost!

This woman is also thinking, "If he's not with me, he's lost." There are some church denominations that believe everyone outside their denomination is lost, but God can't be limited to one particular denomination. Just because somebody isn't with us doesn't mean he or she is lost. Being lost or found is not dependent upon a person's relationship with us, but on his or her relationship with Jesus. Being found is the result of what Jesus did on Calvary's hill. Yet, lost people can be members in the church and have a relationship with us without having a relationship with Christ. *Just because somebody is lost doesn't mean that person is out in the streets.*

But the woman in our story is out in the streets, searching for her lover. She runs into some men, and they have an exchange of words. But then she "passed from them"; in other words, she leaves them. The Shulammite is very vulnerable right now. She and her man have not been getting along; she's lonely, upset and discouraged; she's feeling desperate; she's out on the streets at night looking for love; and she encounters some men. But no matter how lonely and desperate she feels, she still won't go with just anybody. She's already made up her mind after getting her thoughts together, so she no longer has twisted thinking. It's possible to be so vulnerable that you become a victim. Some of us have the mentality that if we can't have the one we want, we will love the one we're with. She's smart enough, however, not to become a victim of her own vulnerability.

There are many sexual predators in this world who can sense vulnerability in others just like hunting dogs pick up the blood trail from a wounded deer. If a dog sees a healthy deer, he won't even bother it, but when he smells one drop of blood from a wounded deer, he'll follow the trail all day to find his quarry. If you feel vulnerable, broken-hearted, and wounded, be careful: there may be someone out there who has sensed your vulnerability and is tracking you, ready to move in and finish your destruction.

Also, settling for the first person who comes along may be a bad idea, even if he or she is a good person. When the Shulammite woman ran into the other men in town, she was not attracted to any of them. They were working, they had responsible positions, and they most likely were dressed in uniforms. She may even have seen them as good, righteous men, but this woman wasn't interested because they weren't right for her. Remember that someone who might be Mr. or Ms. Right for one person can be completely wrong for someone else.

This woman already knew in her mind what she wanted. After setting her standards high, she wasn't about to change them. She had determined that "even though my man and I are not together right now, I am not going to settle for a substitute." She understood that substitutes cannot satisfy. Perhaps some woman reading this has set standards for her own Mr. Right by now: he's got to be a Christian, have a church home, spend time in the Word, live a Christian life-style, talk to her as to a person of value, and have a job. If it takes a while to find someone who meets those standards, it may be tempting to lower them and take somebody who doesn't quite meet them. Substitutes don't satisfy, however; they only frustrate.

The problem comes when someone gets discouraged and tired of waiting for somebody who meets those standards. This applies equally to men as well as women, but in keeping with the continuity of our text, I'll continue to speak about women. Sometimes, if a woman can't find the man of her dreams, she'll settle for someone else—with the idea that she will be able to change him, mold him, and make him into the man she really wants him to be. Let me tell you, that's not going to work. Only Christ can change a person's heart and nature. Second Corinthians 5:17 says, "If anyone is in Christ, he is a new creation." Being "in you" isn't going to make him a new creature! There are a lot of frustrated women trying to make their men over into what they want. Some people can't find their dream partners because their standards are too high for even the best human being to live up to. Many such people have wonderful partners, but rather than appreciate the other as God made him or her, they try to recreate the partner into that impossibly perfect dream image.

In the classic tale *Frankenstein* by Mary Shelley, Dr. Frankenstein is a scientist obsessed with the idea of creating a perfect man. He collects the best parts from dead bodies—an arm here, a leg there, a torso from a graveyard, a head from a dissecting room—which he assembles into human form and somehow uses electricity to bring it to life. The result is hideous, and eventually the monster destroys him. Some people are like Frankenstein, always trying to assemble the perfect lover from the parts of different people: "You ought to work out so that you could have a body like his." "You need a job like hers." "Why don't you have a car like his?" "We need a house like he bought for her." "You should dress like her." "You need prestige like him." "You need money like his." At best, that approach will only create a monster.

The woman in our text could have dragged out the time she spent with the men she met in the streets. Because of her longing for someone to love her, she could have kept company with them for a while to see if—just maybe—she could settle for one of them instead. But she knew what she wanted, and quickly realized that no matter how fine these men were, they were not right for her. She just had to talk a moment with these other men to know, "This isn't right," so she moved on.

Why does it take some people so long to get to that point? If it isn't right, that makes it wrong, so why does a man or woman stay in that situation for so long? How long does it take to realize that a relationship is not of God? How long does it take to recognize that "God has something better for me"? How many phone calls does it take? How many dates? How many dinners? How many midnight walks? How many trips? How many bills do you have to pay? How many times does your car have to be used? How many arguments? How many fights? How many abuses? How long does it take before you decide, "I don't want my kids to look like you, nor act like you. This isn't working"? If you are in a relationship where you know God has said, "This isn't the one," you have to get out. You've already been in it too long. Even though you should never have allowed that emotional bond to develop, now that it is there it will be harder to break, but you still have to move on. You can never receive what God has for you as long as your hands are full of something else.

Once I was watching the Cleveland Browns playing a game against the Pittsburgh Steelers, who had already earned a playoff berth. The Browns had to win this game to also make it into the playoffs, and Pittsburgh was ahead by one point with just ten seconds to go. Cleveland had the ball, and another ten yards would get them in range for a winning field goal. Out of timeouts, they decided to try a "down and out." If they could complete a pass to cover those ten yards and the receiver immediately stepped out of bounds, the clock would stop, and they would have time for one more play—the field goal that would make them the winners by two points.

After the play was called, the receiver went down ten yards and positioned himself to get the ball. The quarterback had passed the ball already, and the receiver caught it. It was a perfect play. Now the receiver just had to get out of bounds, but eleven men on the opposing team tried to hold him back. The Steelers were trying to keep him in bounds, and he was trying to get out of bounds to help them get in a position to earn the victory. The Steelers were saying, "We want you to stay in defeat!" They were trying to hold him in. Finally, the receiver succeeded! He went out of bounds! Unfortunately, the clock had run out. The Browns were defeated because the receiver didn't get out in time. If you are in a relationship that will defeat you, it's time to get out. If you wait too long, you'll discover someday that it's too late. Get out while you can.

When Do I Find My Love?

Scarcely had our woman passed by the other men when she found the man she loved. She said, "When I found the one my heart loves, I held him, and would not let him go...." She was thinking straight now, no longer twisted in her thinking. A lot of single people want to know where she found her lover. Where do you find someone that you can have a royal relationship with? The text doesn't tell us *where* she found him because that isn't the critical point. The text focuses instead on *when* she found him. She didn't find him when she was lying on her back in bed. She didn't find him while she was out in the streets. She didn't find him when she was with other men. She only found him when she had passed by everyone else. She was looking for her lover, but first she had to pass the other men whom she had met on the way.

The only way you are going to find the one you're supposed to be with is by putting everyone else behind you. Until you do this, you'll never be able to receive the one God has placed right out in front of you. You've got to pass by the others and let them go. This isn't only a physical letting-go; it's psychological and emotional, too.

You may say, "I've been out of my surrogate relationship for two years now, and I've gotten past that." That's only partially right. You may be out of the relationship only physically, but not yet emotionally and psychologically. You've heard the saying, "Timing is everything." If God sends you the ideal one right now, and your thoughts and feelings are still focused on a previous relationship, you may not be ready to receive your new love.

The woman in our story goes on to say, "When I found the one my heart loves, I held him and would not let him go." She would not have been able to hold onto this one if she had not let go of everyone else. You've probably heard someone say, "I'm trying to juggle two or three relationships." Juggling is the best you can do if you are trying to have a serious relationship with more than one person at a time. You can't hold on to one without letting the others go. Yet, people who try this juggling act always end up in trouble. Abraham tried to juggle Sarah and Hagar. It didn't work. Jacob tried to juggle Leah and Rachel. It didn't work. Solomon, who tried to juggle an absurd number of seven hundred wives and three hundred concubines, discovered the hard way that "his wives led him astray" (1 Kings 11:3 KJV). It's no wonder that he came to this sad conclusion about life in Ecclesiastes 1:2: "Vanity of vanities, all is vanity" (KJV).

Mother's House

Moving on in our text, watch where the woman takes her lover—to her mother's house. They have been together for two chapters, but this was the first time she has taken him to meet her family. Before this, she didn't know if she was going to keep him; now, she doesn't want to let go of him. She's taking him home to Mother. Now, some of us don't want our mothers to meet the person we're with. We already know what Mother's going to say, and sometimes we just don't want to hear it, even if it's the truth. By letting our family and friends meet the person we're in a relationship with, however, we will obtain a more objective understanding of whether or not the relationship is right.

Sometimes, it may not be that *you* don't want to bring your man home to Mother; it may be that your man doesn't *want* to meet Mother.

Is he telling you that he loves you with *agape* love, but he doesn't want to meet your family? (Agape is an unconditional love which evaluates your needs and does whatever is necessary to meet them. It operates with a spirit of self-sacrifice that does loving acts even when it doesn't feel like doing them.) Yet, your man doesn't want to meet your mother? Something is wrong with a man who doesn't want to meet and thank the woman who brought you into the world.

Brothers, you *need* to go to your woman's mother's house, because there you'll get an idea of what your wife is going to be like in twenty-five years. You'll learn things at her mother's house that you're not going to learn on a date. You have to go to her mother's house to see what kind of environment she has come from, understand why she is the way she is, and learn why she does some of the things she does. You can learn a lot by going with her to her mother's house.

Wait a minute.... *Mother's* house? In those days, didn't men own everything? This woman's daddy likely wasn't there, if her home was her mother's house. When you go with your woman to her parental home, you may learn that she's got an absentee father. Whether he's dead or just a deadbeat, he hasn't been there for her. This has probably had a drastic impact on her life, and it will, in turn, affect how she relates to you.

Wait a minute...*Mother's* house? Remember from chapter 1 that this is the same mother whose sons had caused the Beloved to be burned by the sun. Her brothers had abused her. Her father was absent. The Lover may have represented the first positive relationship she has ever had with a man. He wouldn't have known that— had he not gone to her mother's house.

If you find out that your woman's previous male relationships have been defective, you can then better understand why your woman relates to you in the way that she does. Maybe that's why she is so quick to want to end your relationship. No other man in her life has stayed with her, so now she's thinking, "I'm going to break it off with you before you have a chance to break it off with me. I don't want to be hurt again." But now that you understand where she's coming from, you can say to her, "Baby, I want you to understand something. Your daddy wasn't right. Your brothers weren't right. But I'm not them. I'm somebody new in your life, and I'm not going anywhere! I'm going to be right here for you." You have begun to understand her because you went to her mother's house.

Environment has a lot to do with who you are. You need to know the environment that your woman or your man has been raised in because it does have a critical impact. Someone may say, "Environment doesn't mean anything. I grew up in a messed-up house, and it was nothing...." Let me tell you something: if you grew up in a house where somebody was smoking, it had an effect on you even if you didn't smoke yourself. The very environment that was filled with secondhand smoke was toxic for you. Smoking itself wasn't your problem because you didn't smoke. Somebody else had the problem, but it had an impact on you nonetheless because you were living in the environment. That's why you've got to go to the mother's house—because you want to know what environment your potential mate was raised in. This environment is not justification for messed-up behavior, but it's an *explanation*.

The woman in our text doesn't just want to get the man into her mother's house; she also wants to take him into the room where her mother conceived her. We can view this as more than just environmental; it can represent the genetic influences on her life. There are things her mother has passed down to her through her genes. She may think about her mother: "What she is—that's what I am. Who she is as a person is who I am becoming. Her traits are my tendencies. Her habits have become my hang-ups." This woman wants her man to see what is going on genetically in her life. The Bible speaks of the parents' sins setting their children's teeth on edge. Bishop Paul Morton, pastor of the Greater St. Stephen Full Gospel Baptist Church in New Orleans, talks about generational curses. Some people who are messed up have kids who are messed up; they, in turn, have another generation of kids who are messed up. The good news is that there are generational blessings operating, too. There are good traits mother and father have that they have passed to their children.

You may be lamenting the fact that you see within yourself some aspects that came as a result of your environment, or you may see negative characteristics that came from the generational ties to your parents. But let me offer you a word of encouragement. When you put your faith in Jesus Christ, God becomes your Father, Jesus becomes your Big Brother, and the Holy Spirit becomes your Companion. Titus 3:5 says: "Not by works of righteousness which we have done, but according to his mercy he saved us, by the washing of regeneration, and renewing of the Holy Ghost." Regeneration is re-*gene*-eration! My daddy may have given me some bad genes, but when I got it right with my heavenly Father, He re-gene-erated me, and now I can be like my heavenly Father!

Father's House

Now, of course, just as it is important for the man to go to the woman's family home, she's got to go to *his* family home, too. Sisters, you've got to check out his environment and the genetic influences in his life. But before you go to either his house or her house, you need to go to God's house. Remember chapter one, when the couple made plans to meet for lunch by the shepherd's tent? *You* need to meet where your Shepherd resides. At God's house, you will find what you need to be able to deal with whatever's been happening at *your* house. When we were kids, we used to sing, "Come And Go With Me To My Father's House." There's salvation, joy, and forgiveness at my Father's house. Whatever you need to cope with at your house, you will find it in God's house.

A man recently came to Detroit's Henry Ford Hospital for heart transplant surgery. He got the call from the transplant coordinator on the day of his wedding! When told to "hurry to the hospital right now; your new heart is in," he said, "I can't come to the hospital today, because I'm getting married." The coordinator said, "If you don't come and get this new heart today, we're going to have to pass it on to somebody else."

The man did what he had to do. He went to the hospital, but he didn't go alone. His fiancée, the preacher, and all the wedding guests were called, and the ceremony was conducted right at the hospital. This man had desired to go on with the wedding as planned, but he had to go to the hospital first to get a new heart. Think about it. Their relationship would not have lasted very long because this man had heart trouble, but when he got a new heart, they gained the opportunity to have a longer life together. Be careful about hooking up with folks who have major spiritual heart trouble and aren't willing to go where they can be treated. Remember that if you have heart problems, there is a Great Physician named Jesus who can give you a new heart. You have to believe that Jesus died on the cross and God raised Him from the dead. Then, He will give you a new heart, make you into a new person, and put you in a position to be able to have a living, loving, lasting relationship.

Chapter 8

Putting the Bed in the Right Place

⁶Who is this that cometh out of the wilderness like pillars of
smoke, perfumed with myrrh and frankincense, with all
powders of the merchant?
⁷Behold his bed, which is Solomon's; threescore valiant men
are about it, of the valiant of Israel.
⁸They all hold swords, being expert in war: every man hath
his sword upon his thigh because of fear in the night.
⁹King Solomon made himself a chariot of the wood of
Lebanon.
¹⁰He made the pillars thereof of silver, the bottom thereof of
gold, the covering of it of purple, the midst thereof being
paved with love, for the daughters of Jerusalem.
¹¹Go forth, O ye daughters of Zion, and behold king Solomon
with the crown wherewith his mother crowned him in the
day of his espousals, and in the day of the gladness of his
heart.

(Song of Solomon 3:6-11, KJV)

As I mentioned in an earlier chapter, our Indianapolis church has three locations. Late one Sunday morning, I was driving with Pastor David Page, my former special assistant, from the northeast location in Fishers, Indiana. Normally, there's not much traffic at 11 a.m. on Sunday, but that day we had some problems. Traffic was building up, and people were driving fairly fast down the highway. Then they would come to a screeching halt, maneuvering in strange ways. I thought that someone probably had an accident and other drivers were trying to avoid hitting the cars involved. When we got near the source of the problem, however, I discovered that it was not an accident; instead, right in the middle of the interstate was a king-size bed!

People were putting their lives in danger by either trying to get around that object or coming to a complete stop on the highway. This situation had a strong potential for somebody getting hurt—all because a bed was out of place. The bed had become a dangerous place: it didn't belong in a high-traffic area. Likewise, we also have to be careful about putting our own beds in areas with too much traffic. We need to make sure that we are right where God wants us to be, even when we're in bed. If you are wondering if your own bed is out of place, you need to check and see how much traffic you've got coming and going around your bed. If there's too much traffic, your bed is out of place.

Our text asks, "Who is this that cometh out of the wilderness like pillars of smoke, perfumed with myrrh and frankincense, with all powders of the merchant? Behold his bed, which is Solomon's...." This lover is Solomon, David's son, the king of Israel, and his bed was in the *wild*erness. When Solomon became king, God had appeared to him in a dream and asked him, "What is that you want Me to give you?" Solomon said, "God, what I want from You most of all is for You to bless me with wisdom so that I can lead Your people." This was very pleasing to God, who replied, "Because you didn't ask Me for long life and wealth, and because you didn't ask Me to destroy some other king, I'm going to bless you with what you asked of me; I'm going to give you greater wisdom than anybody else has ever had, or ever will have." So Solomon was the wisest man ever to live on this earth.

But God didn't stop there. He said, "Because you didn't ask Me for wealth, but for wisdom to judge My people, I'm going to give you great wealth, too, riches beyond what any other king has ever possessed." So here is Solomon with a Ph.D. from God—more wisdom than anyone has ever known—*and* he's a multimillionaire. With his new wealth, Solomon built a magnificent home in Jerusalem and acquired a chariot with platinum rims on it. He was a man with prestige and prominence.

Also, Solomon was a political genius. Have you ever wondered why Solomon had seven hundred wives and three hundred concubines? It wasn't because he loved all of them, nor even because of his uncontrollable lust. He married most of these women to form alliances with their fathers, who were kings of various nations.

Wild-erness

Yet with everything Solomon had, his bed was in the wild. This helps me understand that we cannot measure personal success by where someone works, what school he's gone to, how he dresses, where he lives, or what kind of car he drives. Somebody can have all of that at one level and still have a bed in the wild. In fact, anyone could have given his life to Christ, joined the church, finished the New Members Class, formed a ministry, become a leader in the church, and that person's bed could still be in the wrong place. This is the reason why you cannot move so quickly in relationships. You've not only got to find out where the person is, but you also need to know where the person's bed is.

One Illinois woman purchased what she thought was a blank videotape in a Family Dollar Store. When she took it home and put it in her VCR, however, she discovered that the tape had already been used. In fact, someone had used it for filming pornography. She thought the tape was clean, but she didn't find out what it was really like until after she put it in her VCR. Then, a whole lot of stuff was revealed to her. In other words, you can't just go by what a person looks like on the outside, what they wear, and what they drive. A lot of stuff will be revealed to you as you build the relationship.

I keep pointing out that Solomon's bed is in the *wild*erness. By this, I'm talking about his mindset—the wild way he looked at life. On the other hand, I want to make sure that married couples understand this truth: the bed is undefiled in marriage. This means that when you are married, you can be as wild as you want to be in bed. The Bible does indeed teach that sexual activity in marriage is for procreation, but even if you haven't learned anything else from the Song of Solomon, you now know that sex is also for recreation. So when you're not procreating, go ahead and do some recreating.

Have as much fun as you want. You can be as wild as you want to be...or at least as wild as your spouse will allow you to be.

The issue here in this verse is not about being wild in the bed, but about having your bed in the wild. We're talking about King Solomon, whose palace is in Jerusalem, but whose bed is in the *wild*erness. Even though his home is in one place, his bed is in another place. That's what's wrong with so many of us. We've got our residence in one place, but we've got our bed somewhere else. The key is to make sure your bed and your residence are in the same place.

At this point, King Solomon was single; he doesn't get married until verse 11. He wasn't trying to have his bed in the wild once he had a wife in his bed, which doesn't make sense. My mother gave me some advice when I was really young and thinking about getting married: "Jeffrey, whenever you're ready for marriage, you'll have less desire for other women." Don't think about choosing a wife until your mental bed is out of the wild.

As I was preparing this message to preach at my church, I shared a few thoughts with some people. They kept asking, "How did Solomon get his bed in the wild?" The Bible doesn't even focus on that, but rather on how he gets the bed *out* of the wild. I don't know how it got *in* the wild in the first place. Maybe *it* wasn't there at first, but *he* was. Because he spent so much time there, he decided that he might as well start putting some furniture there. Maybe he had become comfortable there—not all at once, but a little at a time—because the longer you stay in an environment, the more comfortable you become with it.

The Bible is quite clear on this point: the key to overcoming fornication, adultery, and other sexual sins is simply to run from them. The Apostle Paul warned both Timothy and Titus in his epistles to them to flee fornication and youthful lust. Paul knew that the *only* way to overcome fornication and youthful lust is to run from them. Maybe you've got a nice home, you're well-educated, you make a lot of money, and you dress really great, but none of that matters when you are exposed to sexual temptation. You can't negotiate with it, sit around discussing it, reason with it, and you definitely can't flirt with it. No, the only thing you can do is run from it.

Notice that this is the only time in the Bible we are told to run from anything. We aren't even told to run from the devil; instead, we are commanded to submit unto God and resist the devil (James 4:7). Then *he* will flee from *us*. Even when the Bible exhorts us to put on the armor of God, it talks about the helmet of salvation, the breastplate of righteousness, the belt of truth, the shoes of peace, the shield of faith, and the sword of the Spirit (Ephesians 6). There's nothing in the armor to cover our backs because God doesn't expect us to retreat. When it comes to youthful lust, however, God says, "Just run. Don't play with it, don't flirt with it, don't talk to it, and don't look at it. Just run." This text helps us to understand the need to be set free from sexual perversion. Sex in itself is not perverted, but there are many forms of sexual perversion available in our society today. Sadly, this is not just taking place in the world, but it is coming into our churches as well. The church, unfortunately, is mirroring the mistakes of the world.

Some people think that I'm out of touch because I preach on relationships and spend so much time in the Song of Solomon, but this topic is so relevant for our day and our time. Let me share with you some statistics that I have found to help you understand the need for us to discuss this. There are eight hundred *million* rentals of pornographic DVDs and videotapes every year. In 2004, companies selling pornography earned more money in the United States than all of our professional baseball, football, and basketball franchises combined.

Pornography has pervaded all of our society. Even if you make up your mind that you're not going to watch any pornography by renting such tapes or DVDs, pornography has permeated the American culture so much that you may unintentionally be exposed to it while watching what appears to be an appropriate television show or music video. Hundreds of thousands of men are addicted to pornography. One out of three females—and more than a few males—have been sexually harassed, sexually abused, or raped. Next time you're in church, think about it. Thirty-three percent of the sisters there have been raped, molested, harassed, or sexually abused in some way.

When my mother was young, the average age for a first sexual encounter was nineteen. When *I* was young, the average age was seventeen. Now, the average age is sixteen. Nearly thirty percent of teenagers between the ages of thirteen and sixteen report being sexually active. Yet, people don't want the church to confront the issue. It isn't just the young people who need to be educated, either. Among the fastest-growing segments of the HIV- and AIDS-afflicted population are women over fifty. That's because they're getting back into the dating scene, either because of divorce or the death of their husbands. But these women haven't dated in over twenty-five or thirty years, and they don't realize how much has changed since then. Many of these women wind up with sexual partners who are on the DL (down low)—men who make everybody think they are heterosexual, while behind the scenes they are sleeping with other men. Our society is messed up, and people are hurt, even dying. How can the church remain silent in the midst of such a social catastrophe?

It might surprise some women to learn that men—not perverted men, but normal, healthy males—think about sex every single day. Most men think about sex every fifteen minutes. It's surprising to a lot of women to learn that *their* man thinks about sex every fifteen minutes. But what's really surprising to a lot of men is the fact that women think about sex only once a week. It's hard for us men to fathom how a woman can go seven whole days without thinking about sex. It's no wonder that married couples have trouble understanding each other!

In a poll, forty-two percent of men and nineteen percent of the women said they have sex on a first date. One out of every three babies in the United States is born to an unwed mother and subsequently more likely to have problems with drugs and alcohol, engage in criminal activity, become a teenage parent, and live in poverty.

These problems are not just issues out in the world that don't really affect us. Unfortunately, the ways of the world have crept into the church. Yet, I believe that there are men and women who are so tired of living life as the world lives it that they want even their sex lives to be pleasing to God. I've got good news. Even for those who have their beds right in the middle of the wild, there is a God who is able to bring them out of their sin and set them free.

Rise Above It

Now, how does God bring us out of the wild? Verse 6 says, "Who is this that cometh out of the *wild*erness, like pillars of smoke...?" Let's stop right there. Do you know how God brought Solomon's bed out of the wild? He brought it out like pillars of smoke; Solomon came out smoking. One characteristic of smoke is that it always rises. (If your house is on fire, you are told to stay low to the ground as you make your way out because smoke always rises.) When you connect with God and trust Him, no matter how deep you're in some problem, you will be able to rise above it. Like smoke, you can come out on top.

I love this about God: when He brings someone out, just like smoke, the person rises up out of the very midst of the fire. No matter how wild or messed up your life is or how many mistakes you have made, God will raise you up—right where you are. You don't have to try to get your life straight and hope that *then* God might help you. He will work with you right now and raise you up, right where you are. He'll raise you up and then bring you out.

Anointing of the Holy Spirit

In the following verses, Solomon is described as one coming out "like pillars of smoke, perfumed with myrrh and frankincense...." Myrrh and frankincense are tree resins that were used to give a nice scent to oils. The Israelite priests used oil for anointing—a sign of things set apart, or sanctified. In the Bible, oil often represents the Holy Spirit. So if we are to be set free, it is not something that we can do ourselves. It only happens when we come under the anointing of God's Holy Spirit. When I allow the Holy Spirit to work on me, He frees me in those areas where I could not free myself.

The best news is that the anointing of God's Spirit is not just for pastors, preachers, priests, and prophets, but for every believer. The moment you believe that Jesus died on the cross to redeem you and God raised Him from the dead, the Holy Spirit comes inside of you. You are thus anointed by the Holy Spirit and set apart for God's use. This anointing is not anything spooky or something to be afraid of.

It simply means that you are sanctified—set apart for a relationship with God and service to Him.

The anointing of the Holy Spirit is not something that happens all at one time. When you accept Christ, the Holy Spirit comes into your life to make you more and more like Christ, but it doesn't happen overnight. You are saved immediately when you trust God for redemption from your sins through the sacrifice of Christ on the cross, but sanctification is an ongoing process. Day by day, year by year, you become less and less like the world, and more and more like Christ.

Some people don't understand this and become frustrated in their walk with the Lord. You may be frustrated right now because someone told you that the moment you accept Christ, you get filled with the Holy Spirit and become instantly perfect. So you're feeling bad, thinking, "I've been a child of God for six months, and I'm still not perfect." Whoever told you that you immediately become just like Jesus when you become a Christian is mistaken. Spiritual maturity takes time.

Let's say that your bed is in the *wild*erness, just as Solomon's was. You're tired of living like this, and you want to be set free. So God says, "I'm going to bring you out, perfumed with myrrh." So, even though you're still in the wild, you now have the anointing of God's Holy Spirit. Your goal is to be like Jesus, but that goal seems so far away from where you are right now. The Holy Spirit has begun the sanctification process, but it doesn't happen all at once. He doesn't pick you up from the wilderness and set you down in a place of perfection, but every day you can get a little closer to Jesus.

Just watch, and you will begin to see changes in yourself. Your desires will change. Some of the places that you used to go to won't appeal to you anymore. You won't find the people whom you used to hang out with to be so much fun anymore. You won't crave those unhealthy things that you used to put into your body anymore. You may have been deep into the wild, so it's going to take longer. But each day, you are becoming less and less like the wild and more and more like the Word of God. One day, if you keep on letting God sanctify you, you'll find yourself fully out of the wild.

Accountability

Although only the Holy Spirit can make you holy, God often uses other people to help you as well. Look at verse 7. Solomon's carriage is coming, and there are sixty courageous soldiers gathered around him—the noblest warriors of Israel. So he's getting some assistance in coming out of the wild. He didn't say, "Listen, I'm a grown man; I can do this by myself." No, he said, "I'm going to need some help," so sixty courageous warriors surrounded him to escort him out of the wilderness.

Do you know why some of us have stayed in our wildernesses longer than necessary? We have failed to surround ourselves with the right people. Because we can't do it by ourselves, we need help. Solomon surrounded himself with the right brothers and got their support. He had sixty men—*warriors* of Israel—who had a right relationship with God to help him. He had the right entourage, or posse.

But how in the world are you going to find sixty men who love God? Where can you go to find sixty brothers who are serious about their relationship with the Lord? I believe you're going to have to make your way to the church. When you come into the house of God, you're going to run into brothers who are serious about helping you come out!

Notice also that it was sixty *men* working together to get Solomon out of the wild—not sixty women. Some sisters think they can help set a man free and bring him out of the wild, but that's just not going to happen. You can't get sixty women around a brother whose bed is in the wild. A man needs brothers who can identify with what he's experiencing. These sixty men were experts in *war*. I believe that these men had already fought the same battle Solomon is now fighting. Because of their experiences, they knew how to get out of the wilderness.

We need men who will not be ashamed to let other brothers know about their past: "Yeah, I was in that same mess. I was just like that, but I fought the fight of faith, and God delivered me." We don't need fake, phony brothers trying to pretend that they are something they're not—that they have always had it together. We need folks who will testify about what God has done because we're all involved in spiritual warfare. We are at war, but some of us don't even know it! That's why it's so hard to fight it.

To fight a war, you must know the enemy's strategy. Perhaps, like Solomon, the enemy can't get you in the area of education because you already have your Ph.D. He can't get you in the area of finances because you're a multimillionaire. He can't get you in terms of your negotiating ability because you are a great businessperson. He can't get you in terms of your influence, since you are a mover and shaker. He can't get you in terms of power, because you're a big baller and shot caller. So the enemy decides to attack you in the sexual area: your bed. He threatens, "You can make all the money you want. You can get all the degrees you want and have all the friends, influence, and power you want, but I'm coming after your sex life. I'm going to bring you down in this area." That's spiritual warfare.

That's why 2 Corinthians 10:4 says, "The weapons of our warfare are not carnal [that means not physical, not discernible], but mighty through God to the pulling down of strongholds" (KJV). That's why the Apostle Paul encourages Timothy to fight the good fight of faith and to endure hardship like a good solider (2 Timothy 4:5, 7). That's why the Bible tells us to put on the whole armor of God (Ephesians 6:11) and assures us that no weapon formed against us will prosper (Isaiah 54:17). In this kind of spiritual warfare, the enemy is not just trying to bring you down; he's trying to take you out. Do you think the enemy is just trying to embarrass you in front of your family and make you look bad in front of your woman? No, he's trying to take you out completely. You have got to gather men around you who can help you out of the mess you're in.

You've also got to stay away from people who will drag you back down. Some people think I'm stuck up because I don't hang out with anybody and everybody. It's not that I'm stuck up; it's that I'm messed up. I'm too messed up to put myself in an environment where I know that I'm going to fail and be tempted to sin. I need brothers around me who know Jesus and the Word. I can't just hang out with anybody!

In addition, I can't choose my friends by the way they look. "Spanky," the clown from Ringling Brothers and Barnum & Bailey

Circus, was arrested in 2004 for possession of child pornography. Here was a man who was not everything he appeared to be. Likewise, as Christians, we need to stop hanging around clowns—falling for their tricks and laughing at their actions. Their smiles aren't real, their hair isn't real, and their noses aren't even real. They are fake and phony. I need real brothers around me, ones who are serious about their walk with God.

Not only are the sixty men in the Song of Solomon people of God and brothers helping another brother, but the text says they are armed for battle, carrying their swords on their thighs. They are experts in war, experienced in battle, so they have their swords at hand. In the Bible, the Word of God is likened to a two-edged sword (Hebrews 4:12). These soldiers keep their swords where they can draw them instantly. Likewise, the brothers around us need to have a solid grip on the Word to help us when we go into battle.

At a convention, Bishop Kenneth Ulmer asked during his sermon: "What is the first piece of armor that the Lord tells us to put on in Ephesians 6?" I had always thought it was the helmet of salvation, but that's not it—nor the breastplate of righteousness, nor the shield of faith, nor the sword of the Spirit. The first piece of armor God tells us to put on is a belt; He tells us to have our loins girded about with truth. We need the belt of truth to hold the rest of the armor in place. If you put on every other piece but don't have your loins girded with truth, you won't be able to hold it together. Many of us are trying to put on the armor of God, yet it slips off because we don't have our loins girded with truth.

In the twenty-first century, we don't talk much about "loins" anymore. But in the first century, that word referred to the body between the chest and the knees. So God is telling us that the first thing we need to do is come to grips with the truth, and then put the truth between our chests and our knees. A lot of us have the Word of Truth in our heads and hearts, and we meditate on it day and night. Many of us have the Word in our hands, so we've got a firm grip on it. But where we often don't have it is around our loins—where we need it the most. We've got to gird our loins with the truth of God's Word.

Notice, too, that Song of Solomon 3:8 says that the warriors were "prepared for the terrors of the night." They knew that terrors would confront them in the darkness of night. With their swords, they were prepared to meet and conquer those terrors. How can we hope to conquer the terrors—the problems, the enemies, and the fears—that come in the nighttime, unless we have the sword of the Word at hand, ready to use?

Also, in verse 9, our text tells us that Solomon made his chariot for himself. It doesn't matter how much anyone else wants to help you come out of the wilderness; until you want it yourself, there is nothing anyone can do about it. I have a close relative who is struggling with drugs right now. Our church has a ministry to help people get off drugs, and some of our members are professionals in that field. Some of them know my relative and have offered to help him, but he doesn't want help—not yet. I want it for him right now, and they want it for him right now, too. But he's got to want help for himself before he can get it. If you're going to be set free, it won't be because your mother, father, spouse or children want it. You've got to want it for *yourself.*

If I get hungry, no matter how much you love me, you can't eat for me. If I get tired, no matter how much you care about me, you can't lie down and sleep for me. If I need to learn something, it doesn't matter how badly anyone else wants me to learn it, no one can learn it for me. In the same way, if I'm going to know Jesus, you can't meet Jesus for me. I've got to meet Him for myself. Just as soon as you make up your mind that you are ready to come out of your mess and say, "I don't want this anymore! God, help me," He will respond by sending sixty people—or as many as you need— equipped with the Word of God and available to help you walk out of your situation.

My friend Ralph West, pastor of the Church Without Walls in Houston, Texas, tells about a time when his sons were much younger. They came into his room and said, "Daddy, we want to try something with you." He agreed. They said, "Put your hands out, and then put your hands together." He did. Then they took a piece of string, wrapped it around his hands, and said, "Daddy, now try and break out of that." He broke the string with no problem.

So his sons said, "Daddy, put your hands back out again." He did, and this time they wrapped the string around his hands two or three times. Then they said, "Daddy, try to break out of that." He did, but it was a little harder than the first time. Then the boys said, "One more time, Daddy." This time, they wrapped the string around his hands several times. When they said, "Now, Daddy, try to break out of that," he couldn't—no matter how hard he tried. He was too entangled.

Some relationships are like that experiment. The deeper you're entangled in something freaky and wild, the harder it will be to break out of that mess when you want to. When you can't break free on your own, your only hope is to surround yourself with men of God who are experts in spiritual warfare, carrying swords of the Word to cut you loose!

To continue in our text, Solomon's mother shows up in verse 11: "Go forth, O ye daughters of Zion, and behold king Solomon with the crown wherewith his mother crowned him in the day of his espousals, and in the day of the gladness of his heart" (KJV). His mother puts a crown on his head. Notice, however, that she did not give him the crown while he was in the wilderness. Many mothers need to say to their sons, "I'm not going to support you while you are still in the wild. I don't support your promiscuity. I'm not going to support your crazy sexual ways. You're not going to bring a woman to whom you aren't married into *this* house to sleep together. As long as you're in the wild, I'm going to hold your crown, because you'd only lose it while you're out there doing wild stuff. But when you decide to come out, baby, Mother's going to be here for you, and she's going to give you this reward."

It's easy to guess why Solomon's mother, Bathsheba, might have felt that way about her son. She probably remembers his father's behavior. She knows his father David had bed issues and that Solomon may be just like him. He had a brother named Amnon, who also has bed issues. When Solomon was a boy, his mother could talk to him about God, but now that he is grown, she just talks to God about him. If your child is grown and doesn't want to listen to you talk about Jesus anymore, you can still talk to Jesus about him.

Tyler Money was thirteen years old when he wanted to play football at Edinburgh High School. He was very big for his age at 6'1" and 285 pounds, so the football team was eager to accept him. He had the talent, the size, and the skills, but he also had an unusually large head. The team couldn't find a big enough helmet for him, so they contacted Division 1 colleges around the nation, but couldn't find one at the college level. Then they called the NFL. Although they called every team, they still couldn't find one that would fit him. Even the one sent over by the Chicago Bears' James Williams, who had the biggest head in the NFL at that time, didn't fit. Tyler had to wait quite a while before a helmet could be especially designed for him. The officials knew that it was too dangerous for him to participate in the game until he got his head right. Before *you* hook up with somebody, make sure that person has come out of the wild, has got his head on right, and has been crowned by God. Then you can have a royal relationship!

Chapter 9

Body Language

∞

¹ How beautiful you are, my beloved, how beautiful! Your eyes behind your veil are like doves. Your hair falls in waves, like a flock of goats frisking down the slopes of Gilead. ²Your teeth are as white as sheep, newly shorn and washed. They are perfectly matched; not one is missing. ³Your lips are like a ribbon of scarlet. Oh, how beautiful your mouth! Your cheeks behind your veil are like pomegranate halves—lovely and delicious. ⁴Your neck is as stately as the tower of David, jeweled with the shields of a thousand heroes. ⁵Your breasts are like twin fawns of a gazelle, feeding among the lilies. ⁶Before the dawn comes and the shadows flee away, I will go to the mountain of myrrh and to the hill of frankincense. ⁷You are so beautiful, my beloved, so perfect in every part.

(Song of Solomon 4:1-7, NLT)

In the Song of Solomon, most of the talking—the verbal communication—comes from the Shulammite woman. In chapter 4, however, it is the Lover who does most of the talking, with only a few words spoken at the end by the Beloved. This intrigued me because it was so different from the rest of the text. It finally dawned on me that although she doesn't *say* anything during most of this encounter, she is giving off some serious body language signals.

Body language is so important. According to various studies, nearly sixty to over ninety percent of our communication is nonverbal. Our body language can speak more clearly than our lips. Even marketing experts understand that the body carries a lot of weight in communicating messages. Advertisements for cars, houses, and just about everything else feature attractive and often half-naked people alongside the product, as if to suggest that if you buy this particular item, bodies like this are going to start showing up in your life.

In everyday life, you can often tell what people are thinking and feeling simply by looking at the signals from their bodies. While preaching, I can watch the body language in the congregation and figure out whether people are grasping my point or not, which lets me know whether I need to move on or stay focused on a point. Body language says a lot.

God understands how important body language is. In Romans 12:1, He says that we are to present our *bodies* unto Him as a living sacrifice. First Corinthians 6:15 reminds us that because our *bodies* are members of Christ, we are never to connect them to a prostitute. Verse 19 of that same chapter tells us that our *bodies* are the temple of God, and the Spirit of God lives in us. What we do with our bodies—body language—is important.

My older sons are starting to date, so I'm trying to teach them that they have to become bilingual. That's because girls will some-times say one thing with their mouths and something else with their bodies. I have told the boys: "Sons, you've got to let whatever comes out of her mouth carry more weight than what you think her body is saying. If a woman is saying 'no' with her mouth, but seems to be saying 'yes' with her body, you've got to listen to what's coming out of her mouth. Once she says 'no,' you cannot go on the other side of that 'no' because to do so would be to violate her... regardless of what her body is saying to you." It would sure help a lot if you sisters would line those two things up. If it's 'no' with your mouth, make it 'no' with your body too. You're confusing the brothers with your mixed signals.

Also, the way we dress, even how we walk or move, and what we shake or don't shake sends a message. We used to scold young men for wearing clothes that fell off their behinds, showing their boxer shorts. Today, some young women dress the same way, showing a whole lot of stuff that we don't want to see. I've been trying to tell the sisters at our church, "You've got to help out your brothers." Yes, these brothers are Christians, but they aren't dead. If something is showing, they are instinctively going to look at it—and that's where the real problems start with body language!

Vision

Body language can be a good thing, too. In our text, this woman is sending a message to her man, and she's not even saying anything. That's why he mentions seven different body parts in the first five verses of chapter 4. She's conveying a message to him without even opening her mouth. Let's look at the physical description that he gives of his woman.

Each of the body parts also carries a spiritual implication. He says first, "Her eyes are like doves." Eyes are physical, but they also signify vision and perception. In this context, he's most likely talking about her peaceful perception of life: "I love the way you see life. I appreciate your world view." It's not about eyesight, but rather insight. Proverbs 29:18 says, "Where there is no vision, the people perish" (KJV). A whole lot of our relationships, friendships, and marriages have been dying because we keep hooking up with people who haven't got any vision. When I talk about vision, I'm referring to seeing things from God's point of view or perspective. Brother, you're going to hurt yourself if you get a woman who's beautiful but doesn't see life clearly. Solomon's woman had peaceful eyes, like doves.

Glorification

He moves on to talk about her hair, which represents her glory. In 1 Corinthians 11:15, the Apostle Paul says that a woman's hair displays the honor God has given her; it is her glory and a covering for her. That's very significant, sisters, because you need to remember that you get your honor from God, not from a man. Quite often, a sister believes that she has to have a certain man, or something is wrong with her. Many women are looking for "the right man" to affirm and confirm them because they haven't realized that God has already given them their glory. Ladies, whether you have a man in your life or not, your hair is a symbol of the covering, or dignity, that

God has already given to you. He gave you that covering before you had any relationship with a man. Even if a man never shows up in your life, you don't have to feel like you're nothing. Why? Because you already have your honor! You already have your glory because you got it from God!

Now let's say a man shows up, and you kick it together for a minute. It doesn't work out, so he walks away. Even so, you don't have to walk around as though you've lost everything. He didn't take your honor with him because he didn't bring it to you. You got it from God.

Also, let me speak a few words about hair, especially to those of us who are of African descent. I'm really tired of hearing people talk about good hair versus bad hair. Whatever kind of hair you have, God gave it to you. Remember that every good and perfect gift comes from God (James 1:17). I learned this a long time ago. My hair was always thick, coarse, and difficult to comb, so people used to say, "You've got bad hair!" Let me help you understand something: just because my hair isn't like yours doesn't mean it's bad. Maybe I have to take a little more time washing and conditioning my hair. Perhaps it takes a little more time to get my hair the way I want it to look, but that doesn't make it bad. Even wine only gets better with time!

But whatever kind of hair God has given you, thank Him for it. If it's short or long, thin or thick, thank Him. If it's easy to handle and just takes a little combing every day, praise God! If it takes you a little more time like it does for me, thank God for that! God is the one who gave you your hair! Appreciate what God has given! Your hair is your glory, sister.

Function

Then the Lover talks about his Beloved's teeth. Even though this is a young woman, he considers it worth mentioning that she's got all of her teeth. In those days, there were no dentists and no fluoride, flossing, or whitening procedures. Teeth didn't often last for a lifetime. This man just appreciates the fact that his woman still has all of her teeth.

Think about what we can learn from our teeth and how they function. Our teeth break down what we eat so we can survive and thrive. Now, the Bible talks about the milk and meat of the Word. The milk involves the foundations of the faith, or the ABC's, that every Christian can handle, including salvation, baptism, and other basic issues. Some of us, unfortunately, never get beyond the "milk." To digest anything more substantial than milk, we let somebody else chew it up for us. At the church where I grew up, one of the deacons would often say, "Break it down, Preacher!" because we had so many baby Christians in the congregation who couldn't chew on the spiritual food themselves. The pastor had to break it down for them to be able to receive it. But the more mature Christians—those with spiritual teeth—can handle the meat of the Word. These individuals are able to get into the Word for themselves and, with the help of the Holy Spirit, chew on it, appropriate it, and internalize it to get the strength they need.

The man in our text is saying to his woman: "One thing I appreciate about you is that I don't have to chew up the difficult things in life for you. You are able to appropriate things for yourself, but it doesn't even stop with the Word of God. Instead of waiting to get an educated man, you got your own education. Instead of waiting for a man with a job to support you, you went ahead and got your own job. Instead of waiting for a man, you went ahead and got your own house and your own car." Sisters, when you learn to get things for yourself, it puts you in a better position to get the brother whom you want. When you've got your own stuff, a brother has got to be strong to have anything to offer you. This brother had a lot, but he appreciated that his woman could get her own stuff, too. In short, she had her own teeth.

Communication

Next, the man starts talking about her lips and her mouth. Remember, this woman did a lot of talking in the first three chapters of the Song of Solomon. Now the Lover is saying, "I appreciate how you talk. I appreciate how you communicate. I appreciate what comes out of your mouth. Your lips and your mouth are beautiful."

This is not a sister who is always putting a brother down, nagging, or using her mouth to spread rumors and gossip. She talks about ideas and things of importance, not just about other people. When she does talk about others, she only says good things; she doesn't constantly pick at other people. Her man says to her, "I appreciate you. I appreciate your mouth—your speech."

The Bible tells us to put away evil speaking and cursing (Ephesians 4:31). No brother wants his woman cussing him out. Nobody wants to be nagged all the time. Even if your husband seems impossible, every now and then he's bound to do *something* right, so find something good to say to him. One thing I've discovered that men need in their relationships with their wives is peace and quiet. Men face constant difficulties on the job, in the community, and trying to get life together. When a husband comes home, he doesn't want to face a lot of difficulties there, too; instead he wants a woman with nice lips and a nice mouth.

Expression

Now the man talks about the woman's cheeks, or "temples." He compares her cheeks to two pomegranate halves. Pomegranates are red and rosy, and their seeds can be very sweet—a vivid description of this woman's facial expression. Remember, with your body language you can send a message without saying a word. When I'm standing in the pulpit and see one of my kids misbehaving out in the sanctuary, I can just give him a disapproving look. I really don't have to say anything. My kids know from my facial expression exactly what I'm trying to communicate.

All families develop their own "body language." A couple can be at a party and, without uttering a word, the husband or wife can look at the other in a way that says, "It's time to go." You can easily tell if somebody you know is happy or sad, at peace or angry, or feeling good or experiencing pain by their facial expression. Your own everyday facial language should reflect godliness and contentment.

Determination

Now the man talks about the woman's neck, which represents her determination and direction: "You have a neck that is like the tower of David." He is saying something very positive to her about her strength of will. Once she makes up her mind to do something, she does it. She has some determination and direction for herself. Determination is a strong and beautiful thing, unless it turns into selfish stubbornness. God uses the neck as an analogy in the Bible to describe the children of Israel in a negative way, frequently calling them "a stiff-necked people." He was talking about their stubbornness at that point in time. But in this context, this woman's neck— her determination—is a strong and beautiful thing.

Also, whatever else a neck does, it mainly keeps the head on straight. However fine all the other body parts are, you are going to have problems if you've got a woman who frequently loses her head, or just doesn't have her head on straight.

Emotion

The last thing the Lover mentions is his Beloved's breasts: "Your breasts are like twin fawns of a gazelle." We might say, "like the fawns of a deer." When we think about baby deer, we often think of them as being cute, cuddly, and playful. Whatever else might be said about a woman's breasts, they are near the heart. Maybe these represent the emotional side of his woman. Perhaps he is talking about the fact that his woman is sensitive and has understanding and compassion for other people.

Perhaps he's also speaking about her nurturing abilities. A woman's breasts produce milk for her children. The Lover knew that this woman not only could bring him pleasure through her breasts, but could also nourish and provide for the children they would have someday.

There's something else about this passage from chapter 4: every description deals with the upper extremities. The man admires his woman's eyes, mouth, cheeks, neck, breasts—all parts of the upper body. He says nothing about her lower extremities, anything below the waist. We can be sure that it isn't because anything below the waist is negative, bad, or dirty—something we shouldn't talk about. No, the whole body is the temple of God. So, even though her whole body is beautiful, her man is only describing the upper portion.

I wondered about that, but then I noticed that in chapter 7, he does, in fact, give a description of the lower parts of her body. It dawned upon me that when he's talking to her in chapter 4, they are still single, and he has not yet seen what is below her waist. In chapter 7, they are married, so he talks to her about her lower body. You only can describe what you have seen, heard, or experienced. If they weren't married yet and had not had any sex in their relationship, he would not have had an opportunity to see those parts.

Some people, even in my congregation, think I'm an old fogy who is outdated and antiquated because I'm always talking about waiting till marriage before having sex, but I'm just preaching what the Bible says. The Scriptures tell us that the bed is pure *in marriage* and undefiled *in marriage*. God created us as sexual beings, but He also determined that there was only one relationship in which we are to give ourselves sexually to another person—in marriage.

God knew what He was doing. I've talked to a lot of people over the years who are hurting and whose self-esteem has crumbled. Believing they could separate the physical from the emotional and spiritual, they expressed their love to someone sexually outside of marriage, expecting to walk away unscathed. But their emotions got in the way; their guilty consciences kept nagging at them; or their partner moved on to someone else, leaving them feeling rejected and betrayed. We have a lot of wounded people in our society and in our churches because they thought they could do things their way instead of God's way, but what they learned is that He made the guidelines for our own good. He created us, He knows us, and He understands how we function as complete persons—body, mind, and spirit. God knows that within a loving marriage, sex is a beautiful thing; outside of that, we leave ourselves open and vulnerable to all sorts of damaging consequences in our body, mind, and spirit.

Part of the problem is that people today are used to rushing into things. That's why many driving areas, including the parking lot at our church, have speed bumps—to keep people from hurrying through at a speed that would bring harm to themselves or others. Before we got the speed bumps, drivers would rush to park so they could get their favorite seats in the sanctuary or try to beat someone to a parking space. Because too many people were driving so fast through our parking lot, an eventual accident or injury seemed inevitable. Installing speed bumps slowed them down some, but almost every Sunday, you can still see a few cars rushing through the parking lot, either ignoring the speed bumps and getting a jolt as they race across them, or swerving into another lane to go around the bumps!

Those speed bumps weren't put there to keep people out or make it difficult for them, but to protect them. If you have a partner who seems to be ignoring God's speed bumps in terms of your relationship, it would be wise to put up some of your own, as the Shulammite woman had done. You need to stop allowing people to rush in too fast, but it doesn't mean that you don't want them to ever come in. "Not now" doesn't mean "not ever." The woman in our text didn't say her Lover could never see her body below the waist; she just wasn't giving him access too soon. She was waiting for things to happen in the order God had prescribed.

Notice that while this man is totally enthralled with the beauty of his woman, during this moment when the passion is so evident, he suddenly says, "Before the dawn comes and the shadows flee away, I will go to the mountain of myrrh and to the hill of frankincense." In the midst of this moment, when he is drawn to her and wants her so much, why would he speak of leaving her presence? Remember, she isn't saying anything with her lips, but her body is speaking to him. On one hand, he is attracted to her just because she is a beautiful woman, and he is a normal, healthy man. On the other hand, we don't know exactly what she did, but she used her body to gently let him know that now wasn't the time. I love the imagery that verse 6 evokes. The man doesn't walk out on her in anger, and he doesn't say, "Okay, I'll just go home and wait." No, he speaks of going to the "mountain of myrrh" and the "hill of incense." It's almost as if she has communicated to him that "before we go any deeper, there are some areas where you need to go higher. You need to go to a whole other level before we go any further in this relationship."

151

It wasn't just any mountain or hill that the man needed to go to: it was the mountain of myrrh and the hill of frankincense. Remember when Jesus was born and kings came from East Africa with gifts of myrrh and frankincense? The Hebrews used myrrh as we use embalming fluid to prepare bodies for burial. When the kings brought a gift of myrrh to Jesus as a baby, it was symbolic of the fact that He was born to die. God already had foredestined in His plans that Jesus was going to die; the crucifixion and death of Jesus did not slip up on God. Jesus came to die. It was His sacrifice that bought our relationship with God. Had there not been His sacrifice, we would not have the relationship, because there is no such thing as a good relationship if somebody has not made a sacrifice. So, symbolically, our text is saying, "Before we can have an intimate relationship with each other, you have got to climb the mountain of myrrh, along with the hill of sacrifice."

What might the Lover have had to sacrifice for the relationship with his Beloved? At the very least, he needed to sacrifice his singleness. If he was not willing to give up his singleness, why should she be willing to give up her virginity? I want to make something perfectly clear here, because I get tired of people talking as if being single is akin to having some disease. Many think that if a person is single, there is something wrong with that individual. People keep asking singles, "Are you married yet?" in the same way they would ask, "Have you gotten over your illness yet?" Being single is *not* a disease, and marriage is *not* the cure.

According to 1 Corinthians 7:8 and 9, the Apostle Paul actually says that it's better to be single, if you can handle the burning of unsatisfied sexual desire. He points out that single people can devote their time to the Lord in a way married people cannot. Single people can offer undivided attention to the Lord. Moreover, they can often witness, teach, preach, and serve without having to think about how that time is going to affect other people in the family. Of course, some singles are caring for their elderly parents or for children in their family. Still others devote time to community involvement. Also, because single people are sole providers, many of them have jobs that demand extraordinary amounts of time. Married people should not assume that the life of a single person is always unencumbered and carefree. There are several advantages to being single, just as there are some advantages to being married. Singleness is not a disease!

Let me help you, though, to understand something. If you can't handle your singleness, you will never be able to handle marriage. If you are looking for some man or woman to complete you, you will be disappointed. Sometimes couples wanting me to marry them tell me that they want to write their own vows. Occasionally, however, one of them will want to say, "You are going to complete me." Wait a minute! If you're incomplete, you don't need a spouse because you are not a whole person anyway. You are only half of a person, and no one can make up for the half of you that is still lacking. When two people marry, it should be two whole people coming together and becoming one!

Some people are determined never to get married. It's not because they feel God calling them to serve Him more effectively through singleness. They just aren't willing to walk away from anything in order to walk into a loving, intimate, marital relationship. Some married people have never truly given up their singleness, yet they are wondering what's wrong with their marriage. To have an intimate, healthy sexual relationship with someone that brings honor both to that person and God, you have to be willing to give up your singleness by offering it on the mountain of sacrifice. When you're willing to sacrifice your singleness by practicing some self-denial for the person you love, only then can you walk into a loving relationship.

Think about the difference in perspective from the mountain as opposed to the valley. A brother who is looking at you from the mountain of sacrifice will see your head first. A brother who is looking at you from the valley will see you from your feet up. Such a "lowdown" brother will think more about what's in your lower anatomy than what's in your brain. But a brother who has climbed the mountain of sacrifice has a different perspective on life. He wants to know what you think and will desire to share his life with you.

Intercession

Remember that the Lover was going to the hill of frankincense as well as the mountain of myrrh. Like myrrh, frankincense was used in embalming, but it was also used as an incense to scent fires burned before sacrificial altars. The Jewish high priests burned frankincense during their intercessory prayers on behalf of the people. Extremely expensive—in the same market as gold, silk, and jewels—it was another gift that was brought to Jesus when He was born, representing His identity as our High Priest and His ongoing intercession for us. As our High Priest, Jesus can identify with our hurts and our pains.

In the Scriptures, frankincense was literally considered prayer. As the aroma of the smoke rose up to God, it was just as if He accepted the sacrifice and directly responded to the prayer of intercession. The Lover is climbing not just any mountain, but a spiritual mountain that symbolizes sacrifice and intercession. In essence, he is saying, "I'm going to climb the mountain of spirituality, to be spiritual with you." Sister, you need a brother who is spiritual and can get in touch with God. It doesn't matter how big your house is, how much money your husband makes, or how big a car you drive. When issues and trials come your way, you need a husband who will say, "Wait a minute, let's take this to Jesus. Let's take this to the Word of God, and see what God says."

In this verse, the Lover says, "I am willing to climb these mountains before I try to climb on you." This is not to say that he doesn't want to get below her waist. Believe me, he does! Why do we keep thinking that the people in the Bible were any different from you and me? This woman wanted what every sister wants, and this man wanted what every brother wants. Every Christian sister wants a spiritual man who's willing to make sacrifices for her and prove his love to her. Every brother wants sex. In other words, these two are saying, "You give me what I want, and I'll give you what you want." It's a perfect partnership, with the Lover saying the words of the Diana Ross song, "Ain't no mountain high enough, ain't no valley low enough, to keep me from you!"

Illumination

Notice the symbolism in verse 6: "Until the day breaks, and the shadows flee." This woman is not going to enter into a more intimate relationship with her man until then. When does the day break, and the darkness leave? When the sun rises. This woman is not entering into any relationship in the dark. After having been burned in the past, she isn't going through that any more. She wants to know what's going on in her relationship by seeing her man for who he is and wanting him to see her for who she is. Some people get to know others in the dark, sleep with others in the dark, and get married in the dark. When the light dawns, they finally wake up and cry, "Oh, my God, what have I done?" We need to stop rushing into relationships by letting some light in on them before it's too late.

One thing I don't understand is why anybody would hang out in a nightclub looking for a husband or wife. Have you ever seen how dark it is in a club? You can't really see the person you're with. On top of that, the atmosphere is dense with smoke. Everything that's going on there is cloudy and muddled. Also, the music is so loud that you can't really hear what anyone is saying, so you don't know if the person you're with can really communicate with you or not. If someone is drinking, you don't know if he or she is telling the truth or lies to you. Why would anyone go to a dark place like that, expecting to find someone they can live with in the light of day? It doesn't make sense. No wonder so many people wake up with a deep sense of regret that no "morning after" pill can erase.

Now let's look at our last verse for this chapter: verse 7. The man says to his woman, "You are so beautiful, my beloved, so perfect in every part." He's telling her, "You are so fine. There is no flaw in you." He started off in verse 1 telling her how beautiful she was. Then he broke it down by describing her eyes, her hair, her mouth, her cheeks, her neck, and her breasts. Now he says, "You're not just beautiful, you're *all* beautiful." When you're in the dark, all you're looking for is legs, limbs, and lips. But when the sun comes up—when the Son rises in your life—you understand that a sister is more than just body parts such as lips, hair, and breasts. She's not just a body on the outside, but she's a soul on the inside. When you see that, you start respecting and loving her for who she is—not just on the outside, but on the inside.

Through it all, keep in mind that body language is important. Think about the messages you are sending with your body. What you do on the outside can let people know what's on the inside, revealing the part that is not visible to the eye. But if you're not careful, your body can send out wrong messages.

While you're thinking about your own body language, learn to accurately read the body language of others. Brothers, while you're checking out the body, remember that every woman also has a soul. Moreover, you need to let the Son of God arise in your life. You must find your way to the mountain of myrrh, where you lay down your life, and to the hill of frankincense, where you sacrifice and intercede for the person you love. You need to at least begin to understand how important the spiritual aspect is in a loving relationship. Once you do, your marriage will never be the same.

Yesterday, the sun was shining, and it was a beautiful day. My car had been dirty for so long that I couldn't wait to wash it. The weathermen said that it wasn't only going to be sunny that day, but all week. I said, "Great!" I was happy and eager. I was at the car wash at 8 a.m., the first customer there. I wanted the car to look good because it had been dirty far too long.

On the way to the car wash, the indicator light came on, telling me I was low on fuel, but I wasn't trippin' about it. I can go a few miles with my car after that light comes on, so I wasn't going to be deterred or delayed. I just wanted my car to look good. After I left the car wash, I rushed to the office because I wanted everybody to see how good my car looked when they came in. It was shining and looked really good. I still hadn't taken time to get gas, but I knew my car so I didn't worry. I was just feelin' good about how it looked.

A couple of the other pastors and I made a few calls to visit some people who were sick, and then we had a lunch appointment. We did all of that in my car, because *my* car was looking so good. I knew that I still had time to get fuel, so I wasn't worried. After work, I had to pick up my son K. J. from school, and then I helped him with his homework. He had a basketball practice at 7 p.m., and I had already decided that I would stop for gas right after that. I said to myself,

"I'm going to stop at that station right before I get on the highway to go to my house. No problem. I know I'm low on fuel, but I'm sure I can make it. I'll be fine." Besides, I was still thinking about how good my car looked. K. J. was in the back seat and I was planning to stop at the station, so everything was fine.

There was one problem. I got so involved in talking on my cell phone that I forgot about getting gas until we were already on the highway. Even though I had known that I should have met my car's need for fuel, I had gotten distracted and missed the opportunity.

My car has a button I can push to display exactly how much gas is left in the tank, along with an estimate of how far the car can go on it. By now I was worried enough to check. It showed half a gallon of gas and ten miles left, but the next gas station was more than ten miles away. Now I'm not so confident. My car still looked great on the outside, but there was something definitely not right on the inside.

Now I started thinking, "I'm about to run out of gas. I've got this boy with me. I'm on the highway, about ready to get stranded out here, so I'm not going to make it to my destination. I'm going to be embarrassed. Everybody who knows me is going to be driving past, saying 'Isn't that Jeffrey Johnson out there walkin' on the highway with his son?' I'm going to try to hide like I don't see anybody." I'm really thinking I'm not going to make it.

But then I started thinking, "I've got to pray." I'm praying. I'm looking at my gauge. I'm praying. I'm realizing how far I am from my destination. I'm praying. Now I'm finally getting close to the exit where the gas station is, but the gauge says there are zero gallons in the tank, and zero range. I have no fuel. My car should have stopped by now, but it's still moving. I should have been stranded by now, but my car is still going. I should be out walking by now, but I'm still riding in my car.

I made it to the gas station—not on the fuel, because I didn't have any—on God's favor. Do you know why I didn't have any fuel on the inside? Because I was more concerned with making my car look good on the outside. I never took the time to stop at the place to get filled on the inside. Some of us are so concerned with how we look, what we drive, what we wear, where we work, and who we're with, that before we know it, there's nothing of God left in us. If we could look at a gauge, we'd see a zero amount of the Holy Spirit and zero range. The only reason we've made it this far is because of the favor of God! I made it to that gas station on God's favor; I was able to get filled up there and go on. Are *you* filled up so you can make it to the destination God has set for you, or do you need to stop, seek God's favor, and allow Him to fill you once again with the Holy Spirit?

Chapter 10

Goodies

[8] Come with me from Lebanon, my bride,
come with me from Lebanon.
Descend from the crest of Amana,
from the top of Senir, the summit of Hermon,
from the lions' dens and the mountain haunts
of the leopards.
[9] You have stolen my heart, my sister, my bride;
you have stolen my heart with one glance of your eyes,
with one jewel of your necklace.
[10] How delightful is your love, my sister, my bride!
How much more pleasing is your love than wine,
and the fragrance of your perfume than any spice!
[11] Your lips drop sweetness as the honeycomb, my bride;
milk and honey are under your tongue. The fragrance
of your garments is like that of Lebanon.
[12] You are a garden locked up, my sister, my bride;
you are a spring enclosed, a sealed fountain.
[13] Your plants are an orchard of pomegranates
with choice fruits, with henna and nard,
[14] nard and saffron, calamus and cinnamon,
with every kind of incense tree, with
myrrh and aloes and all the finest spices.
[15] You are a garden fountain, a well of
of flowing water streaming
down from Lebanon.
[16] Awake, north wind, and come, south wind!
Blow on my garden, that its fragrance
may spread abroad.

Let my lover come into his garden
and taste its choice fruits.
¹ I have come into my garden, my sister, my bride;
I have gathered my myrrh with my spice.
I have eaten my honeycomb and my honey;
I have drunk my wine and my milk.
Eat, O friends, and drink;
drink your fill, O lovers.
(Song of Solomon 4:8–5:1 NIV)

Continuing in the Song of Solomon, let's skip to verse 11 of chapter 4. The Lover is still talking here, saying to his Beloved: "Your lips drop sweetness as the honeycomb, my bride; milk and honey are under your tongue. The fragrance of your garments is like that of Lebanon." Verse 16 says, "Awake, north wind, and come, south wind! Blow on my garden, that its fragrance may spread abroad. Let my lover come into his garden and taste its choice fruits." Chapter 5:1 replies, "I have come into my garden, my sister, my bride; I have gathered my myrrh with my spice. I have eaten my honeycomb and my honey. I have drunk my wine and my milk. Eat, O friends, and drink; drink your fill, O lovers."

When I was a kid, I used to love to be in the kitchen with my mother. I was like my third son Jalon, who likes hanging out in the kitchen with his mother. When my mother was preparing meals for us, I liked to lick the spoons and bowls to get a foretaste of the dinner that was to come.

Every now and then, my mother baked a German chocolate cake, which was my favorite. When Mother fixed that, I licked the bowl clean of the batter that didn't make it into the pan, and then tasted the coconut frosting even before we put it on the cake.

Of course, I couldn't help asking Mother, "Can I have a piece of this German chocolate cake?" She would answer, "You can have some, but you can't have it right now because it would spoil your appetite. There are some other things I'm preparing that I want you to eat first." She wanted me to have the cake, knowing that I had an appetite that craved it; that was why she made it for me. She wasn't telling me that I couldn't have it. She was just saying that *first*, before I could eat a piece of the German chocolate cake, there were other things I had to internalize so I could benefit from them. Had I not listened to my mother and focused only on the cake, it would have been unhealthy for me. Not only would it have been unhealthy, but I would have gotten out of shape. If I kept eating it, it would have made me sick.

Do you know why some of us have unhealthy walks with God and end up in unhealthy relationships? Do you know why some of us are out of shape spiritually and always down, depressed, and sick of life? Often it's because we don't want any of the other things that are healthy for us; instead, we want to focus only on the goodies.

You can guess what "the goodies" of life are. In verse 16 of our text, the woman invites her husband to come into her garden and eat from her choice fruits—to enjoy the physical pleasures of her God-given sexual attributes. Every woman has such a garden, but we brothers have to be careful not to focus so much on the goodies in the garden that we forget the other things we should internalize first. You may have noticed that the goodies in chapter 4 are at the end of the chapter. God says, "First, you need to figure everything else out, then you can be blessed by the goodies." So let's go back to verse 8 and see what this man has to figure out before he can enter into the Shulammite woman's garden.

A Better Home

There was not just one mountain, but an entire range of mountains in and near Lebanon; verse 8 specifically mentions Mount Amana and Mount Senir. Mount Amana was in the Lebanon Mountains, a range known for its tall cedars with lumber fit for building palaces, temples, and huge ships. Even Egyptian pharaohs imported this cedar wood to build their homes, as did King Solomon. He didn't just want a *big* home; he wanted a *better* home—quality, not just quantity. Likewise, before we enter into the garden of physical love, we first have to go to a higher level to get the right material. Earlier, we saw the man going to the mountain of myrrh and the mountain of frankincense, the places of sacrifice and intercession. Now we hear of another trip into the mountains, but this time the Lover isn't going alone. He is taking his Beloved with him.

When a man and woman are on different spiritual levels, it can cause problems and frustration in a marriage. When each person is looking at life from a different perspective, there is a constant tug-of-war as both people are pulling in opposite directions. That's why 2 Corinthians 6:14 says that Christians ought to be equally yoked together—not unequally yoked with unbelievers. So, it isn't just the man who needs to go to another level; the woman needs to go to the mountains as well.

In addition to Mount Amana, the passage mentions Mount Senir, which is another name for Mount Hermon, a three-peak mountain in Israel. On the slopes of this mountain were orchards and vineyards where fruit was plentiful. If our relationships are going to be fruitful, we need to go higher and get closer to God in order to honor Him and bless each other.

Once the couple makes it to the higher level, you might think that now they can relax because they have nothing left to worry about. You'd think that the man would say, "I've found the woman who loves me, and I know that I love her, so everything is going to be fine." But no, the text starts talking about lions and leopards. No matter how high you go, there will always be problems to contend with, as well as enemies trying to destroy all that you have built up. Some of my Charismatic friends say, "At every level, there is a new devil." There will always be people trying to destroy, devour, and devastate what you're trying to develop. Even when you are in the house of God, studying the Word, and trying to get your stuff together so you can go to another level, you'd think that you would be safe there and just bask in the presence of God. But, no. Remember that the devil goes to church, too. Even there, you will find lions and leopards— people with animalistic attitudes and beastly behaviors.

You can tell a lion from a human being because lions are only interested in the body. When a lion comes after you, it is not concerned about your emotions, feelings, mind, or heart, nor does it care about your background, family, dreams, goals, or soul. Lions only want your body. This should serve as a serious warning to those of us who are married. We've got to be careful how we treat our spouses in the home, because while they are out in society, they keep running into those lions and leopards who are only concerned with their bodies. At work, in the neighborhood, and even at church, they constantly meet up with lions eyeing their bodies. What's really tragic is a married person who comes home and, instead of a loving spouse, finds a lion there just ready to pounce. Before asking about how the day went and trying to be a source of encouragement and support, the hungry ol' lion is just wanting to get at the other's body. With all the lions out in the community, our spouses have enough to deal with. Surely, we are not going to act out of instinct rather than love when they come home.

We've got to remember that when we deal with lions, even in mountainous areas, we sometimes don't see them or know they are there because, as it mentions in the text, there are lions' dens. If a lion is in his den, he's there but you can't see him. Sometimes lions will crouch down in the high grass or in the brush, waiting for the right opportunity to jump out at you. In Genesis 4, God warns Cain about sin crouching down at his door just waiting to pounce on him as he comes out of his home. The old folks used to say, "Father, I thank you that you have kept me from both seen and *unseen* dangers."

It doesn't matter how high you go in life, there will always be some lions and leopards trying to destroy your stuff. Some of us think, "Finally, I've reached a certain height financially. I've attained a high-level position, and I'm in a mountaintop relationship with my spouse. Therefore, I'm safe, and nothing can touch me now." We're learning from this text, however, that there are some mean cats even in high places. Even so, we still have to make our way to the high places, because it's necessary to go to the mountains before we can enter the garden.

There is something else I've learned about mountains: it takes time to climb them, and you have to do it very carefully. I went mountain climbing in Phoenix once. (I'm trying to do some things before I get too old to do them.) Now this wasn't the kind of mountain with steep, straight cliffs for which you have to use ropes and serious climbing gear. What I discovered while hiking up this mountain was that it just wasn't going to happen quickly. I couldn't just jump from the bottom to the top. I had to take it one step at a time, being careful with my footing because if I wasn't, I could slip all the way back down to where I started.

163

Likewise, you've got to reach certain heights, but you cannot rush it. You've got to take it one step at a time. The first step in making it to the top of the mountain we're talking about here is friendship. Then we move from friendship to dating, from dating to engagement, and then from engagement to the top of the mountain — marriage.

You start climbing the relationship mountain by talking with someone you don't even know yet. From those early conversations, you may discover that you have no interest in climbing the mountain with that person. You may find that you don't really like this person because he or she doesn't value any of the things that are important to you. Perhaps he or she is not a Christian or has no goals in life, no moral base, or no God. If you discover this when you are only casual friends, nobody gets hurt. You haven't invested a lot of time and emotions into this relationship, so you haven't given yourself fully to this person. Since it's just a casual friendship and both of you knew from the onset that it could deepen or eventually dissolve, that's okay; you haven't begun the climb yet.

On the other hand, if you do learn at the friendship level that this is someone you could be interested in and wouldn't mind going a little higher with, you can begin dating, but that doesn't mean you rush straight for the top of the mountain. Again, you have to take it one step at a time. Eventually, as you get to know the other person and share who you are with him or her, you may find your deeper emotions coming into play. If you both have put God first in your lives and have similar goals and the same vision, you will learn that you can talk together about things that matter and find yourselves sharing in a close, personal way.

As you are taking one step after another, if all goes well, you both come to the realization that you want to spend the rest of your lives together. You have developed such a love for each other that you don't want to ever be apart, so you get engaged. But even after you become engaged, you are still only engaged. You're not married yet. You also have to take this stage one step at a time, and the next step isn't into bed. Until you've both agreed to "forsake all others, cleaving only unto him/her," you're not ready to share your goodies with each other.

While we're on this topic, let me say this: don't let someone use you by discussing an engagement with you just to get you into bed. I've seen that happen too often. The woman starts telling everyone that she's engaged, but there is no ring or wedding date—nothing tangible. It's just talk that's designed to get a woman to let her guard down and invite the man into her garden before he ever has a right to be there.

Sadly, I have heard some single Christians say they never want to be married. They have been turned off by seeing too many marriages fail. After having been burned themselves by past relationships, they also don't want to risk committing themselves to one person for the rest of their lives, fearing that they will be hurt. Let me help you to understand something. When a single Christian says, "I don't want to be married," in order for that person to remain obedient to God, he or she has to also be willing to say, "Therefore, I will never have sex again in my life." Sex is only designed for people who are married. You can't please God if you remain single but not celibate. Unless you have the gift of celibacy, it's going to be really difficult—almost impossible, in fact—for you to deal with the burning passion that will continue to rage within you.

Before we go on to discuss marriage, I'd like to note something about mountains in the Bible. Whenever the Scriptures mention going up into the mountains, it means that God is getting ready to do something special. When Abraham went up Mount Moriah, it meant finding a miraculous ram in the bush so he didn't have to sacrifice his son. When Moses went up Mount Sinai, it meant receiving the Ten Commandments from God. When Elijah went up to Mount Horeb, it meant discovering that God doesn't always show up in wind, earthquake, and fire; sometimes He shows up in the stillness with a small voice. When Jesus went up the Mountain of Transfiguration, it meant revealing the radiant glory of God through Him. When He went up to the Mount of Olives, it meant His ascending into Heaven. If you are not willing to go up to the mountain, it means that you are likely going to miss out on a blessing of God. The mountain always precedes the garden.

Equally Yoked Together

Notice in our text that the man keeps calling his Beloved "my sister, my bride." I love that. He is not marrying his biological sister, so this is not some incestuous relationship. This is the way we talk about relationships in the Body of Christ—in the Christian family. She is his spiritual sister, sharing his relationship with God. If God is the heavenly Father of both of them, that makes them brother and sister. It also makes them equally yoked together. In essence, the Lover is saying, "Because you are my sister in Christ first, I can also make you my spouse."

Sister, don't ever allow a man to make you his wife if he hasn't first recognized you as his sister. If he isn't a child of God, you'll never have a truly fulfilling marriage with him. We have to get away from the ungodly practice of believers marrying unbelievers or adherents of different religions. The Bible tells us in 2 Corinthians 6:14 that we are not to be yoked together with unbelievers because righteousness and wickedness have nothing in common and light and darkness cannot fellowship together. It would be like Jesus having fellowship with Satan. How can you take your body, the temple of the Holy Spirit, and connect it with somebody who has no relationship with God?

I can already hear some single person saying, "But maybe hooking up with me is what will make him/her become a Christian." Stop using marriage as an evangelistic tool! God has never told you to win somebody over to Him by marrying him or her. If you are a Christian, you need to date a Christian, be engaged to a Christian, and marry a Christian. If you are a Christian, you need to have a baby only with another Christian, and only after you are married.

God's Daughter

The woman in our text can feel comfortable in her relationship because the man who calls her "my bride" has first called her "my sister." She is his sister first, and then his spouse. Think about it. If a man cannot treat you like a sister, why would you want to be his spouse? Before this woman invites her man into her garden, she realizes that he respects her as his sister, or God's daughter. Brothers, you had better be careful about how you treat God's daughters.

If you have a daughter of your own, you will immediately understand what I'm talking about. If somebody abused your daughter, beat her up, or treated like dirt, would you not use everything legally in your power to protect your daughter? Would you not come alongside your daughter, standing between her and whoever was hurting her? Would you not use everything in your power to make sure that this mess came to an end? Now if we respond like that as human fathers, how do you think God, with His eternal love for his daughters and His infinite power, is going to respond? Men, treat your woman like your sister first, then like your spouse. Treat her as God's daughter even before you think of her as your wife.

Now in verse 9, the man says, "You have stolen my heart." Here is a brother who wasn't actively looking for marriage or even for a serious relationship. He was minding his own business and doing his own thing, but then he met this woman and, before he knew it, realized that she was the one for him. She has stolen his heart. He doesn't feel or think the way he used to; he doesn't want what he used to want. How did she steal his heart?

Perception

The old school said, "The way to a man's heart is through his stomach." The new school says, "You've got to go even lower than that." But this text says it happened with a glance of her eyes. Verse 9 says, "You have stolen my heart, my sister, my bride; you have stolen my heart with one glance of your eyes...." The Bible talks about the singleness of the eye, which refers to perception and purpose. What I believe he's saying is, "You have stolen my heart by the way that you looked at me. I love the way you perceive me—the way you view me." Think about how she has viewed him since they first met. She saw him first as a shepherd, one who leads and protects. Then she saw him as a king, a man of royalty and prosperity. After that, she saw him as a shade tree, one who wouldn't let her get burned again. Next, she saw him as a fruit tree, one who is productive, even when other trees are doing nothing. She sees him in a very positive way. He says, "It is because of how you see me that made me love you."

Sister, how do you see your man? How do you perceive him? When you look at him, what do you think about? I'm not asking about what you say to him because what you say and what you think can be two different things. I didn't study psychology for a long time, but I do know that the way you think about a person determines how you relate to him or her, no matter what you are saying. If you think that I am inferior to you, you may call me "Mr. Johnson," but you will still treat me as though I am less than you. If you think that I am a dog, you will relate to me as though I exhibited beastly behavior and animalistic attitudes, even if you never tell me what you think. If a man thinks you are a whore, he may call you his queen, but he will treat you like the image he has in his mind. The Beloved thinks highly of her man. He sees in her eyes what she thinks of him, and he loves what he sees. With her eyes, she has stolen his heart.

Environment

In verses 10 and 11, he goes on to talk about her fragrance: "How much more pleasing is our love than wine, and the fragrance of your perfume than any spice...the fragrance of your garments is like that of Lebanon." He is talking about her aroma from her perfume, which creates her individual fragrance. He is speaking of that which is physical to help us to understand that which is spiritual. Physically speaking, we all know about the fragrances of cologne and perfume, but some of us don't understand about attitude and disposition. So in a way that we will understand, he is really saying, "Your attitude and your disposition are so sweet; it's like the way a beautiful fragrance changes the environment. When you come into a room, it's as though you are wearing some sweet perfume because you affect your environment in such a positive way." This causes me to ask my sisters another question: What kind of attitude do you have in the home? This woman stole her man's heart by the positive way she looked at him and expressed what she thought about him by her sweet attitude and disposition. She had a way of making life sweeter for him.

A lot of us are interested in the sex event, but we don't think much about the environment. There is a big difference between the act and the environment, but the environment affects the action. Some of us never get everything God intended out of the event because we have not yet learned how to deal positively with the environment.

My wife and I attended the Super Bowl of 2005 in Jacksonville, Florida. The game was scheduled to start Sunday evening at 6:30 p.m., and all weekend long I overheard people complaining, "Why are they starting so late? Why can't they start the game at one o'clock in the afternoon, or at three o'clock? Why wait till 6:30 p.m.?" The reason was that the Super Bowl coordinators spend the weekend setting the environment for the event. They understand the value of hype—"foreplay" before the game. So, all during that weekend there were Super Bowl parties, Super Bowl dances, celebrity appearances, tailgate parties, special dinners, and even church services—all to create the right environment. Why were people making sacrifices by flying in from around the world and spending lots of money to go to the event? Because they knew the environment would be worth it.

Do you want to know why some of our sex events aren't worth much? Because we haven't done much in preparation. One thing that stands out in my mind about that Super Bowl was the line-up of performers—Alicia Keys; Black-Eyed Peas; Paul McCartney; and Earth, Wind and Fire. Indeed, many people elsewhere in the country saw them on television, but those of us who were there also saw the stage being set up. (I was impressed by how quickly that went.) In other words, there's a problem in a relationship when people want to perform but haven't taken the time to set the stage.

In verse twelve of our text, the man finally starts addressing the goodies—the garden: "You are a garden locked up, my sister, my bride; you are a spring enclosed; a sealed fountain." Here is a sister who took the garden God gave her and locked it, sealed it, and secured it. She had decided, "I'm going to put a lock on this treasure. I don't want to be a supermarket. I want to be a private garden." A supermarket and a private garden both have fruit, but at the super-market, just about anybody can go in and get something. They all come in touching, feeling, smelling, and sometimes even tasting the fruit before they buy it. Some people actually put fruit in their carts, push it around for awhile, and then say, "I don't really want this!" so they put it back where they got it. Some women let too many men come into their gardens who act like the fruit is theirs before it really is. Unlike a supermarket, a private garden is exclusive, inaccessible, and available only to the one chosen to have access. The fruit isn't picked over: it hasn't been handled, tasted, and smelled by everyone who came by. It's fresh and untouched.

You may be thinking, "It's too late for me; I've messed up. I've lived a promiscuous lifestyle. I've given my life to Christ now, but I haven't lived with a private garden mindset. I lived with a supermarket mentality regarding what God has given me. It's too late." With God, however, it's never too late. He will give you another opportunity; that's the good news of the gospel. You just need to change the way you do things. You have to put a "no trespassing" sign in front of your garden. You don't have to try to get the key back from every man you've given it to; just change the lock. When a man comes back and tries the lock but can't get it open, let him know that your garden is private now.

Verse 13 says, "Your plants are an orchard of pomegranates with choice fruits...." The garden is *planted*. In other words, somebody took time to create this garden. Likewise, God has a purpose for your garden. There is somebody that God has for you. When you learn to trust God and live life His way, you will be blessed. According to Psalm 1:2 and 3, when you fall in love with the Word of God, and in that Word you meditate day and night, you will become a tree planted with purpose by the rivers of water, giving forth fruit in its season. Do you want to know why some sisters keep opening up their gardens? Because they become envious of another sister. They see that she is being productive and has gotten married, so now they are trying to go outside the will of God to get what the other sister has received from God. Yet, it doesn't work like that. What you won't get is what she got. You can't get on your own what only God can give you. You need to learn how to wait on the Lord, and be of good courage. He will strengthen your heart!

Variety

There's something else about this garden. It's both pleasant and pleasurable. Look at all the stuff that's in this garden. It's got spice, choice fruits, incense trees, honeycomb, henna, nard, myrrh, saffron, aloe, honey, calamus, pomegranates, and cinnamon. Have you ever seen a garden with so many different kinds of plants in it? This is a garden with creativity, diversity, and variety. So, in verse 16, when the Beloved invites her husband to come in and taste its choice fruits, he's got plenty to choose from. He doesn't have to eat the same thing every time he goes in. In fact, he can't wait to go back because he never knows what he's going to get the next time he goes there.

But he's not the only one who gets to experience diversity and variety. In verse 16, the woman says, "Awake, north wind, and come, south wind! Blow on my garden, that its fragrance may spread abroad. Let my lover come into his garden, and taste its choice fruits." By saying to her man, "Awake, north wind, and come, south wind," she's letting him know that he doesn't have to come in the same way every time. "Sometimes you can come in from the north; sometimes you can come in from the south. You don't have to be in the same position every time you come in. It's your garden. Come in however you want." There is variety for the woman as well when her husband comes into her garden.

Now, look back at verse 11: "Your lips drop sweetness as the honeycomb, my bride; milk and honey are under your tongue." Look again at verse 16: "Awake, north wind, and come, south wind! Blow on my garden, that its fragrance may spread abroad. Let my lover come into his garden and taste its choice fruits." Then read verse 1 of chapter 5: "I have come into my garden, my sister, my bride; I have gathered my myrrh with my spice. I have eaten my honeycomb, and my honey; I have drunk my wine and my milk." There's an awful lot of eating going on in these verses. Some people say the milk and honey under her tongue represent a passionate kiss. Some say it's a reference to Palestine, the Promised Land, flowing with milk and honey. Whatever the reference, you've got to admit that there's a lot of eating, right?

The Bible makes it clear that when God created sex, it was not just for making babies. It was also good for recreation, release, and enjoyment. Whatever else we get out of the Song of Solomon, we see that sex is fun.

Many people ask, "In marriage, are all forms of sex okay in the sight of God?" When it comes to creativity in sex, that is a matter between you and your spouse as you express yourselves lovingly to each other. You and your spouse have to decide together what is right for you. In making that decision, you have to be careful because you don't want to do something that makes your partner feel that he or she is doing anything sinful or demeaning, however much you enjoy it. If it makes the person you love feel like a prostitute, why would you want to do it? If it makes that person feel guilty, why would you insist on doing it? How can you develop something positive if the one you are making love to sees your actions as negative?

There has to be a lot of communication as your relationship develops. You can't just say, "No, it makes me uncomfortable and I'm not going to do it." You need to think through your feelings and express them to your mate. Why do you think it's wrong, or, why do you think it is right? On what do you base your response? What is your experience? What have you been taught? What have you heard? You need to communicate.

First Corinthians 8 talks about believers with weak consciences and puts the responsibility on those who have greater freedom in Christ not to wound their consciences. Therefore, you shouldn't pressure or coerce your mate to do something that will leave him or her hurt or wounded.

At the same time, I would encourage you to think about the way the Bible talks about sex. Think about the freedom of both communication and behavior between the Lover and the Beloved in the Song of Solomon. It would be healthy for some of us to be a little more adventurous with our marital partners. Why settle for a bologna sandwich every night when you can feast on all kinds of wonderful delicacies? Ask God to help you understand why you are so hesitant when it comes to sex. Ask God to help you see lovemaking between you and your spouse from *His* perspective. Ask our God "who richly provides us with everything for our enjoyment" (1 Timothy 6:17) to show you if your thoughts about sex are coming from somewhere other than Him. Ask Him for the freedom to lavish love upon your spouse in ways he or she will appreciate and enjoy. Keep talking to God and to each other.

Communication

So much of this is about communication. Many people, even those who have been married for years, are frustrated in marriage and particularly in their sex lives. Why? Because their spouses aren't meeting their needs. If that's you, does your spouse *know* he or she isn't meeting your needs? Do you expect him or her to auto-matically know what you like and don't like, and what you want to do and don't want to do? Your spouse can't read your mind; you're going to have to give some direction. You're going to have to open your mouth and let your spouse know exactly what you want and expect. Just look at how the Lover, even as he is making love to his wife, continues to talk about what he sees, hears, smells, touches, and tastes.

Have you ever had your back itching in a place you couldn't scratch? When this happens, you turn to your spouse: "My back is itching, and I can't reach the spot. Please scratch my back." What usually happens? The person goes all over the middle of your back, trying to figure out where the itch is, while you keep saying, "No, it's not there! No, to the right. A little to the left and up a bit. That's it. Okay, right there. Now harder, harder, harder! Okay now, slow, soft." It may take a while for them to find the itch, but it feels so good when they do!

You may be frustrated because you've got a sexual itch that you can't scratch yourself. You need to turn to your spouse and say, "Listen, I've got an itch that I can't scratch." Then you need to guide them, telling them where you need their touch, what feels good, and what isn't quite getting it. Be specific. Only you know what you're feeling and what you need to feel satisfied. You've got to communicate.

There is one more thing this text can teach us. Many words used in the passage are often representations in the Scriptures of the Holy

Spirit: water, spring, blow, and wind, for instance. Whatever else this text is teaching us, it's also teaching that our relationships with each other are never going to work right till we have the proper relationship with God. We need God's wind, God's breath, God's spring, God's water, and God's stream. We need the Holy Spirit of God in us so that we can get right with God. Then after we get right with God, we've got to work on getting right with ourselves. I've got to love God first, but then I also need to love and appreciate myself. We need to develop an appreciation for who and how God has made us, sanctified us, and set us apart unto Himself. When we get it right with God and ourselves, then we are in a position to get it right with others.

Chapter 11

Let's Talk about Sex

² I slept but my heart was awake.
Listen! My lover is knocking:
"Open to me, my sister, my darling,
my dove, my flawless one.
My head is drenched with dew,
my hair with the dampness of the night."
³ I have taken off my robe —
must I put it on again?
I have washed my feet —
must I soil them again?
⁴ My lover thrust his hand through the latch-opening;
my heart began to pound for him.
⁵ I arose to open for my lover,
and my hands dripped with myrrh,
my fingers with flowing myrrh,
on the handles of the lock.
⁶ I opened for my lover,
but my lover had left; he was gone.
My heart sank at his departure.
I looked for him but did not find him.
I called him but he did not answer.
⁷ The watchmen found me
as they made their rounds in the city.
They beat me, they bruised me;
they took away my cloak,
those watchmen of the walls!
⁸ O daughters of Jerusalem, I charge you —

if you find my lover,
what will you tell him?
Tell him I am faint with love.
            (Song of Solomon 5:2-8, NIV)

S ixty-five percent of new marriages end in divorce. This means
that for every 1,000 new marriages, 650 of them will end in
divorce. One out of every twenty teenage girls now gets pregnant
before getting married. Fifty percent of teenagers are having sex.
One and a half million abortions take place every year; half of the
ones having them are teenagers. Ten million Americans every year
are diagnosed with sexually transmitted diseases. More than thirty
million people already have herpes. Millions have contracted HIV/
AIDS. Each year, one hundred thousand forcible rapes and seven
hundred thousand sexual assaults are reported. Yet, often we want
the church to sit back quietly with its head in the sand, acting as
though nothing is going on.

I believe it is time for the church to speak out regarding sex. As
I've mentioned before, it seems as if everyone is talking about sex—
except the church. People on the street talk about it, the movies talk
about it, pop songs talk about it, television talks about it, and the
Internet talks about it. The church needs to speak the truth about this
subject from the Word of God because the truth will make us free.
So let's talk about sex.

Just last month I was preaching in Dallas, Texas, and a group
from my church went to visit other ministries in the area. While we
were there, a tragedy took place. A south Dallas man was seriously
injured in a home fire, suffering second- and third-degree burns over
seventy percent of his body. The firefighters showed up, put out the
fire, saved his life, and then conducted an investigation to try to find
out what happened. How did this man catch on fire? What went
on in his home? They discovered that when the man went to sleep,
he was smoking a cigarette. As a result, his bed caught on fire, the
flames quickly spread through his home, and he was burned. He was
injured because he was doing something in bed that he had no business doing. Likewise, there are some of us who keep getting burned

in one relationship after another. If the truth be told, it is because we keep doing things in bed that we've got no business doing.

We see some strange things happening in this passage of Song of Solomon. But first, let me point out that in this section of verses, the couple is still single. Remember, this is a book of poetry, not a chronology. It's a song, so it doesn't follow a special timeline. They just sing what they feel. Even though verse 1 of chapter 5 says "my bride," that verse is part of the previous section. As we begin with verse 2, we're starting a new section in which the two lovers are single.

Undressed, Unsure, Unconscious

This being the case, I wonder what this man is doing in this woman's house at this time of night. As the text begins, he's knocking on her door. Since he's probably been to her house numerous times, she is used to having him come over for a visit, but this is the middle of the night. Verse 2 says, "My head is drenched with dew, my hair with the dampness of the night." If dew is gathering, it must be sometime between midnight and sunrise. Why is he knocking on her door at this hour?

She certainly wasn't expecting him. Here she is, undressed, awakened from her sleep, and feeling groggy, unconscious, and unsure. She's trying to figure out, "Should I open the door, or should I not open the door? Should I let him in, or should I not let him in?" Certainly, her Lover would know her schedule by now. It seems that he deliberately waited until she was undressed, unconscious, and unsure before knocking. If she had been covered, conscious, and sure, would he have been there at this particular time? Look closely at the second part of verse 2: "Open to me, my sister, my darling, my dove, my flawless one. My head is drenched with the dew, my hair with the dampness of the night." This verse uses seven personal pronouns! The only one whom he's interested in right now is himself. He's not thinking about her, her family, her emotions or even her soul. There he is, knocking on the door, spouting out *seven* personal pronouns. In the Bible, the number seven represents a state of completion, so not only is he selfish: he's *completely* selfish. He's only concerned with what he can get right now.

Let me slow down for a second, because we're not talking about an evil man here or a sexual predator. We're talking about a good, spiritual man, but even good people do bad things now and then. This is a good man, acting out of character in the middle of the night. While she's undressed, unsure, and unconscious, he's trying to get in.

Intellectual Decision

Groggy as she is, the woman is trying to figure this out. She's got an intellectual decision that she has to make here. I love the fact that this sister was trying to think this thing through. Here is a man she knows is good, surprising her in the middle of the night, his head drenched with dew. Do you know how long it would have taken for his head to get *drenched* with dew? Not only is he out in the middle of the night, he's been out *all* night. He didn't just get there; he's been out there for a while. Now he's knocking on his Beloved's door, and she's trying to figure out if she should let him in. His head is full of dew, meaning that his thought process has been affected by the world.

Now, you may have had your head messed with by the world, too. It didn't happen suddenly, like a rainstorm that drenches you all at once but like the process of dew—subtly, slowly, gradually. When you stay in the wrong environment with the wrong people for too long, you start thinking like them. It's so slow and subtle that for a long time you think it's not affecting you. You are deceived into thinking that you are the same person that you were two years ago when you opened yourself up to that environment. When you first started hanging out at that club, it wasn't a problem for you because you were still filled with the Spirit and grounded in the Word of God. But, the longer that you've been hanging out there, the more it's been affecting you. If you are the only Christian in the crowd you hang out with, it's good for you to be salt in the world and to let your light shine in dark places. But what if your salt has lost its savor, and your light has become overcome by darkness?

Gradually, over time, as you stay in an unhealthy environment, you are going to be corrupted by it. Listen to how the conversations go and what you talk about, look at where you hang out, and think about how you and your friends treat other people. You may think, "I'm still a believer!" but eventually the company you've been keeping starts messing with your head. The jokes you entertain, the conversations you hold, the gossip you listen to, and even the music slowly but surely influences how you think.

I'm very concerned about today's music—not all of it, because there's some good stuff out there. Yet, we have to admit that we are living in a day and time when the music that many people in our society are listening to is not promoting a positive worldview. This kind of music degrades women and encourages violence, sexual promiscuity, and drugs. If we expose ourselves to ungodly music over and over again, it is going to have a negative impact on our thinking. Now someone will be quick to say, "Well, I do listen to it, but I just listen to it for the beat. I really don't like or appreciate the lyrics, but I do like to dance to the rhythm. I'm just listening to the music, not to the words." Your mind, however, can't function like that. God has given you such a wonderful tape recorder in your head that everything you hear you are picking up, whether it's consciously or subconsciously. You can't take the music in and leave the lyrics out. Even though you may think the music isn't getting to you, just like dew, it slowly, subtly, gradually seeps in. Then, one day you wake up, and you are filled with it. That's what happened to the Lover in our text.

So here he is, knocking at his Beloved's door in the middle of the night. Sisters, if any man comes knocking on your door at three in the morning, however well you may know him, don't let him in. It doesn't matter if he is saying through the door, "My sister, my darling, my dove, my flawless one...." He may look fine from the other side of that door, but don't let him in. No man who is full of the Holy Spirit is going to be there at that hour, sweet-talking you like that! He may be full of alcohol or drugs, lust, ego, or selfishness, but it's not the fullness of the Spirit prompting him to try to seduce you.

Now that the woman is in this predicament, she has to think her way through it and make a decision. There is something I almost missed when I first read through this text. The way I read it initially, the woman realizes that her lover is knocking at her door, trying to get in. He's calling out to her, asking her to open the door, and she calls back to him: "I have taken off my robe—must I put it on again? I have washed my feet—must I soil them again?" At first, I thought she was hollering back to him through the door. But, no, she's not talking to *him*; she's talking to *herself*. She's thinking out loud, using her intellectual capacities to make a decision: "Should I let him in, or should I not let him in? Should I open the door, or should I not open the door? No, I can't let him in because I'm not dressed. If I let him in when I don't have any clothes on, one thing's going to lead to another...." (If we're honest, we've all had some sort of conversation like that with ourselves.) This wasn't some thug standing outside her door; this is her man. This is someone she loves and someone who loves her, someone who usually has his life together and possesses all of these great qualities that she appreciates. She knows, however, that if she opens that door, the temptation will be too much for her.

We all have to realize that there is a certain level of temptation that will get all of us to sin. It doesn't matter how holy we are, how many tongues we speak in, who anointed us, what church we go to, how big our Bible is, how many crosses are hanging around our necks, or whether we are wearing our "What Would Jesus Do?" bracelet. If we put ourselves in compromising positions, the temptation will be great enough to entice us to give in. We have to make up our minds that we are not going to put ourselves in a situation that will cause ourselves to fall. That's why I encourage young, single people to double-date. If young men and women hang out by themselves, it's too easy to find themselves before long in some dark room with the shades pulled, the candles burning, and just the right music on the CD player. They are just setting themselves up for a fall!

The Shulammite woman also knew that if she opened the door, she was going to get her feet dirty. Houses in those days had dirt floors, so if she walked from her bed to that door, she would get her feet dirty. Again, we are still looking at all of this text symbolically. Remember when Jesus was washing the disciples' feet? In essence, Peter said, "Wait, Jesus, you're too holy to wash my feet. You can't do this. You are the King of kings and Lord of lords. You can't wash my feet because I'm less than you." Jesus replied, "If you won't let me wash your feet, you won't have a part in the kingdom." So Peter said, "Don't just wash my feet; wash my head and my hands; wash all of me." Jesus said, "If I only wash your feet, it will represent your lifestyle, so it will represent all of you."

In other words, this woman is saying, "If I get out of bed right now and open that door, it is going to make my lifestyle dirty." There are some doors you can't open without getting dirty. She says to herself, "I have already washed," which is past tense. If you were once dirty, but you have let God clean you up, you don't want to get dirty again—not for anybody. She is thinking, "I'm not getting dirty for anybody. I don't care who's on the other side of the door. I don't care how fine he is. I've made up my mind."

Some of us confess our sins, say we're sorry, and cry big croco-dile tears: "God, I'm sorry. I shouldn't have done that. I shouldn't have gone there. I shouldn't have said that. I shouldn't have behaved like that." While we're asking God to forgive us, we really mean it. But once He forgives us, we run right back out, go right back to the same places, and get back in the same messed-up relationships that got us dirty in the first place. Jesus said that it's like a dog going back to its own vomit. When I was a kid, I had a bunch of dogs—but not all at the same time. I learned something about dogs. Dogs will often eat things they have no business eating; they ingest things they shouldn't be ingesting. They get something in them they're not supposed to have, and then it begins to make them sick. They mope around, roll around, and act all sad and crazy because they've got something in them that they shouldn't have, and then they are sick. All of a sudden, they'll vomit it up. But then dogs get back to feeling good and after a while, they forget what made them sick. So they go right back to their own vomit and ingest the same thing again that made them sick before.

Jesus said that's how some of us are. We're out in the world, living a sinful life, taking into our bodies and our minds things we shouldn't be taking in. At some point, we make up our minds that we don't want to live like that anymore. So we go to the house of God, confess our sins to Christ, unite with the church, become active in the church, get a new Bible, buy a cross to show the world what we stand for now, get involved in one of the ministries at the church, and, two or three months later, we're feeling better. We've gotten out of the mess we were in, and we've gotten the mess out of us. But as we start to feel better, we forget what it was that made us sick. Then we end up going right back to ungodly relationships and unrighteous places, and end up in the same dirty situations.

Not all women are like the one in our text. Her initial thought was that she couldn't open her door to a man because she wasn't dressed. Did you know that there are some sisters who feel that they have to be *un*dressed to open a door? They feel that they can only relate to a man on a sexual level. So, every time they open the door, they are undressed—ready and willing for something to happen, because they don't know how else to relate to a man. If you are like that, and the only reason a man is attracted to you is because you are ready and willing, you might as well break off that relationship right now. Sooner or later, you are going to have to put your clothes back on. If you don't know how to continue a relationship when you are dressed and doing things that are positive and productive in your life, then that relationship isn't any good for you anyhow. First, you have to get it right with your clothes on! Then later, after you have entered into a marriage covenant before God, you can get it right with your clothes off.

Emotional Decision

Watch, though, how the brother at the door isn't giving up. He is trying to entice her with his words—"My sister (you know how close we are); my love (you know how I feel about you); my dove (come on, baby); my flawless one (I know your character and your purity, and I respect that)." When his smooth words don't work, he goes from knocking and talking to action by trying to push his way in. The woman says, "My lover thrust his hand through the latch-opening...." Now you would think that this would upset her and she would get angry: "That's my door. I'm not opening it because it would be inappropriate to open this door at this time. How dare you think you can barge into my house anytime you want to! Now I'm definitely not opening that door!"

You would think that his behavior would cause agitation on her part. But instead, she is getting sexually stimulated because he's trying to force his way in. Why? Because she's flattered. No longer thinking with her intellect, she's operating now on pure emotion. She somehow thinks his persistence is a sign of his passion. Now in this day and age, a woman thinking like this one would probably grab her cell phone next to her bed, call up her best friend and say, "Girl, guess who's outside my door? No, right now; he's out here right now. He's trying to push his way up in here." Wait a minute. That is not a sign of his love for you! Your feelings are fooling you. The enemy is trying to destroy what you have. Women, just because a brother is persistent doesn't mean he cares about you. If a brother is violating your boundaries, it doesn't show how much he cares about you; instead, it shows his disrespect for you.

Sister, before you open that door and get dirty again, you need to understand something. One of the things that attracted this man to you was the fact that you were clean: he called you his "flawless one," or, as the King James Version puts it, "my undefiled." You haven't come to the door undressed or opened your garden to other men. If you open that door, his feelings for you are going to change, and he won't see you in the same way. Even though you are doing what he wants you to do at that moment, you would become defiled in his eyes, just like so many other women he knows.

But the Beloved is no longer thinking with her head. There was a wrestling match going on between her mind and her heart. Her head was saying, "Girl, don't you open that door," while her heart was saying, "Girl, don't you let that man get away." She put her heart above her head, and now she's no longer trying to reason things out with her intellect. Operating now on feelings, she gives in and heads for the door.

But by the time she gets to the door, her Lover is gone. We aren't told why the man finally left, but we can only imagine that the woman was asking that question herself. She had to be wondering where he was going and why he left. There are several possibilities. Maybe he left because he got too cold. (He did have all of that dew in his hair in the middle of the night.) Perhaps he was cold in temperament. Some brothers are so cold that if you don't open your garden for them, they aren't staying around. Maybe he left because there was no communication between them. She talked to herself, but she didn't talk to him. He might have left because she took too long to make up her mind, and he didn't feel that she wanted him. Perhaps he left because there were some other doors he wanted to knock on. There are so many possible reasons for the decision he made.

We don't know why he left, but watch what she does. She goes after him. After throwing some clothes on, she went running around in the streets looking for this man. When she was thinking, she was safely lying in her bed. Now that she's operating on emotion, she's out running around in the streets. Likewise, we have to be careful not to let our feelings fool us. There are some good sisters in the church right now hanging out in the streets, trying to figure out why their men did not stay. Here in Song of Solomon, we see this good woman looking for a man in bad places. In this text, she comes to other men, the watchmen of the city, who beat her, hit her, violate her, take her cloak, and humiliate her.

I can't proceed further without saying this to any men reading this book: if you have a problem with laying your hands violently on any woman, something is wrong with you. There is not a sister anywhere in the world who deserves to have her man beat her. If you have a problem in that area, you have to get help. Understand this: The problem is not *your woman*; the problem is with *you*. There is something wrong with a man who is willing to hit a woman, especially the one whom you said God has given to you. Also, sister, there is something wrong with *your* thinking if you stay with a man who keeps beating you. Don't say, "Well, maybe I shouldn't have done this, or maybe I should have...." Stop making excuses for him! If he's beating you, the problem isn't with you; the problem is with him!

Now the Shulammite woman finally gets past those men and finds some of the women in the city. She begins to ask them: "Have you seen my man? Do you know where my man is?"

Do you know what the other sisters are thinking? "If he's your man, why don't you know where he is?" Notice the irony. She has no idea where he is, but he knew exactly where he could find her. He knew she would be at her home in the middle of the night. She doesn't know where to begin looking for him. Why is she accountable and responsible, but he's not? How is she going to be involved in a healthy relationship if he knows where she is, but she has no idea where he is? Something is wrong. She has stopped thinking, has started operating according to her emotions, and has ended up in the streets looking for a man.

When I was a kid, Courtney Gordon, David Green, some other friends, and I in our little neighborhood formed a club, and we had a secret handshake. It was an exclusive club; not just anyone could get in there. David, Courtney, and I were the leaders of this group. We had a little place where we hung out, and if you didn't know the password, you couldn't get in. It didn't matter what else you had or didn't have, what you looked like or didn't look like: without the password, you couldn't get into our club.

Sisters, you need to get a password; then, you need to let these brothers know that they can't get in without the password. None of this, "My sister, my love, my dove, my flawless one." No, that's not it. You can't get in with that! Also, sister, you've got to stop giving men keys to your place. For some women, it's like their bedrooms have revolving doors. Men just keep coming and going out. Sister, you need to put a lock on your door and tell the man you love, "You can get in here freely and often, but you have to say the password. That password is 'my wife.' When you can call me that, you can come in. Till then, it's not happening."

Chapter 12

AWOL

[8]O daughters of Jerusalem, I charge you—
if you find my lover,
what will you tell him?
Tell him I am faint with love.
[9]How is your beloved better than others,
most beautiful of women?
How is your beloved better than others,
that you charge us so?
[10]My lover is radiant and ruddy,
outstanding among ten thousand.
[11]His head is purest gold;
his hair is wavy
and black as a raven.
[12]His eyes are like doves
by the water streams,
washed in milk,
mounted like jewels.
[13]His cheeks are like beds of spice
yielding perfume.
His lips are like lilies
dripping with myrrh.
[14]His arms are rods of gold
set with chrysolite.
His body is like polished ivory
decorated with sapphires.
[15]His legs are pillars of marble
set on bases of pure gold.
His appearance is like Lebanon,
choice as its cedars.

¹⁶His mouth is sweetness itself;
he is altogether lovely.
This is my lover, this my friend,
O daughters of Jerusalem.
¹Where has your lover gone,
most beautiful of women?
Which way did your lover turn,
that we may look for him with you?
²My lover has gone down to his garden,
to the beds of spices,
to browse in the gardens
and to gather lilies.
³I am my lover's and my lover is mine;
he browses among the lilies.
(Song of Solomon 5:8 – 6:3, NIV)

S ong of Solomon 5:8 reads, "O daughters of Jerusalem, I charge you—if you find my lover, what will you tell him? Tell him, I am faint with love." This is about a man who is AWOL—Absent With Out Leave, like a soldier who is missing from his or her assigned post.

David Copperfield is one of the greatest magicians who has ever lived. Some suggest that he is even greater than the legendary Houdini. I've never had the chance to see Copperfield perform in person, but I have seen him numerous times on television. Once, I saw him make an elephant that was more than 2,000 pounds disappear. One moment the elephant was there, and the next moment it was gone. On another occasion, I saw him make a 737 airplane disappear, and in one of his greatest feats ever, he made the Statue of Liberty disappear. He truly is one of the greatest illusionists of all time.

But greater than David Copperfield and Houdini is the greatest illusionist of all—Satan, our adversary. The Bible says he is able to deceive the very elect of God, those of us who are Christian believers. Jesus said that Satan is a liar and the father of lies. He is the daddy of deception, the master of illusion.

One of the worst tricks that he has pulled in the twenty-first century is to make men disappear. One minute a man is there, and the next minute he's gone. One moment a husband is there, and the next minute he's gone. One minute a father is there, and the next minute he's gone. One minute a man is in church, and the next minute he's gone. The enemy has a way of making men disappear, making them go AWOL.

Even some women have been deceived by this enemy to the point that they are now saying, "I don't need a man." He has fooled us into thinking that manhood is unimportant, so some sisters feel that they don't need men in their lives. Also, some men feel that their absence doesn't mean anything. They don't believe that their absence has a negative impact on the lives of those with whom they are supposed to be in a relationship—their wives, their children, their parents, their friends, and others. That's part of the reason some statistics show:

- Sixty-five percent of new marriages end in divorce.
- By the time children are eighteen, fifty percent of them will have lived in households headed by single females.
- Fathers spend an average of seven minutes a day with their children.

Some men and women do not understand the importance of the father's presence in the lives of their children. They don't realize that children who grow up without their fathers being present in their lives are more likely to drop out of school, do drugs, and abuse alcohol. Teenage girls who lack the presence of their fathers in their lives are more likely to get pregnant before they get married. Both boys and girls who have absent fathers are more likely to end up in poverty. It's time for men to stop being absent without leave. Men, your children need your nurturing, as well as your name.

We could ask men why they are not in the lives of their wives, children, churches, and communities. Yet, if we asked a hundred men, we would probably get a hundred different answers or reasons. In this chapter, however, I'm not trying to deal with *justification*; I'm talking about *rationalization*. I'm not trying to justify why a husband is not there for his wife, why a father is not there for his children, or why men are not there for their churches and community. I'm talking rather about the reasons they give. If we can figure out the reasons why men disappear, we might be able to also figure out ways to get them to reappear. It's time for men to stand up and be the men they're supposed to be by returning to their families, their churches, and the life of their communities.

Locked Out

In chapter 5 of Song of Solomon, we read about a man who has disappeared. One moment he is there; the next moment he is gone. It seems that the reason he left was because the woman he wanted had locked him out. He was knocking on the door, but she would not let him in, so he walked away. I wonder if that's why there are some men who are not where they are supposed to be. I wonder if they've been left out, locked out, and shut out.

Now, based on the previous chapter, someone will argue, "But wait a minute! He came at the wrong time. You pointed out how he showed up in the middle of the night with dew on his head, trying to sweet-talk and push his way in. He came at the wrong time." But remember, I'm talking now about how a man rationalizes his actions, not whether they are justified or not. It's true that he did come at the wrong time, but I wonder what would have happened if she had communicated with him. It might have worked out better if she had said to him, "I have feelings for you and I'd like to be with you, but we've got to do things the right way. You seem to be looking for a shortcut in our relationship, but I'm not willing to do that. I'm not ready to go to that level with you because I don't think it's the right time or the right way." But she never said anything. When a brother is being locked out, left out, and shut out, how long do you think it's going to be before he walks out?

Let me make sure that I'm being understood. I'm not only talking about locking a brother out physically. He can be right there in the same house, in the same room, and even in the same bed, but still be locked out. Some sisters have locked brothers out psychologically and emotionally. He's been trying to talk his way in with loving words such as "My sister, my love, my dove, my flawless one," but he doesn't even get the time of day from her because his woman refuses to communicate with him. She's content to keep him outside, but how long does she think he will stay there, waiting? It doesn't matter how attractive you are or how much you seem to be in control, if you lock him out long enough, he's eventually going to leave.

The sisters who are especially bad are those who shut their brothers out for superficial reasons: they don't drive a certain kind of car, live in a certain kind of house, wear the right clothes, make a certain amount of money, or hold a certain kind of position. Now that wasn't true of the woman in Song of Solomon. When we hear her talking about her man in verse 10, there is no mention of a house, a car, money, clothes, or a job. She was focused on who he was—not what he had. But too many sisters today are more concerned about what a brother has, rather than who he is. In short, their priorities are all messed up.

By verse 7, the Shulammite's man was gone, so she is running around the streets, looking for him. She goes to the watchmen, who were the policemen of that day. She lets them know, "I'm trying to find my man. Will you put out a missing person report on my man? Can you please put out an APB, an All Points Bulletin, or a BOLO, a Be On the Lookout, for my man? I don't know where he is, and I'm trying to find him." Now before the police officers will file a report like this, they need to know some details. If it's a missing infant or child, they file the report and start the search immediately. When it's a teenager or an adult missing, however, they need to know the circumstances under which the person left. What's the environment like at home? What's been happening in the home? What was going on the last time that person was seen? The person may not be lost at all. He may simply have left or run away.

This woman is asking the police to help her find the very same man whom she has been shutting out. My grandma used to say, "Sometimes you don't appreciate your water until your well runs dry." While the woman had her man, she locked him out. But now that he's gone, she's trying to get him back. She's on the lookout for the same man she shut out. She's trying to find what she already had at one time.

Let me illustrate. I now wear contact lenses, the disposable kind that you can wear for thirty days and then just throw away. When I used to wear glasses, I kept losing them. One day I couldn't find them anywhere. I looked in drawers, in my closet, in my car, in the glove box—everywhere I could think of. Finally, I called my sons together and said, "You've all got to help Daddy find his glasses. I'm going to give a reward to whoever finds my glasses first." Immediately, and in unison, they said, "Daddy, they're on your face."

Okay, now don't act like you've never done that before. I had gotten so comfortable with them and so used to them that I started taking them for granted. When I first got them, I could feel them and used to adjust them every now and then, but now I had gotten so used to them that I didn't even think about having them on. Some sister is treating her *good* man like that right now. She has gotten comfortable with him and used to him paying the bills, supporting her, being there for her, opening the door for her, helping her with her coat, and treating her like a queen. She's gotten so used to him that now she takes him for granted. The next thing you know, she's out looking for him. He may still be right there, but she has gotten so used to him that she treats him like he isn't even there.

Still Beautiful

The Shulammite woman goes to the other women because the watchmen didn't help her. She says to the sisters of the community in verse 9: "I need for you to help me find my man. If you find him, tell him that I'm lovesick and overwhelmed. Tell him I want to get back with him."

The sisters compliment her by calling her "the most beautiful among women." This is important. Remember that when she first met her lover back in chapter 1, he said to her, "How beautiful you are, my darling! Oh, how beautiful!" In chapters 2 through 4, when everything was good between them, he called her his "beautiful one," and repeatedly told her how beautiful she was. Now, her man is gone. He walked out on her, so she is alone in the world. Things aren't good for her right now. Her world has been turned upside down, and she is crushed in spirit. But yet, the other women in the community call her the "most beautiful among women." Even though her man is not in her life right now, she is still beautiful. In other words, she was beautiful before she met him, she was beautiful while they were together, and even now, after he's gone, she's still beautiful. Let me put it in our vernacular. She was fine before she met him, she was fine while they were hooked up, and she's still fine even when he's gone. Her beauty, the way she carries herself, and her spirit have nothing to do with her relationship to a man.

Sister, stop thinking that a man has made you! No, God has made you. I love this, because when you look at the situation, you see a paradox. When they first got together, the Lover *did* add something to her. But when he left, he did not take anything from her. It's hard to come to grips with this, but when a good man comes into your life, he does add something to you. If it doesn't work out and he leaves, however, he does not take anything from you. It is God who makes you who you are. In Him, you live, move, and have your being. It's not in your man, not in your husband, and not in your ex: it is in God.

Let's back up for a minute to look at the treatment the watchmen give the Shulammite. The sisters are complimenting her and supporting her. On the other hand, when the watchmen find her, they hit her, hurt her, and harass her. Remember that in this chapter, I am not talking about justification. There is no way that they can justify their behavior toward her. Make no mistake: there is no reason for a man to hit, harm, harass, or humiliate any woman. This is unequivocal. You can't justify it or come up with any reason for it.

I'm bringing the watchmen up again, though, because I want you to see the contrast. In verse 10, she begins describing this great man she's looking for. Before she gets to the good man in verse 10, however, she runs into those bad men in verse 7. If she doesn't get away from the men who hit her, hurt her, humiliated and abused her, she'll never be able to get a man who can help her. Sister, you've got to figure out a way to get away from the bad men in order to get a good one. If you stay entangled with the bad ones, you'll never be able to get the good man God wants you to have.

It's rare for a woman to marry the first man she has a relationship with. You may have found a good man now and are married to him, but he most likely wasn't the first one you got to know. There were other brothers before him that you got to know, dated, and maybe even considered marrying, but you had to let go of them before you could find the best man. That's what other sisters have to learn. Too often, if you hang around a bad brother too long, you will find yourself in love with him and saying things like, "He really means so much to me, and I think I can change him. I'm just going to be patient with him. I really think it will work out."

Sister, you're never going to get the good man God wants you to have because you have let yourself become entangled with less than the best. Paraphrasing the advice Kenny Rogers once gave in a folk ballad, you've got to know when to hold them. You've got to know when to fold them. You've got to know when to walk away. And, sisters, you've got to know when to run. As long as you remain entangled with bad people, you'll never get the good one.

If you are one of the women who has found a good man, you may occasionally run into one of the men from your past. It may be the one whom you thought, "This is going to be the one," even though you knew he wasn't right for you. Your mother told you he wasn't right for you, your daddy told you, and the brothers and sisters in the community told you—everybody told you. You knew it yourself, but you tried to make excuses for him. He continually dogged you, but you kept trying to hold on. You wanted somebody who didn't want you. Then when he left, you got mad at God: "God, why are You letting this happen to me? Why didn't You let us be together? You could have made it happen. God, You should have. He wasn't perfect, but You could have helped me to change him." There was a lot of trauma and drama when he left, right? But that was back in the day. You got it together after that. Now you've got somebody with sense in your life who loves you. You've got something good going on.

So one afternoon, you're out at the mall, and you run into that character again. Of course, when you see him now, you're not trippin' because that thing is over. (One of my friends who studies psychology says that it takes about twelve months to get over somebody you are entangled with, but if within that twelve-month period you hook back up for even a minute, your twelve months start all over again.) In this case, you're long past your twelve months. You've got your new person—a good man—and everything is fine. So you run into this clown at the mall and talk for a minute. Then you walk away, thinking, "That dude is crazy; he's out of his mind.

He's still strung out, still doesn't believe in God, and still doesn't know Jesus."

Then you have another conversation with God: "Oh, God, thank You so much for doing the thinking for me when I couldn't think for myself. Thank You for breaking it off when I couldn't break it off. Thank You for not letting me stay entangled with someone who doesn't even know You. Thank You, God." I truly believe that every now and then, when God lets one situation end in your life, it's because He's getting ready to open up something much better for you. Just let it go! You've got to know when to walk away.

One Size Doesn't Fit All

Now the Shulammite woman is talking with these sisters in the community, asking them for help. Watch what the sisters ask her in verse 9: "How is your beloved better than others, most beautiful of women?" In other words, they're asking her, "You want us to look for him? What makes him different from anybody else? Before we waste time trying to find him, is he worth looking for?" What they're implying is that all men are just alike. They are essentially asking her, "Why are you going to waste time chasing this one and running after him? Just take one of these that's available because they are all just alike. They all think alike, they all want the same thing, they are all interested in the same stuff, and they are all intimidated by relationships. None of them will make a commitment to one woman. None of them can handle a woman with more education or one who makes more money. They can't deal with a woman who can think and make decisions for herself. They just want someone weak whom they can misuse and abuse. Why should we look for this one when they are all the same?"

Unfortunately, some sisters still believe this way today. They think that all men are just alike. To these women, they are all dogs that are just interested in sex, none of them can commit to one person, none of them can be accountable and responsible, and none of them understand intimacy. Every time I hear a woman talking like that, I am offended. Are all men are the same? Of course not— just as all women are not alike. Not all men have a relationship with God, but some of us do! Not all men have a job that they go to faithfully every day, but some of us do! Not all men love their wives the way Christ loves the church, but some of us do! Not all men take care of their children and are an integral part of their lives, but some of us do! Not all men own their own houses and cars and have their finances in order, but some of us do! We're not all alike. We're not all alcoholics or drug addicts, or in and out of jail. One description doesn't fit all!

This is how the Shulammite woman responds: "My man is worth looking for because out of ten thousand men, he stands out." Think about it. Her man loves God, works, pays his bills, and takes care of his responsibilities. There may be ten thousand good men, but he is chief among them all. Sisters, that's why you can't rush into a relationship. Don't let a brother start coming into your garden whenever he wants to. Where does he rank among ten thousand? You're going to run into a lot of men who aren't going to value you or appreciate your garden. When some of these brothers walk out, you need to let them go!

Men, too, need to learn how to let go. A while back, here in Indiana, there was some news about a family that really got to me. I felt so deeply for them that I spent a lot of time in prayer on their behalf. The incident happened in a small town of only 2700 people in rural Indiana. A man and woman had just divorced, and the woman got a new boyfriend, which made the ex-husband angry. He may not have wanted her, but he didn't want any other man to have her, either. The ex-husband borrowed a gun, went to his ex-wife's trailer, and started shooting up the car in front of the trailer. The new boyfriend came outside to see what was going on, and the ex-husband shot and killed him. Then he went into the trailer, shot his ex-wife in the head, turned the gun on his own two kids and shot them in the head, killing them also. The man was walking home with the gun in his hand as some policemen approached him. He took the gun, pulled the trigger, and killed himself. Two men, a woman and two children are all dead, just because a man didn't know when to let go. When it's over, it's over. Let it go.

Altogether Lovely

In our text, the sisters in the community want to know why this missing man is worth looking for. The woman starts telling them about the Lover she wants back in her life. Beginning with verse 10, she starts talking about him in great detail. She speaks symbolically about some of his physical attributes:

- Head: his intellect, or how he thinks
- Eyes: his vision, the way he sees life, his worldview, or his outlook
- Cheeks: his disposition
- Lips: his conversation, or how he talks
- Arms: his mission, or how he reaches out to other people
- Body: his inward parts, his appetite, his desires, and his sexual being
- Legs: how he walks, or the direction he's going
- Appearance: how others perceive him
- Mouth: the way he communicates

Notice that she talks about his head before she talks about the rest of his body. We need to stop trying to deal with people from the bottom up. No matter how it looks from that perspective, if there's something wrong with the head, it affects the rest of the body as well.

Then, the Shulammite sums it up in verse 16 by saying, "He is altogether lovely. This is my lover, this is my friend, O daughters of Jerusalem."

Lover and Friend

Look at what she's saying here: he is both her lover and her friend at the same time. This is very significant. She's got a lover and a friend, and he's one and the same person. There's nothing better than having a spouse who is both a lover and a friend. You need that in marriage, but you had better be sure to cultivate the friendship before you become lovers. You can always teach someone how to love you: "Touch me here. I like it when you do that. That's perfect...." Becoming friends is much more complicated. Friendship has to do with shared interests, mutual values, the same standard of morality, loving and serving the same God, and walking in the same direction. This woman is blessed because she has all that is necessary for an intimate friendship, and that same man is her lover, too.

This man who is both a friend and a lover is someone she finds to be altogether lovely. When she sees him in his totality, he is altogether lovely. She isn't talking here about separate body parts, different facets of his personality, or individual actions and behaviors: she's referring to his total being. She's saying, "I've seen enough. I've been with him long enough. I've seen him in one situation after another. I've seen the way he has dealt with this person and that person. I've heard him speak from the depths of his heart. I've watched how his mind works. I *know* this man, and he is altogether lovely."

Too many of us look only at an isolated incident and base our judgment about a person on that one situation or that one characteristic. Some of you women, for instance, are in relationships with dogs. The man you are with is evil, and you know he is evil. Even Jesus refers to someone like that as a dog when he warns, "Give not that which is holy unto the dogs" (Matthew 7:6 KJV). The man you're with has got animalistic attitudes and constantly exhibits beastly behavior. You know he isn't right, and nobody has to tell you because you know it. When you look at him in the totality of who he is, you see evil. But every six months or so, he does something nice for you, an isolated incident of goodness. So, in spite of the evil you see in him every day, because he does those good things every now and then, you deceive yourself into thinking, "Everything is going to be all right. He may not be perfect, but there's some good in him." You make excuses for him and, by doing so, you only make a fool of yourself.

Then there are women on the other end of that spectrum. You've got a good man. He isn't perfect because Mr. Perfect doesn't exist, but you have a brother who is good. He loves God, loves the church, supports the ministry, and supports you. He comes alongside to care for you, takes care of the kids, and, in totality, is a good man. But every now and then, he does something you both know is not right.

Now you've taken those isolated incidents of badness and judged him as though he's good for nothing. Yet, you can't base your assessment of a person on a few isolated incidents; even good people can do bad things now and then. One of the things I've told my wife as we develop our marriage and continue to build our relationship is, "Baby, don't judge me on account of what I did yesterday, or what I did once last month. Judge me on the basis of the twenty years we've had together." In the spirit of the moment, I told her also not to just look at all the mistakes I've made over the twenty years we've been together, but to "count your blessings, name them one by one. Count your many blessings, see what I have done."

Grant Hill, one of my favorite basketball players, came back to the NBA for the 2004-05 season. His is one of the greatest stories in NBA League history. He had been out of the game for four years after breaking his ankle. After four major surgeries, dozens of pairs of crutches, and a near-fatal infection, he battled his way back onto the court and soon made the 2005 All-Star team as a starter, which meant that he was one of the Top Ten players in the NBA.

Grant's wife, Tamia Hill, a great singer who was nominated for a Grammy, was interviewed during that All-Star Game in Denver. When asked about all that Grant had undergone during the previous four years, she told the interviewer, "I'm so proud of my man, and everything that he went through." Then she told this story:

It happened when they were in the midst of their ordeal in Detroit, where Grant used to play. They had rented a car, and she was driving because Grant's foot was in a cast. He had just come out of surgery and been fitted for new crutches. It was freezing cold, sub-zero weather. Low on fuel, she had to get out of the car to pump the gas. While Grant Hill sat in the warmth of the vehicle nursing his wounded foot, there was the beautiful, Grammy-nominated Tamia Hill out there in the cold, pumping gas. She said that some bystander, seeing a big, strong man sitting in the warmth and comfort of the car while she was out in the cold pumping the gas, walked up to her and said in reference to her husband, "Ma'am, I don't mean to get in your business, but I think you can do a whole lot better than that." She said that as the man walked away, she began to laugh because she was thinking, "That's Grant Hill in the car." She realized that "he must not understand who I'm riding with."

She knew that the stranger was only seeing an isolated incident and didn't know who Grant Hill is. He didn't know that Grant Hill is a devoted Christian who gives millions of dollars to worthy causes to be a blessing to others. Not only that, he was given a great legacy by his family. His father, Calvin Hill, a Yale graduate, was an All-Pro football player back in the day, and is currently a consultant for the Dallas Cowboys. His mother, who got her bachelor's degree from Wellesley and her master's degree from the University of Chicago, is the vice president of a corporate consulting agency and has previously held numerous positions, including acting as the Special Assistant to the Secretary of the Army.

But Grant Hill himself has made the sacrifices and put forth the discipline to make it to the top of his profession, earning a degree from Duke University. He also loves his wife and takes care of his children. Yet here is a stranger, somebody on the outside, looking at an isolated incident and thinking his wife could do better than that. All she could do was laugh as she thought, "My man had been broken. But my man taught me that you can battle your brokenness and come back better than when you got broken!" If you've got a good man, it doesn't mean that he isn't going to be broken sometime, but you can help him battle through his brokenness! God can make him better than when he got broken.

The Place of Intimacy

After the wonderful description of her Lover that the Shulammite woman gave to the sisters in her community, they asked her, "Where has your lover gone…which way did your lover turn, that we may look for him with you?" In other words, "We've not seen the kind of man you're describing, not out here." Remember, they are in the streets. They knew they wouldn't find him in the same places where they might find other women's lost men. They knew they weren't going to find him in someone else's hotel room. He wasn't going to be in a club or in a bar. He wouldn't hang out in a strip club or be found in a crack house. A good man like that wasn't going to be found in the company of a lot of men with baser passions. They knew better than to look for a holy man in hellish places, realizing that such a fine man wouldn't be found in a foul location. They knew where they wouldn't find him, so they asked her where she had seen him last: "Which way did your lover turn?"

In chapter 6, verse 2, she responds by saying, "My lover has gone down to his garden, to the beds of spices, to browse in the gardens and to gather lilies. I am my lover's and my lover is mine. He browses among the lilies." Do you mean that he is in his garden, among the lilies—in the place of intimacy, responsibility, and accountability? This brother was right where he was supposed to be. Why couldn't she find him? Because she was in the streets. He was not the one out of place; she was. The sisters' question is symbolic because they are saying, "If you want a man like this, you need to go the same direction that he went. You aren't going to find him out in the streets." No holy man wants to marry a hellish woman. If you want a godly man, you're going to have to walk in godly ways yourself. The Lover was right where he was supposed to be, but she was out in the streets stalking him. Sister, any brother whom you've got to stalk isn't really yours. If love can't keep him with you, he's not yours. Get a brother you can trust. Stop stalking him. Stop following him. Stop calling him every two minutes. If he's yours, he's yours! If he's not, he's not.

Remember what I told you about David Copperfield? He made the elephant disappear, an airplane disappear, and the Statue of Liberty disappear, but when he was interviewed, he said, "I'm not a magician. I'm an illusionist." He said, "I didn't make those things disappear. I made them appear as though they had disappeared." Wait a minute. If he is an illusionist, then I must have been *dis*illusioned, because he's saying those things were right where they had always been. Do you know what the enemy Satan does to you and me? He disillusions us. We have Christ, but often he makes us think we don't have Him. Even now, you may be mad at your heavenly Father and ready to walk out on God because you think, "Jesus is not there for me." You've gone through one problem after another, and you've thought God was gone. No, He didn't leave you. Satan is an illusionist, and he has left you disillusioned. Jesus is always right where He has been. He's the same yesterday, today, and forever. He is right there with affinity and intimacy, just for you. Jesus is alive and well, and He's with you!

Chapter 13

The Diary of a Mad Black Woman

[4]You are beautiful, my darling, as Tirzah,
lovely as Jerusalem,
majestic as troops with banners.
[5]Turn your eyes from me;
they overwhelm me.
Your hair is like a flock of goats
descending from Gilead.
[6]Your teeth are like a flock of sheep
coming up from the washing.
Each has its twin,
not one of them is alone.
[7]Your temples behind your veil
are like the halves of a pomegranate.
[8]Sixty queens there may be,
and eighty concubines,
and virgins beyond number;
but my dove, my perfect one, is unique,
the only daughter of her mother,
the favorite of the one who bore her.
[9]The maidens saw her and called her blessed;
the queens and concubines praised her.
[10]Who is this that appears like the dawn,
fair as the moon, bright as the sun,
majestic as the stars in procession?
[11]I went down to the grove of nut trees
to look at the new growth in the valley,
to see if the vines had budded
or the pomegranates were in bloom.
[12]Before I realized it, my desire set me

among the royal chariots of my people.
[13]Come back, come back, O Shulammite; come
back, come back, that we may gaze on you!
Why would you gaze on the Shulammite
as on the dance of Mahanaim?
(Song of Solomon 6:4-13, NIV)

Y ou probably recognize the title of this chapter. I borrowed it
from a play written by Tyler Perry, an awesome man who went
from homelessness to making over seventy-five million dollars from
his plays and movies. When I first heard the title of his play, *The
Diary of a Mad Black Woman*, which later was adapted into a movie,
I couldn't help but think about this woman in the Song of Solomon.
We know that as a Shulammite, she is of African descent, a woman
of color. In chapter 1, she talks about being black and beautiful. In
spite of that, in chapter 5, as she was out looking for her man in the
streets in the middle of the night, some other men saw her.

In Song of Solomon 5:7, the Shulammite woman said, "The
watchmen found me as they made their rounds in the city. They beat
me, they bruised me; they took away my cloak, those watchmen
of the walls!" They beat her, bruised her, and even *took her cloak*.
In those days, women would only appear in public fully covered,
including their head; single women would often even wear a veil as
a sign of chastity and virtue. The only women who walked around
without their outer garments were women of the night—prostitutes.
So when these men stripped this woman of her covering, they were
treating her like a prostitute.

Try to think about how this woman felt. This was not a super-
woman who had special powers to defend herself. She was a woman
who felt both the pain and the shame of the attack on her. It wasn't
even just one man who wronged her, but it was *men*. These weren't
just street thugs who hurt her and put her to shame; they were officials of the city, men whose job it was to watch over and protect
the people. Think how it feels to be mistreated by men whom you
thought that you could trust. There was more than one man, but none
who helped her; instead, they all brought her injury and shame. She
was hurt and humiliated, but she also felt betrayed.

At some point in our lives, probably all of us have been wronged by someone in the community who should have been protective and helpful: a coworker or supervisor, a parent who should have been nurturing and loving, or a best friend in whom you trusted and confided. So then the question arises: how do we respond when we are wronged? Now some people are so holy that they would tell you we should never get mad at anyone, but the Bible never told us not to get angry. The Bible tells us that it is possible to get angry and not sin (Ephesians 4:26), but, at the same time, it teaches us that we cannot overcome evil with evil, but we can overcome evil with good (Romans 7:21). It would have been only natural for this woman to want to get back at the men who hurt her. Most of us have felt like that at some point. Someone did something to wrong us by either saying something evil or mistreating us in some way. Our immediate thought was, *how can I get them back?*

Let It Go!

I know that I've felt like that before. When somebody wronged me or really hurt me, I wanted to get back at him. That's a natural response. An eye for an eye *feels* right when someone has purposely brought us pain. But then I have to remember what the Word of God says in Romans 12:19: "Vengeance is mine; I will repay, saith the Lord" (KJV). God doesn't want us to do wrong by trying to get back at somebody who wronged us. We've got to leave that up to Him. So, I've learned to stand back and watch God work. My part in the process is learning how to forgive people. If we don't forgive others, we're only hurting ourselves, not them. It doesn't matter who they are or what they did, we have to forgive them; God gives us no other option. When we hold grudges, refusing to forgive people, we literally put ourselves in bondage.

You may be in so much bondage right now that you can't move forward into what God has planned for you because you're still holding a grudge over a wrong that someone did to you in the past. Your lack of forgiveness is keeping you from being set free and moving on. Let me be clear about this. When I talk about forgiveness, I'm not saying, "Just forgive and forget." Forgiving isn't something you *just* do. It's hard to do because it goes against all of our natural tendencies. It takes the grace of God working within us to enable us to forgive someone who has truly wronged us. At the same time, I don't believe we're expected to forget. If it's in our memory, we can't just pretend that it isn't. We don't have to dwell on it, but we can't forget that it happened. Even if we could forget, that would only make us vulnerable, tending to let the same thing happen again. If I forget what the person did the first time, I wouldn't recognize the warning signs if he or she came back to do the same thing over again. What I must learn to do is to let go of the offense so that it doesn't stand in the way of my relating to that other person.

You have probably heard about the foolproof way to catch a monkey. I've never tried this myself, but I've heard that it works. A piece of fruit—an apple, banana, or whatever—is placed in the bottom of a vase and left in an area that monkeys are known to inhabit. Before long, a monkey will use its sense of smell to find the fruit. The monkey then goes over and sticks its hand down inside the vase to get the fruit. As it tries to pull the fruit out, its hand can't get back through the opening because it is holding onto the piece of fruit. The monkey refuses to let go of the fruit, so it sits there stuck, trying to get the vase off and the fruit out while the captors come out of hiding and cage him.

You are probably thinking, "But that doesn't make sense. Why doesn't the monkey just let it go?" That's my point. Yes, someone wronged you. Yes, someone hurt you. But if you want to avoid being in bondage and have the freedom that God desires for you, you just have to let it go.

Pretty and Pleasant

The Shulammite woman had let it go. By chapter 6, verse 6, she's back with her lover, and he again reviews all of her attributes, just as he did in chapter 4. He says things such as: "You are beautiful, my darling, as Tirzah, lovely as Jerusalem, majestic as troops with banners." From verse 5 through verse 9, he gives a vivid description of his woman. I'm not going to get into detail because it is the exact description that he gave in chapter 4. But think about this. All of the beauty she had in chapter 4, both inside and out, she still has in chapter 6. Even after the brothers abused, mistreated, insulted, and humiliated her in chapter 5, she still has her beauty in chapter 6. That's because she made the decision not to allow what happened in the previous chapter of her life to keep her from receiving the blessings that God had for her in the next chapter. Some of us get stuck in chapter 5 of our lives and never move on to chapter 6. We're still dwelling over what someone said or did. We refuse to forgive, so we can't go on.

Not only did the woman's lover talk about how beautiful she was outside, but he said to her, "You are beautiful like Tirzah." Tirzah, an ancient city in Israel, means "friendly" or "pleasant." Even though she went through that terrible ordeal in chapter 5, she was still pleasant in chapter 6. The man also likened her to Jerusalem, which means the City of Peace. In spite of what she went through on the outside, she still maintained peace on the inside. Check her out: she's pretty, pleasant, and at peace. Likewise, you shouldn't allow what you've gone through to cause you to lose sight of what God has done in your life. You don't have to let a bad experience from the past make you negative and bitter, robbing you of future happiness.

All Things Work Together for Good

I want to make a point here, but I don't want to be misunderstood. God sometimes allows things to happen in our lives because He knows that He can work *all things* together for our good, even though it seems anything *but* good at the time. Notice that I did not say that God initiates evil; He did not set this woman up to be beaten and harassed. I don't believe God would do that. It happened because of the evil that is within the heart of human beings who do such things; however, God did not stop that event from happening. If God allows something to happen in our lives that hurts us or brings us pain, it is never without a purpose. He never allows one of His children to suffer for no reason.

Whenever God allows something to happen in our lives that is hurtful, it is because He can use that ordeal for a higher purpose. It doesn't matter what it was or how bad it seemed at the time. It may have been a terrible relationship—a bad marriage or divorce. Your father may have run out on you, or your mother was no good. Perhaps your job got downsized, and you were laid off. All kinds of things like this can happen, and they leave you wondering why God didn't step in and stop it from happening. There are some things we can never understand in this life from our vantage point. One reason that God *sometimes* allows things to happen is because He knows that He can use that disastrous situation to build our character.

I mentioned in an earlier chapter how much I like German chocolate cake. As I eagerly watched my mother make that cake, I saw her sift the flour; add butter, vanilla extract, and the eggs; and mix all the ingredients together. Then she would put the mixture into the pans that she had already greased and place them in a preheated oven for a set amount of time to let them bake. That aroma would spread throughout the entire house. I could hardly wait for the cake to be ready.

But as much as I love German chocolate cake, I don't like the individual ingredients that are used in making the cake. I can't just sit and eat flour because I don't like it. I can't eat a stick of butter; I don't like butter like that. I don't even like eggs by themselves, oil by itself, or pure sugar on its own. I don't like all that stuff individually, but somehow Mother knew how to measure it all together just right. She knew how to add just enough of this, not too much of that, just a pinch of this, and a little of that. She knew how to beat it until the consistency of the batter was just right. After pouring out the mixture, she put the pan into the oven that was already preheated. Mother wasn't going to let the cake burn; she was just letting it stay at the right temperature just long enough to become what it was supposed to be. She kept a watchful eye on that cake while it was in the oven. Every now and then, Mother would open up the oven, pull that rack out a little bit, take a toothpick and stick it in the cake, and then take the toothpick out and look at it. I'd say, "Momma, is it ready yet?"

"No, not yet," she'd reply as she put it back in and close the oven door. A little while later, I'd be in the next room, but I heard her open the oven door, so I came running into the kitchen, asking hopefully, "Momma, is it ready?" "Boy, it's not ready. I'll let you know when it's ready!" She put it back in and kept going through that process until it was finally ready to take out of the oven. Then she would take it out and put all the topping over it. It was the best cake ever.

Just as it takes a lot of different ingredients to make a great cake, it also takes a lot of different life experiences to help you to become the best person you can be. You may not like the individual things that go on in your life—the tragedies, the troubles, the pain, the heartaches, the people walking out of your life or the ones dogging you—none of those "taste good" in themselves. But God somehow knows how to blend all of those things together in your life to help you become what you were destined to be.

Even when you feel the heat in a bad situation, it will only make you better; it won't destroy you. God knows how much you are able to bear, so He won't let you stay in it too long. Through that process, you rise as you were intended to do. When you come out, God adds a sweet topping so you will be at your best. He is using a process that others may have intended to hurt you to bless you. God didn't allow it to destroy you, but to enable you to fulfill your destiny.

One of a Kind

As we read on, look how special the Shulammite woman is in the eyes of her man. In verse 8, her Lover says that out of sixty queens, eighty concubines, and countless virgins, "my dove, my perfect one is unique." See how much he delights in her and appreciates her. He sees not only her beauty and charm—which would likely be true of all the other women chosen to satisfy the king's desires—but he also sees special qualities in her that the others don't have. Of all the women he knows, she is unique. He recognizes that God made her one of a kind. By implication, he may also be pointing out the fact that even though the king may have a multitude of women, he is satisfied with this one. He doesn't need other women because this one woman supersedes them all. Although the king may continue to be frustrated and dissatisfied going from woman to woman, trying to find someone who will satisfy him, this man has found all that he needs in just one woman.

Too many of us males in the twenty-first century have misunderstood what real manhood is all about. Somehow we have mis-defined the word, and now there are brothers who think their manhood is determined by how many women they can use and maybe even abuse. Men will even boast about how many children they have with different women. Something is very wrong with that misconception of manhood. Real manhood is based first on your relationship with God, through His Son Jesus Christ. It is in Him, not in women, that you find your purpose, your personhood, and your practical lifestyle.

But I've got a question for some sisters because there's one thing I can't figure out. This text talks about one man with sixty queens, eighty mistresses, and then a whole bunch of young women. All of them are sharing one man. In that society, they may not have had much choice, but why would a woman today be willing to share a man? The Shulammite woman and her man are showing us that it is possible for a man to be satisfied with one woman, and a woman with one man. That was surely the way God intended it. He gave Adam only one wife, not multiple wives. Also, Genesis 2:24 says that a man will leave his father and mother and cleave to his wife, not wives, and they will be one flesh. It was always God's plan for the two to become one, not for a bunch to become a messy situation.

Adam and Eve is one of the best illustrations in the Bible about marriage. When you look at this couple, you see all of the hell that they went through. The enemy deceived Eve, and Adam allowed himself to give into the temptation to disobey God. They lost their home, going from life in paradise to life even as we know it today. They went from having perfect bodies to bodies that would age and die. They lost one son because another son murdered him. They went through so much stuff, but notice that they never got a divorce. Do you know why? Because they had a connection underneath the skin. Their relationship wasn't superficial because they were united in a special way. God had put Adam into a deep sleep, took one of his ribs, and made this woman to be his companion...bone of his bone and flesh of his flesh.

Think about it. God took out only one rib because He intended to make only one woman. All a man needs is one woman. Too many of us have complicated our lives because we've got too many ribs out there trying to be one flesh with us. One of the functions of the ribs is to protect the heart. If, for some reason, you lose some of your ribs, your heart becomes more vulnerable. Now there's somebody who has got a rib at the church, a rib out in the 'hood, a rib in Chi Town, a rib back in college, and a rib back in high school. You're missin' a bunch of ribs, and yet you wonder why your heart keeps getting broken. But God has designed us so that one woman and one man can satisfy each other.

So what would make women share a man? One reason might be that the women may not know they are sharing the same man. There are a number of men who have several women, and each one of them thinks that she's the only one. In some cases, however, it isn't really that they don't know about each other, it's that they don't *want* to know. They've seen the signs and figured it out, but they act as though they don't know. They've become so comfortable that they would rather just leave well enough alone.

There are still other women, however, who know what's going on, but they have a problem with low self-esteem. In short, their self-image is damaged. They think that having even part of a man is the best they can ever hope for. That could possibly have been the case in biblical times when women were not only considered less than men, but they were even considered to be property of men. They were on the same level as animals and other possessions. But we aren't living in those days anymore: this is the twenty-first century. The only person you belong to is Jesus because He is the only one who purchased you with His blood on Calvary. Don't ever allow your self-esteem to get so low that you let anybody treat you any less than the daughter of God who you truly are. You deserve your own husband; you don't have to share him with anybody else. Moreover, you are just as unique as the Shulammite woman. Understand who you are; you are the only one like you. You are invaluable and cannot be replaced.

Artists will tell you that an original is worth much more than any copy. When God made you, He didn't make you just like anybody else. He created you as a very special, never-to-be-repeated miracle of human personality. He made you an original. When He designed you, He did not make a mistake. He didn't make you too tall or too short, too wide or too thin, too dark or too light, too outgoing or not outgoing enough. When God made you, He knew exactly what He was doing. As soon as you stop trying to be what somebody else wants you to be and start being the woman God made you to be, then you will begin to see yourself as a person of value. When you respect yourself, other people will respect you, too. Don't let low self-esteem cause you to share a man.

A third reason some women share a man is because of finances. Even now, some woman is likely saying, "I don't care what you say. He's paying my rent. He's buying my kids clothes. He's helping me with my tuition. He's helping me get my car. I don't care who else he's with, as long as he pays the bills." I would urge you to stop and think about what you are saying, as well as the position in which you are putting yourself. Remember, in chapter 5, the men of the city pulled off the woman's cloak and were trying to treat her like a prostitute. She was not a prostitute, even though they were trying to treat her like one. Now someone may read that word *prostitute*, and think, "Well, I'm not a prostitute! Just because somebody else's husband is helping me with my rent and my car and putting a few dollars in my pocket doesn't make me a prostitute."

When I was a student at Bishop College—this was many years ago—there was a story spread around the campus about a young man that asked a coed this provocative question: "Would you sleep with a man just once if he offered you a million dollars?" Then he said, "Wait a minute, before you answer, this also comes with a guarantee that you won't get any disease, you will not get pregnant, and he will walk away and you'll never have to see him again."

The coed said, "Let me get this straight. All I've got to do is sleep with him once, right? No disease…guaranteed, right? No baby? And I'll never hear from him again?" "That's right," the young man answered. "For one million dollars, would you do it?" She thought for a minute and then responded, "You know what, I think that if there were absolutely no strings attached and I could be assured of no bad consequences, I *would* sleep with somebody just once for a million dollars."

The young man asked, "Well, would you sleep with me for twenty dollars?" She replied indignantly, "No! What do you think I am?" He said, "Well, that's already been established; now we're just negotiating the price."

Dr. John B. Mangrum, who used to be the Dean of Religion at Bishop College, says that prostitution is when you are selling what you ought to be giving away in love. Now, if that's prostitution, then not all prostitutes are on street corners; some are even members of the church. If you are sleeping with someone because he is helping you pay your light bill, it means you're selling what you ought to be giving away in love.

What I love about the woman in our text is that even when other men tried to treat her like a prostitute, she didn't start acting like one. She went on to become the beautiful, blessed person God wanted her to be.

But there are still more reasons why some women will put up with being one of many instead of the only one. Some women are simply so very lonely that they would rather have what Stevie Wonder calls "a part-time love" than no love at all. They think, "Even if that person belongs to somebody else and is not mine; even if he shows up for only twenty-five minutes, does what he's going to do, and heads on back to the one he's married to; that still seems better to me than spending an entire night alone."

There was a popular song a few years ago that had the message, "If loving you is wrong, I don't want to be right." It goes on to say that even though her parents and friends tell her that it's wrong for her to be having an affair with a married man, she would rather be wrong than to sleep alone at night. She doesn't care if he has a wife and two children. She needs him, too, and doesn't see why she should have to give him up. How can I say this delicately? It's wrong! It's wrong! It's wrong! It's wrong for the man who is sneaking away from his wife to be with another woman. It's wrong for the woman who is sleeping with a married man. I know you're lonely and want someone to love you. I know you want the benefits of marriage, but you can't get what you're looking for with someone else's husband.

Recently, I was talking to Pastor James Anthony Jackson, senior pastor of New Beginnings Fellowship Church, one of our church plants. I'm very proud of what God is doing there: lives are being changed, souls are being saved, and Pastor Jackson is doing a wonderful job serving God in that ministry. He was telling me about an illustration he used at his church based on the movie *Rush Hour*, the first one of the series starring Jackie Chan and Chris Tucker. The movie begins with the young daughter of a Chinese consul in Los Angeles getting kidnapped. The consul calls on his friend (Jackie Chan), an inspector in Hong Kong, to come help find his daughter. He hooks up with an LAPD officer (Chris Tucker), and they spend the entire movie trying to find the young girl. They are fighting here and there, kicking over tables, going into dangerous places, and putting their lives on the line. When they finally find the girl, she is wrapped in an explosive vest, but their connection with the bomb squad is able to set her free. Of course, the Jackie Chan character is elated. After all of their hard work and all that they went through, the little girl is finally safe.

When Jackie sees her; he's so happy that he runs up to her and gets ready to hug her, but what does she do? She hits him and says, "What took you so long?" She is implying, "I knew you were going to show up. I knew you were going to come. I knew I was going to make it. But, I want to know, what took you so long?!" What she did not realize was all the things Jackie had been doing behind the scenes to save her life. All she saw was the difficulty she was in and the final outcome in which she was rescued. She didn't get to see all that had to happen to give her that happy ending. This illustrates what God is trying to say to someone right now: "Stop asking Me what's taking so long. You have no idea what I'm working out, you have no idea who I'm partnering you with, and you have no idea about all the things that have to happen at just the right time and in just the right way in order to set you free. Be patient. Give Me time to work. Don't get in the way by trying to do it yourself. You'll only hinder Me from working."

I want to encourage some mad Black, White, Hispanic, and Asian sisters—*all* sisters in that situation—to wait upon God instead of trying to make something happen yourself with someone who doesn't belong to you. Instead of spending your time and effort on somebody else's man, you can be investing it into your relationship with God. You can be preparing yourself for the man God has for you, because even though God may not come when you want Him to, He's always on time!

Still Shining

There is something else in this text too that we see when we get down to verse 10. Keep in mind all that she has suffered through in the previous chapter. But when we get to chapter 6, verse 10, we read that all of the women in the community—the maidens, the queens and the concubines—call her happy, or blessed, and say, "Who is this that appears like the dawn, fair as the moon, bright as the sun, majestic as the stars in procession?" I love that. Here's a sister whose very countenance lights up her environment and changes it for the better. When she walks into a room, people notice because she comes in with illumination. She's like the moon, the sun, and the stars. After all the suffering she went through in the previous chapter, she is still shining. She didn't let anyone take her light from her. They could hurt her, and even humiliate her, but what she had on the inside continues to shine.

Those around her said she's as fair as the moon. As you know, the moon doesn't generate its own power to shine all by itself. The moon can only receive its light from the sun and then reflect it back to Earth. Even though you can see the moon in the daytime, it shines best at night. Do you know why some of us who went through our own chapter 5 are still living dark, discouraged, depressed lives? It's because we keep trying to deal with it by ourselves. We keep thinking we don't need anybody or anything. We feel that we don't need the church or God. We keep trying to generate enough power within ourselves to overcome our troubling issues, but it's just not going to happen that way. We need the power of the Son of God in order to shine the way that God wants us to shine. When we start depending on His power and receive power through the Holy Spirit, then we begin to reflect the Son's light in our lives and release it into the lives of other people.

When my son Jalon was much younger, I bought him a pair of glow-in-the-dark basketball shoes that soon became his favorite pair ever. Even though he was afraid of the dark then, he would put on those basketball shoes and turn out the light because he wanted us to see his shoes glow in the dark. On the first Sunday after he got the shoes, it was time for us to go to church, and there was Jalon, wearing his glow-in-the-dark shoes. That particular Sunday, he was singing in the Joybelles, the children's choir, so his mother said, "You aren't wearing those shoes to church." "But, Momma," he pleaded, "I want to wear these glow-in-the-dark shoes." "No," she told him, "you're not going to wear those. You're going to wear your church shoes because you're in the program. You can't wear those."

It was one of those long Sundays when we had to be there all day and all evening, from morning till night. When we got home that night, Jalon eagerly rushed to change out of his church shoes and, even though he had just put on his pajamas, he got his favorite shoes and put them on. In just a few seconds, he came running to me, saying, "Daddy, something is wrong with my shoes." I said, "Son, those are the best shoes I've ever seen in my life. Those shoes are great. There's nothing wrong with those shoes." "Yes, there is, Daddy. They aren't glowing!"

Now, the problem was that when his mother made him change shoes that morning, she had taken his good shoes out of the closet for him to wear and put his basketball shoes back in the closet since he didn't need them that day. But, as I tried to explain to my young son, those shoes had to spend a significant amount of time in the light before they could glow in the dark. Since they had spent the day in a dark closet, they couldn't be expected to glow that night because they had no light within themselves. They needed to absorb the sunlight in order for them to shine in the dark.

The same is true for us. We can't keep hanging out in dark situations and dark places, doing dark things, and then expect to shine. But if we spend time soaking in the light of Jesus Christ, we'll begin to shine the way God designed us to.

But wait a minute. Not only is this woman compared to the moon, she is also described as being as bright as the sun. The sun is not just light, but it also generates heat. She's not only glowing, but she's also warm. She didn't allow her calamity in the past to make her cold in the present.

Unfortunately, some woman may freeze out her man in the present because of something that another man did in her past. A woman like that may have a good man now. He's not perfect, because none of us is perfect, but he's a good man who loves God, works hard, and is generous and loving. Yet, the woman has a defense mechanism that keeps him at a distance. Because someone else has hurt her in the past, she is not going to risk letting that happen again, so she freezes out even the man she loves.

It's strange how the past affects present behavior. Because of their past, some women think that any man who speaks to them is flirting with them. They need to learn that every man who says hello isn't hitting on them; sometimes, they are just saying hello. Some women think because sometime in the past someone has hurt them, that now everybody is trying to hurt them. Don't let the evil that someone did to you in the past determine how you will live in the present. Don't try to freeze someone out today because of what someone else did yesterday. You still have to maintain your warmth, like the sun.

I remember one Sunday morning a few years ago when the temperature in Indianapolis registered a wind-chill of -35 degrees, the coldest I had ever seen, though I've lived here all my life. People were even warned to stay inside, not because of hazardous driving conditions, but the cold weather itself. In spite of the announcements, I left my house early to go open the church. Now, if the officials had ordered people to stay off the streets because it was too hazardous to drive, it would have been different. But we weren't going to cancel church just because it was cold outside—I don't care how cold it gets. So, I got out early and was driving to church.

Normally on a morning like that, I would see city trucks spreading salt to protect drivers from ice on the roads, but this morning I didn't see any trucks out at all. It was cold and slippery, yet there was nothing being done to deal with the elements. I kept wondering where the Department of Public Works was and why they weren't getting out there to salt the roads to get rid of the ice problem. I found out later that they didn't bring the trucks out because it was too cold. Anytime it drops below -20 degrees, the salt has no effect, so they don't even try. They don't go through the motions by just showing up; they don't even get up. There's no reason for them to try to do anything because if it's too cold, what they do isn't going to make any difference.

Sister, don't be surprised if you've gotten so cold that the man in your life doesn't even try anymore. He's already found out that no matter what he does, it doesn't make any difference because you're just too cold. You've got to let the Son of God warm your heart and be what God wants you to be in the present by showing warmth and light to the man He has given you.

The text says, too, that the Beloved is as majestic as the stars. Remember that just a short while ago, she was down in the streets, being mistreated and abused by the watchmen. Even though she wasn't a low-down sort of person, she was being treated that way. But look at her now: she is as majestic as the stars. Once she was down in the streets; now she is high up in the heavens. Once there were men who looked down upon her, but anyone who looks at her now has to look up. Do you know why? God has a way of turning things around. Even when people have humiliated you, He can raise you up to the heavens. That's why Maya Angelou can say with confidence, "Still I rise." God is able to show up in your situation and raise you up from the streets to the stars, from the gutter to glory.

New Growth

A lot of what happens to us in life depends upon our expectations. Look at verses 11 and 12. The Shulammite woman says, "I went down to the grove of nut trees to look at the new growth in the valley, to see if the vines have budded or the pomegranates were in bloom. Before I realized it, my desire set me among the royal chariots of my people." Think about what she's saying. She went down to the grove of trees to see if there was anything blooming and any new growth *in the valley*. She went expecting to find new growth. After all she had been through, she believed that it had to result in new growth. She couldn't have gone through all of that suffering for nothing, so she went down to the valley to see what her suffering had produced.

You need to know that God never lets you go through anything without a purpose or reason. Seasons change, and you may have just gone through the winter of despair, which means that now you're about to enter into the spring of hope. Spring is that special time of year when we see new growth, trees budding, and flowers blooming. That's what God is about to do in your life. You may feel that you've been through hell with all that you've had to face, whether it was a financial problem, that difficult situation on the job, the horrible thing that person did to you, or some trying ordeal that you went through with your family. God was just using it to bring some new growth in your life.

Look where the woman was looking for growth—down in the valley, which represents difficulty. She said, "I'm not just expecting growth. I'm expecting growth in the valley." It's one thing to be committed to God in the good times on the mountaintop when everything is going well. Folks smile in your face, pat you on your back, and everybody loves you. Your job is secure, the bills are paid, the kids are on the honor roll, your husband is being loving and supporting, or your wife is trying hard to meet your needs. All of that's fine, but can you still be committed when you're in the valley? Can you stay loyal to God amidst difficulties such as living from paycheck to paycheck, working at a job that may be downsized, or suffering abandonment from someone who ought to be in your life? Every now and then, God has to take you through the valley of the shadow of death to get you to a table He's prepared for you on the other side.

The Shulammite woman says, "Before I realized it, my desire set me among the royal chariots of my people." Listen to what she's saying: "I went through the valley, but before I realized it, God had raised me up. Before I knew what was happening, I was hanging out with royalty, and didn't even know it." Look at the wording carefully. She says, "Before I realized it...." That means that God had already done it. He had already raised her to a higher level, but she didn't even know it. Sometimes when God is taking you through the valley, He doesn't say anything until you come out. You may be in a valley now, wondering where God is, and why God won't do something.

Ask Joseph in the book of Genesis. His brothers were jealous of him, threw him in a pit, and then left him there. Other folks found him in the pit, pulled him out, and sold him into slavery in Egypt. As a slave, he ended up working at Potiphar's house. Then Mrs. Potiphar lied and said Joseph tried to rape her, so he was imprisoned for something he didn't do.

But even in jail, Joseph trusted God and was a leader. Even there in his valley, he interpreted dreams for one of the king's men. That man forgot all about Joseph and the promise he made to try to help him get out. But when the king had a dream, the king's man told him about Joseph, who could interpret dreams. Joseph was brought out of prison, interpreted the king's dreams, impressed the king, and was given the second highest position in Egypt.

Even though God has been silent all of this time, just look at all that happened to Joseph while He stayed silent. Now, God helps Joseph to understand what he then told his brothers: "You intended it to harm me, but God intended it for my good...." Had his brothers never thrown him into the pit, the other people would have never found him and sold him into slavery. He would have never ended up at Potiphar's house, Mrs. Potiphar would never have lied about him, and he would never have gone to prison for something he didn't do. He would never have interpreted the king's cupbearer's dreams, never have been called upon to interpret dreams for Pharaoh, never have come out of prison, and his family, as well as all of Egypt, would have starved to death. But, as he sits next to the king, God assures him: "They meant it for evil, but I was working behind the scenes for your good."

Chapter 14

Going to the Next Level

¹How beautiful are thy feet with shoes, O prince's daughter!
The joints of thy thighs are like jewels, the work of the
hands of a cunning workman.
²Thy navel is like a round goblet, which wanteth not liquor:
thy belly is like an heap of wheat set about with lilies.
³Thy two breasts are like two young roes that are twins.
⁴Thy neck is as a tower of ivory; thine eyes like the fishpools
in Heshbon, by the gate of Bath-rabbim: thy nose is as the
tower of Lebanon which looketh toward Damascus.
⁵Thine head upon thee is like Carmel, and the hair of thine
head like purple; the king king is held in the galleries.
⁶How fair and how pleasant art thou, O love, for delights!
⁷This thy stature is like to a palm tree, and thy breasts to clusters of grapes.
⁸I said, I will go up to the palm tree, I will take hold of the
boughs thereof: now also thy breasts shall be as clusters
of the vine, and the smell of thy nose like apples;
⁹And the roof of thy mouth like the best wine for my beloved,
that goeth down sweetly, causing the lips of those that are
asleep to speak.
(Song of Solomon 7:1-9 KJV)

Let's begin this chapter by looking at verses 7 and 8 of chapter 7 of Song of Solomon: "This thy stature is like to a palm tree, and thy breasts to clusters of grapes. I said, I will go up to the palm tree, I will take hold of the boughs thereof: now, also thy breasts shall be as clusters of the vine, and the smell of thy nose like apples."

"I will go up to the palm tree...." In this chapter, we are going to talk about "Going to the Next Level." One of the things that I'm hoping that we will accomplish by the Spirit of God and the power of His Word is for us to overcome the mindset of mediocrity.

There are so many of us who are content with being mediocre, or just being average. We just do things the way they've always been done because we've entered into a comfort zone. We've gotten satisfied with just being average, saying to ourselves, "As long as I'm better than two or three other people, at least I'm not as bad off as them." That kind of thinking helps us to justify going through life being average. So we end up with mediocre friendships, lifestyles, relationships, marriages, and we're happy just being mediocre parents and raising mediocre children—all because we've just become so satisfied with being average.

For many of us, everything that we're going to possess, we already have. Everything that we're going to learn, we already know. Every place we're going to go, we've already been. We're content with mediocrity, so instead of going to another level of living, we just keep recycling the same experiences. We end up repeating the mediocre life experiences we've always had, rather than going to another level with God. Someone has suggested that if you choose the good in the face of the best, you sin all the more. God always wants us to go to another level—to move higher and to excel.

Higher and Higher

My friend, Bishop Paul S. Morton, says, "Being average is like being on top of the bottom." I don't know about you, but I don't want to be on the top of the bottom. I feel like the Apostle Paul—I may not be perfect, but "I press toward the mark for the prize of the high calling of God in Christ Jesus" (Philippians 3:14 KJV). I want everything that God has for me. If it's more knowledge, I want it. If it's more possessions, I want them. If it's more character, I want it. I don't want to settle for a mindset of mediocrity.

As we do a mediocre job, working in our mediocre careers, we take that same mindset into the church. We don't give God our best because we're just average. We give God mediocre praise and offerings, we live mediocre lifestyles, and we have mediocre walks with God. We have settled into a comfort zone of being just average, but I believe it is time for us to go to another level by getting everything God has for us, doing everything God wants us to do, pressing toward the high calling of Christ, and carrying a sense of excellence about us. Don't ever get satisfied with where you are.

Our grandparents used to say, "Every day with Jesus is sweeter than the day before," and "Every round goes higher and higher." Second Corinthians 3:18 tells us that we are being transformed "from glory to glory" (KJV). We should do this not only in our walk with God, but in our relationships with one another as well. The Bible says we ought to love God with all our heart, mind, soul, and strength, and then love our neighbors as ourselves (Luke 10:27). So we should, therefore, have a sense of excellence in terms of our friendships, our partnerships, our relationships as singles, our marital relationships, and our parental relationships. That is what the man is seeking in the Song of Solomon, chapter 7. He says that his woman is like a palm tree, and he wants to climb it. His aspiration is to go higher in that relationship.

As I thought about that, I began to wonder, how do we do that? How do we enhance our relationships? How do we take our relationships to a higher level? If you are a single person, and you are in a relationship with someone whom you believe God has chosen for you, how do you go on to marriage? If you're married and you want your marriage to thrive, not just remain in a survival mode from one year to the next, how do you make that happen? Chapter 7, verse 1, gives us some insight into this. The man says to his Beloved, "How beautiful are thy feet with shoes, O prince's daughter! the joints of thy thighs are like jewels, the work of the hands of a cunning workman."

One thing I appreciate about this man is that even after seven chapters, he's still growing closer and closer to his woman by getting to know her better. He's still getting a sense of communion and unity with her by continuing to learn more about her. We know that is true because in chapter 4, when he gave a description of the Shulammite woman, he only talked about the features of her upper body. But now in chapter 7, he starts talking about her feet, her thighs, her navel, and her belly. This means that he's still learning about her and getting closer to her, even after seven chapters.

There are some people who have been dating the same person for five years, but don't know any more about each other in the fifth year than they knew in the first. There hasn't been a sense of growing and knowing, getting close, having communion, and establishing concord. There are some people who have been married for fifteen years, but don't know any more about their spouses in the fifteenth year than they knew in the second. Somewhere down the line, they just didn't care about getting to know who the other person was. Now they've lost sight of the things that once attracted them and eventually led to dating and marriage. No matter how long you've known your spouse, there are still things you haven't learned and ways that you can get closer. As the man in our text gets closer to his woman, he still compliments her even after seven chapters. When he met her in chapter 1, he was telling her how beautiful she was. Six chapters later, he's still telling her how beautiful she is. He keeps finding different areas in which to compliment her. If you want your relationship to be enhanced and grow, you can't always point out the negative traits in your partner; there has to be something good that you can compliment. Every now and then, you have to highlight the positive.

Compliments

Notice in verse 1 that as the Lover begins to compliment his woman, he acknowledges that she is a created being. He speaks of her thighs as "the work of the hands of a cunning workman." He recognizes that God created this woman, and praises God for His wisdom in the way that He did it. For example, he says that her thighs look "like jewels."

There is no sense in anyone trying to remake what God has made. Perhaps that's the main problem in our relationships. We look at someone God has made and try to recreate that person after our own image—in the way we want him or her to be. But this man says in effect, "I appreciate who you are. I appreciate the way God has made you. I appreciate His ingenuity and wisdom in putting you together. He is a craftsman, a cunning workman."

The fingerprints of God, brother, are all over your woman. The Bible says in Psalm 139 that when God made us, He shaped and formed us in our mothers' wombs. He made your woman by hand. That's why David says, "I will praise you, because I'm fearfully, and wonderfully made." Do you know the people who have issues with praising God? It's the same ones who don't know that they've been fearfully and wonderfully made. Once you know that God made you, then you don't have an issue with praising Him. Some people give praise that belongs to God to other people instead, because they think those other people made them. But don't fool yourself. It is God that "hath made us, not we ourselves" (Psalm 100:3 KJV). Your man didn't make you. Your woman didn't make you. Even your mother and father didn't make you: neither did your supervisor, your professor, your principal, your coach, or any other human being. God has made you. It is in Him that you live, move, and have your being (Acts 17:28).

Here is a man who appreciates that in his woman. He knows it is God who put her together, and the closer that he has gotten to her, the more he appreciates her. They are so close now that he even knows her feet and thighs, along with her navel and belly. He knows her and is close to her now. He's intimate with her. Even though he has gotten this close, he still finds beauty in her. Some people are pretty at a distance, but the closer you get, the less attractive they are. In fact, some are downright ugly. I'm not talking about physical beauty, but in totality. I'm talking about their character and their personality.

I once got to know one of my childhood heroes. When I was a teenager, there was a preacher I greatly admired and respected. He mentored me through his preaching of the gospel and taught me about presentation. Meanwhile, he edified me and built me up. When I was tempted to give up my plans for ministry, he reminded me "what God has for me is for me." After I was grown up and my ministry began, I had the opportunity to work more closely with him. We worked on a couple of projects and programs together, shared a few meals together, and got to know each other socially.

At one time, he had looked good at a distance, but the closer I got to him, the clearer I could see how ugly his character actually was. The man I had seen in public, at a distance, was not what I saw in private, up close. It was such a disappointment that I almost wished I had never met him.

This man in our text, however, is letting his woman know that as he is getting closer to her, he sees even more how beautiful she is; every part of her is beautiful to him. He begins to speak of his closeness to her, and compliments her about how good she is. One thing that surprised me is that he started off with a description of her feet: "How beautiful are thy feet..." (verse 1). I have to admit that bothered me. How beautiful are your *feet*? Remember, the last time he described her, he started from the head and worked his way down. Now, he's starting from below, and working his way up. He says, "How beautiful are thy feet with shoes...." What he's saying symbolically is that, "I like how beautiful your feet are, even when they are covered. I appreciate you even when you aren't bare." Many relationships remain superficial because people can only appreciate each other with their clothes off. There is something wrong with a man and a woman who can only connect when they're undressed. Sister, if a brother can't connect with you with your clothes on, why are you letting him see you with your clothes off?

The Lover in our text continues to describe in detail all of the fine aspects of his Beloved's body, then sums it up in verse 6: "How fair and how pleasant art thou, O love, for delights!" He's saying that she is not only beautiful, but pleasing; it is a pleasure for him to be with her. This is important, because there are some women who feel that they are so pretty that any man should be pleased to be in their presence. But, sister, it doesn't matter how pretty you are on the outside, if you aren't pleasant on the inside, it's nobody's pleasure to be with you.

I am reminded of a woman in Carmel, Indiana, who went to have cosmetic surgery because she wanted a makeover on the outside. Tragically, she died on the operating table. Of course, her husband was extremely upset and angry and wanted to hold the doctor accountable, but the doctor explained that she died because of a heart condition. Here was a woman who was spending time and money to change some external things without realizing that she had a fatal flaw on the inside. Some people spend a lifetime focusing on their outward appearance, but they never take time to make sure their hearts are good.

Continuing on in the text, the man works from the feet up to the woman's thighs. He specifically mentions the joints of her thighs, comparing them to jewels. He doesn't only notice the skin on the outside, but recognizes the value of what is on the inside. Sister, you need the kind of brother who not only can compliment you on your physical appearance, but also looks beneath the surface and recognizes that there is more than meets the eye.

Our joints allow movement and motion. They connect the other components so that the leg can function and not be just a stiff or dangling limb. Just as the joints unite the ligaments, cartilage and muscles to allow the limb to be of value to the body, there is deep within this woman—in a place not visible—a strength of character and determination that has allowed her to hold her life together in the midst of all that she has gone through. She has been in the streets, has had one bad experience after another with men, and has been on the mountain top and in the valley, but after all the hell she's been through, she's still got it together.

That's what the Holy Spirit is able to do in our lives. He gives us strength and holds our lives together. When you believed that Jesus died on the cross and that God raised Him from the dead, and then turned your life over to Him, He not only gave you eternal life, but He also began working inside of you through the power of His Holy Spirit. So, when life with all of its troubles pulled you one way and then another and your relationships stretched you to the point that you felt you were going to break, the reason you were able to hold it together was because of the Holy Spirit. You can look around and see other folks who went through the same experiences and didn't make it, but there you are, going against all the odds. You're still keeping it together, thanks to the Holy Spirit dwelling within you.

When I was a kid, my family was poor, so I owned hardly any toys. My little cousin used to have a lot, so when we wanted to play with toys, we went over to his house to play. One of his toys was a Bozo the Clown punching bag. It was a tall plastic figure that was round on the bottom and weighted with sand so that when we pushed him down, he'd come right back up. We could even hold him down, but no matter how long we did that, he just sprang back up as soon as we let go. Now my cousin and I didn't just hold him down and push him down—we were out to defeat this clown. We would stick him, hit him, kick him, judo-chop him, double-team him, and beat up on him, but no matter how long we kept him down, Bozo came up standing. No matter how tired we got from our efforts, he kept on smiling. Only later did I learn that not only did he have that round base and hard plastic on the outside, but also that sand on the inside. It was the material filling the inside of Bozo that kept him coming back up again, no matter what we did to him.

When you are filled with the Holy Spirit, it doesn't mean folks won't hurt you, team up on you, or try to put you down and keep you down. But even after they get finished doing all that, you're still going to be right there, standing victoriously. Because the joy of the Lord is your strength, those people are even going to see that they didn't remove the smile from your face. They can do what they want to you on the outside, but you've got something on the inside that just won't let you stay down.

Commitment

But we're not just talking here about keeping it together; we're also talking about going to another level. If you are going to take your relationship to a higher level, it will require more than just getting closer and paying compliments. You have to be willing to make a commitment. In verse 7, the man is talking about the woman being like a palm tree. Notice his choice of words in verse 8: "I *will* climb the palm tree; I *will* take hold of its fruit." He is determined to make this climb because he is committed to her. He's saying, in effect, "No matter what has gone down in our relationship in the past—and I know we've had our ups and downs, our ins and outs—we've come through too much, baby, to let it go now. I'm willing to go to the next level with you. After the hell we've been through, we're not going to let this thing go now. We're not going to let the enemy steal this away from us now. Look, I'm here, and I'm willing to commit to making this climb. I'm willing to commit to going to the next level."

This text shows us that this man and woman were not on the same level; perhaps that is why they had so many issues. It's frustrating when a man is at one level, and his woman is at another. One is trying to go up higher, while the other one is content to keep things just as they are. The woman might be wondering, *How are we going to go to another level together when we aren't even on the same level now?* We can see that he's not at her level from the wording of the text. When he first starts describing her in verse 1, he talks about what he's seeing: her feet. Had he been on her level, he would have looked into her eyes and described them to us. Also, he makes it clear that he was going to have to climb to reach her fruit. Had he been on the same level, he could have simply reached out and received the fruit from her. He faced the fact that he was going to have to climb the tree first. Even though they may share the same faith, they are unequally yoked together. He realizes that it is time for him now to get to the level where she is and he is supposed to be.

He admires what he sees in her, which is the reason he calls her a palm tree. Listen to what he says, in essence: "Your stature, your character, your values, your morals, your spirituality—you are like a palm tree that stands tall and firm." He specifically chooses a palm tree to describe her because it is able to weather the stormy times. The Caribbean is full of palm trees. Even though hurricanes frequently sweep through that region, the palm trees aren't going anywhere because they are able to handle high winds and hard times. Florida is so beautiful to me, partly because its natural landscape is sprinkled with so many palm trees. They've been through so many hurricanes with winds up to 150 miles per hour. When the winds were over and the storms were gone, the palm trees were still standing because they can handle hard times. We need to try to live our lives like palm trees, so that even when storms and adversity come our way, we may bend, but we never break.

Other trees may be uprooted, houses destroyed and buildings flattened, but because the palm tree is so flexible, it just lets the storm pass by and then stands up tall again. As a child of God, storms may come your way. You may get sick, you may lose your job, and someone may still hurt you. When that stuff blows in, however, you can let it bend you, but you don't have to let it break you. Just as the sun shines after a storm and the rays of that sun cause the palm tree to stand back up, so also will the rejuvenating light of the Son enable you to rise again!

Climb

Not only does the Lover say his woman is like a palm tree, but he also observes that there is fruit on her tree. His desire to experience that fruit gives him a strong incentive to climb. He knows that if there is fruit on the tree, it is a sure sign that there is also a sturdy system of roots underneath. Without roots, the tree cannot bear any fruit. It's the same for the spiritual realm. When we are rooted and grounded in Jesus Christ, God will plant us by rivers of water so that the subterraneous roots draw the water out that gives life to our branches in order to produce fruit.

When the sap begins to flow, I feel just like Ray Charles: "I'm gonna make it do what it do, baby!" When people begin to dog me, baby, I just do what I do. It isn't me; it's the Holy Spirit in me holding me together. Next time someone acts like a fool at your job because they're jealous and envious about what God is doing in your life, just tell them, "I just make it do what it do, baby! It's not me, it's the Holy Spirit!" You're rooted and grounded in Jesus. If you want to produce fruit and desire some love in your life, along with joy, peace, patience, kindness, goodness, faithfulness, gentleness, and self-control, you need to stay rooted and grounded in Christ. Those godly qualities, as you know from Galatians 5:22 and 23, are the fruit of the Spirit. Just as the Lover saw the fruit his Beloved was producing, so people should also be able to see that fruit growing on the outside of our lives. If they don't, that's because nothing is going on inside.

The fruit and the palm tree-like character of the Shulammite woman were quite evident to her husband. Her strong character qualities of steadfastness and productivity motivated him to want to climb higher to reach another level. He appeared to be thinking, "I've got to climb, because my woman and I are not at the same level. She's like a palm tree with fruit, and here I am, just interested in feet and thighs." But he must have reached the level she was on by verse 9 because that's when they start kissing. If he had kissed her in verse 1, he would have been kissing her feet! Now he is face-to-face with her because he was willing to make the climb; now they are equally yoked together.

When the Bible says not to be unequally yoked together with unbelievers, it doesn't mean that you both have to hold the same college degree to have a good relationship. It's not saying that you both have to be in the same tax bracket to have a good relationship. You don't even have to hold the same status in society to have a good relationship. You just need to be on the same plane spiritually. You've got to worship the same God, have faith in the same Jesus, be filled with the same Holy Spirit, and be reading the same Word. Since they were on different levels, for their relationship to work, either the Shulammite had to stoop down to his level, or he had to come up to hers. She made up her mind not to lower herself; if he wanted to get her fruit, he had to rise up to her level.

Sister, stop lowering yourself so somebody can get your fruit. If your fruit is as sweet as you say it is, there are brothers who would climb the highest mountain, trudge through the lowest valley, and swim the widest river to get to you. If your fruit is sweet, you don't have to lower yourself to give it away. This couple ends up on the same level, but it's because she waited patiently for him to come up to the level where she was. She didn't lower herself to be with him.

Now some foolish brother will think, "I don't have to work to get to any other level. I'm content right where I'm at. I like feet and thighs. I don't have to give my life to Christ; I can just stay as I am and enjoy the women who are on my level." But what you don't understand, brother, is that the sweetest fruit is at the top of the tree, where it's exposed to the sun. Brothers, don't settle for a woman at a lower level just because you can get her. Two people living life below the place God wants them to be and where they could be in Christ are going to discover that eventually feet and thighs aren't enough. When their heads finally get involved, they may find out that neither one of them is worth spending a lifetime with. Start at the top: get to know the other person eye-to-eye and head-to-head. Don't settle for less than God's best.

There's some good news in this passage of Scripture. Even though the brother started low, he didn't stay low because of his aspiration and determination. He said, "I will climb." This wasn't just some emotional decision; it was an act of the will. When you will yourself to go on to another level, God gives you the power to do it. This man teaches us that just because you start low doesn't mean you have to stay low. He ends up face-to-face with the woman he loves, and that's how they are able to kiss in verse 9. Notice that he says, "The roof of your mouth is like fine wine." The only way he can know this is if he's got his tongue in her mouth. He's kissing her face-to-face because he chose not to stay down low.

That's the good news of the gospel: God arranges things so that we don't have to stay down. He gives us another chance after raising us up. If you still think that the fruit is sweet down low, wait till you come up high. Every day with Jesus *is* sweeter than the day before. When you put your faith in Jesus Christ, He's able to raise you to another level. You don't have to stay where you start.

Look at Gideon. When God spoke to him because He wanted to use him, he was troubled because he had a self-esteem problem. He basically said, "My tribe isn't anything, and I'm the worst one in my tribe." But God let him know that he didn't have to stay at the level where he started. He used Gideon to bring one victory after another to His people. Look at David. He started off as a shepherd boy caring for his father's sheep. The family wouldn't even let him stay in the house for the family business meetings, but God raised him up to be the greatest king of Israel. Look at Moses, who started off as the baby son of a Hebrew slave, drifting down the Nile. God pulled him out of that situation, placed him in Pharaoh's house in Egypt, and then raised him up to deliver God's people out of bondage.

In more recent times, look at Wilma Rudolph. She had such a severe case of polio that the doctors told her she would never be able to walk. Not only did she start walking; she began running as well. God then raised her up to receive a gold medal for her athletic prowess at the Olympics. Look at Madame C.J. Walker, a Black woman living during the Jim Crow days in Indianapolis. Folks told her she was never going to do anything or be anything, so they wouldn't even give her a chance. Determined to create her own economic opportunity, she began her own hair care and cosmetic business, soon becoming the first African American female million-aire. Look at Sean "P. Diddy" Combs. He began life labeled as "learning disabled," so he had to ride a special bus to school because he couldn't be with the other kids. Today, he is one of the most influ-ential men in America, as well as being one of the richest Black men in the world.

Look at Dave Thomas, a high-school dropout who began Wendy's Restaurants and went on to become a multimillionaire. Look at Oprah Winfrey, who was sexually abused as a child and told during her first job in her chosen field that she didn't have what it takes to make it in the media. Today, she is one of the best- known celebrities on television and one of the most prominent women in the world.

Look at me, Jeffrey Johnson, born in poverty and raised in a broken home. God raised me up, and now (as all pastors feel about their own church) I pastor one of the greatest churches in the world.

Finally, look at Jesus. He was tortured, killed, and buried in a borrowed tomb, but God raised Him from the dead and made Him the Savior of the world. God can raise you up!

Chapter 15

I Ain't Got Nothing but Love for Ya

¹⁰ I belong to my lover,
and his desire is for me.
 ¹¹ Come, my lover, let us go to the countryside,
let us spend the night in the villages.
 ¹² Let us go early to the vineyards
to see if the vines have budded,
if their blossoms have opened,
and if the pomegranates are in bloom—
there I will give you my love.
 ¹³ The mandrakes send out their fragrance,
and at our door is every delicacy,
both new and old,
that I have stored up for you, my lover.
                    (Song of Solomon 7:10-13, NIV)

In Song of Solomon 7:10, the Shulammite woman begins, "I belong to my lover." I have to admit that her declaration somewhat disturbed me. Living in the twenty-first century, our way of thinking says, "I don't belong to anybody. I'm my own man," or "I'm my own woman." Yet, this woman says here unapologetically, "I belong to my lover."

Then, I was disturbed even more as I thought about it, because we aren't supposed to belong to anybody but God. In 1 Corinthians 6, it says that we have been bought with a price, and our bodies are the temple of the Spirit. In other words, we don't even belong to ourselves, but to Christ, the One who bought us. But wait a minute here. In 1 Corinthians 7, it goes on to say that when a couple marries, the wife's body doesn't belong to her but to her husband, and the husband's body doesn't belong to him but to his wife. This sounds confusing. Which is it? Do we belong only to God, or do we belong to our spouses? I believe the answer isn't either/or; it's both/and.

We Belong to God

We belong both to God and to our husband or wife. Actually, we belong to God twice. He owns us once by creation: "…it is He that hath made us and not we ourselves" (Psalm 100:3 KJV). He also owns us through redemption. Jesus is the One who shed His blood on Calvary to pay the penalty for our sins. In 1 Timothy 2, the Apostle Paul notes that Jesus paid a ransom for all of humanity. We were being held as hostages in bondage to sin, and as Romans 6:23 explains, "The wages of sin is death." Jesus paid the penalty for our sin with His own life—His own blood. First Peter 1:18 and 19 says, "For you know that it was not with perishable things such as silver or gold that you were redeemed from the empty way of life handed down to you from your forefathers, but with the precious blood of Christ, a lamb without blemish or defect." That's how we belong to Him.

Thirteen or fourteen years ago, I heard an old preacher give this illustration, and I've been using it ever since to tell how we are owned once through creation and again through redemption. A boy who had a great talent with arts and crafts designed and made a beautiful little sailboat. When he finished it, he took the boat to a lake and began to play with it. He was having a great time giving the boat a push and watching it sail, carried along by the wind and the currents in the water. But suddenly, the waves caught the sailboat and took it farther and farther away from him. He stood there watching as the little boat sailed out of sight and was lost.

The little boy was distraught because he had very lovingly and painstakingly designed this boat with his own two hands, and now the waves had taken away his treasured possession. He walked home in tears.

Not long after that, as he was walking down the street one day, he saw a toy sailboat in a store window. He went over to the window and looked more closely. It was *his* boat—the very same one he had made and lost! Excitedly, he ran into the store and said to the owner, "I came to get my boat. The boat you have in the window is mine. I made it, and I'm here to get it back."

But the owner of the store said, "Wait a minute, son. I don't know what you're talking about. That boat is for sale; it's got a price tag on it." "But sir," the boy insisted, "I made that boat with my own hands. I designed it myself and put it together myself. It's *my* boat." Look," replied the owner, "I don't know who made that boat, whether it was you or somebody else. What I do know is that if you want it, you're going to have to pay the price for it."

So the little boy went out and raked leaves, cut grass, picked up trash, and did everything he could to make the money to buy it back. He saved every penny he earned, and even though it took a while, he finally went back to that store and bought his own boat back. As he walked down the street and held the boat up in the air, he said, "You are twice mine. I made you with my own hands, but the waves took you away. Now I have bought you back."

God has done the same thing for us. He created us, but we drifted away from Him. Yet He loved us so much that He sent His Son Jesus to die in our place so that we could serve Him here on earth and then spend the rest of eternity with Him in heaven. Since we belong to God, we must put God first. In Exodus 20:3, God said, "You should have no other gods before me." Anything or anybody who becomes more important to us than Jehovah becomes our god, and He isn't going to put up with that. As our senior saints remind us: "He's God all by Himself," or as it says in Deuteronomy 6:4 and 5: "Hear, O Israel: The Lord our God, the Lord is one. Love the Lord your God with all your heart and with all your soul and with all your strength." As a matter of fact, Jesus said, "You can't have two masters, because you'll love one and hate the other" (Matthew 6:24).

You have to make up your mind. If you belong to God, then act as though you belong to God. In the Old Testament, Elijah asks, "How long will you waver between two opinions? If the Lord is God, follow him; but if Baal is God, follow him" (1 Kings 18:21).

We have to stop trying to go both ways. Joshua said, "Choose for yourselves this day whom you will serve…. But as for me and my household, we will serve the Lord" (Joshua 24:15). In the book of Revelation, when Jesus is speaking to the Church of Laodicea, He says that God would rather that you be hot or cold. When you are lukewarm, or trying to go both ways, He will spit you out of His mouth. Several times in the Old Testament, we read that God is a jealous God. This is not in the same sense as human jealousy because God is not insecure or worried about His competition. He *owns* us. He expects us to love Him, worship Him, honor Him, praise Him, and obey Him because He is worthy of all that; He *alone* is worthy! When we dishonor Him by turning our backs on Him and treating Him in a way that is unworthy of Him, He becomes angry. We are twice His, so how can we disrespect His love for us so badly? If we recognize that we belong to God, first through creation and then through redemption, we have to keep Him as the only one on the throne of our hearts.

But what about the verses that say we belong also to our spouses? If you are single, everything is just between you and God; your body belongs to Him alone. But when you're married, your body belongs to your spouse. The Bible makes it clear that the husband's body doesn't belong to him, but to his wife. The wife's body doesn't belong to her, but to her husband. Just as you don't play around on God, you don't play around on your spouse, either. If you made that commitment to your spouse, then be committed. If you are ever thinking about getting married, it should mean that you have narrowed your focus down to one person. You aren't trying to get anybody else, and you aren't letting anybody else get you. Why? Because you belong to the one you marry.

In the same verse (verse 10) that the Shulammite woman says, "I belong to my lover," she also says, "His desire is for me." She says, "I belong to him. His desire is for me." That's the joy in this text: the joy of marriage. It's a joy when the one you desire, desires you; when the one you belong to, wants you. Many people can tell you how horribly frustrating and deeply painful it is when the one you belong to desires somebody else, or the one who belongs to you is giving himself or herself to someone else. There is no joy in that—only hurt, anguish, and eventually death to the relationship. But God never intended for it to be like that!

God also never intended for you to desire someone else's spouse. If you have a desire for somebody else's husband or wife, that is outside of the will of God. Someone will argue: "But I can't help what I like because I can't control my desires. I didn't mean to want somebody else's husband [or wife]. It just happened, and I can't control myself." I beg to differ with you. You can control your desires.

I started this chapter talking first about belonging to God because that's where our desires arise. Once I get that relationship right and I'm redeemed, the Spirit of Christ lives within my heart, motivating, guiding and empowering me, so my very desires are changed. Once God is on the throne of my life, everything else begins to fall into place. If I discover that I am desiring someone who belongs to someone else in marriage, then I need to go back and recheck my relationship with God because He doesn't contradict His own Word. When I've got it right with God, I'm not going to be trying to get what isn't mine.

Remember Psalm 37:4: "Delight yourself in the Lord and he will give you the desires of your heart." Don't misinterpret that verse. It doesn't mean that God will give you everything your heart desires. Sometimes we desire things we have no business desiring and want to get something we aren't supposed to have. In this situation, we are trying to hook up with somebody we have no business hooking up with. If that particular text meant that God gives me everything I desire, then, whether it's good for me or not, whether it's morally right or not, whether it's God's will for me or not, it's mine. We know that isn't what this verse is saying at all.

This verse is instead telling us that God gives us not the fulfillment of the desires, but the very desires themselves. When we are delighted in the Lord—loving Him, spending time with Him, listening to Him, and finding joy in His presence—He guides our thinking and the desires of our hearts. We begin to want what God wants for us and desire what He desires for our lives. When that happens, we discover that we do see our desires fulfilled as well because God's will has become our will. In other words, what He wants for us has become what we want for ourselves. If I find myself wanting somebody I shouldn't want or being flattered by the fact that someone wants me when I belong to someone else, I need to get back to my first Love, who is Christ, and let Him show me where I allowed myself to lose my focus on Him. Then, I need to repent of my sins, ask Him to renew a right spirit within me, and allow Him to deal with my heart.

Desire with Direction

Watch what happens next in the text, after we learn that she belongs to her lover and that his desire is for her. The two determine to walk in the same direction. She says to him, "Come, my lover, let us go to the countryside, let us spend the night in the villages." They were no longer taking separate walks. If someone says that he or she desires you but isn't willing to go in the same direction, that person isn't someone you want to hook up with. Desire isn't enough to make a good marriage. Amos 3:3 asks, "Can two walk together except they be agreed" (KJV)? If I'm going to the countryside, but my spouse insists on staying in town, how can we be one?

Now we're not talking here about one spouse wanting to go to St. Elmo Steak House for dinner one evening and the other wanting to go to White Castle. We're talking about life choices, about moving together in the same direction in life. Desire without direction can't accomplish anything. If you're seeking God's will and walking where He wants you to walk, but your spouse is listening to the enemy and refusing to go that direction even though he or she knows that way is from God, your life is going to be in a perpetual state of chaos.

Some young person will say, "But I love this person, and this person loves me." Please hear me; love alone isn't reason enough to get married. Love may be the foundation for marriage, but when you build a house, just pouring a foundation isn't enough. You have to put something on top of that foundation. Let me make this plain: if you love someone but that person has no work ethic, you're going to find that love won't pay the bills; in fact, love is going to run out on you real soon. If you love someone but find out that person doesn't have the same morality or the same values as you have, that foundation is going to start shaking very quickly.

Freedom and Openness

In essence, the Shulammite woman says, "I'm glad your desire is for me, but now I need for you to be moving with me in the same direction. Come, let us go to the countryside." You have love, but now you need some direction in your relationship. I find it significant that they are going to the countryside. When you think of the countryside, you picture in your mind wide-open spaces, vast fields with no restraints, and no restrictions. Before you get married, you'll have restraints and restrictions in your relationship with your future spouse—if you are doing things God's way. But once you are married, those boundaries come down because there is freedom and openness in marriage. The Shulammite woman is saying, "Let's go in a direction where there will be freedom and openness in our marital relationship." If you can't be open and honest with the person whom you say you love, you can make love with that person all day, but you still won't experience intimacy. You cannot get close to people whom you lie to. You can have sex with them, but you can't have any intimacy or emotional closeness with them.

Look at Adam and Eve, for example. Remember that Adam and Eve are our frame of reference when we're going through the Song of Solomon. I believe in "the law of first mention" when trying to understand a passage of Scripture. That is, to know how something is supposed to be, you go back to the first time God mentions it because that is His design for it. The first time God mentions marriage, family, and the man-woman relationship, it's with Adam and Eve. The Bible says in Genesis 2 that God bring them together. They didn't have a father nor mother; instead, they were clinging to each other and the two became one. They had openness and freedom, with no restraints and no restrictions. They were naked, but not ashamed. They were able to reveal to each other their most intimate and private areas of their lives without any shame in their game.

Do you know why there was no shame? Because they had created an environment where they could be open and honest. That's what every couple needs. Desire is fine, but you've got to create an environment in which you can be open and honest with the one you love without getting your head cut off. If your spouse gets verbally or emotionally attacked while trying to be open and honest with you, guess what? Very soon you're going to find your marriage restricted and strained. Married couples have to enjoy an environment of freedom to flourish.

Fruitful and Flourishing

In verse 12, the woman says, "Let us go early to the vineyards to see if the vines have budded, if their blossoms have opened, and if the pomegranates are in bloom." She's talking about being fruitful and flourishing. In other words, she's saying, "It's cool that your desire is for me, but I want us to move in a direction where we're not just surviving, but thriving. I want things to be blossoming, blooming, and growing."

How do we cause our marriages to flourish? Too often people look around and decide that the grass is greener in someone else's yard. Sometimes it only seems that way because they are looking at it from a distance; if they saw it up close, they'd realize it isn't what it appears to be. If, on the other hand, it really is true that the grass is actually greener, do you know why that is true? It's because that couple is making the effort to plant grass seed, cultivate the soil and water the ground. We reap what we sow: if we're not sowing anything, we're not going to reap anything. If we aren't planting anything, we can't expect anything to grow.

Here's the key to sowing in marriage. You should sow based on the needs of your spouse. If she needs affection, give her affection. If he needs praise, give him praise. If she needs to hear the words, "I love you," then say them. If he needs some variety in the bedroom, be willing to experiment with him. Do you know what you're going to reap if you sow to meet the other person's needs? You are going to reap the harvest of your needs being met as well. But if you're not planting anything, cultivating the ground or letting your plants die of thirst, don't expect anything to blossom and grow.

What the woman wants is a fruitful relationship. She says, "I want to make sure that what we have flourishes, and what we have is fruitful." Remember, the fruit that makes relationships sweet is the fruit of the Spirit: love, joy, peace, longsuffering, gentleness, goodness, faith, meekness, and self-control. We need to make sure that the fruit of the Spirit is operating in our lives. Desire is wonderful, but it takes direction to get us somewhere. We need to move together toward a closer walk with God, with the fruit of the Spirit growing in our relationship.

If your relationship isn't working, don't waste time trying to figure everything out on your own. One day, my wife went out to get into her vehicle and found out that she had a flat tire. She drives a big ol' Suburban that we've had now for five years. When she saw that she had a flat tire and told me about it, I wanted to change it for her; I had a desire to change the tire. She had things to do, errands to run, and I wanted to make sure she could accomplish her goals.

Now, I'm the man of the house, and I'm going to change the tire on this big ol' SUV. But even though we've had the Suburban for five years, we had never had a flat before. I didn't even know where the spare tire was. Naturally, I assumed it was in the trunk. In the trunk of the car I drive, there's a flap you lift up, and the tire is right there. So, I opened those big back doors, and there was her cargo space. I lifted up that mat, but there was nothing under there. Now I was thinking, "They sold me an SUV with no spare tire." I was looking everywhere for it, and finally discovered that the spare tire is *underneath* the vehicle. So, I got under the vehicle and unscrewed all of those screws, thinking that once I did that, the tire was just going to fall down, and I'd have access to it. For some reason, the tire didn't fall.

Now, I really had a desire to get that tire changed; I *wanted* to change that tire. I still hadn't figured out just how to do that, but I decided that since I was having trouble getting access to the tire, I could at least go ahead and jack up the vehicle. I didn't know where the jack was, either. After searching for a while, I finally found it in a special compartment under the flooring in the trunk, but I couldn't figure out how it worked. Now, don't sit there shaking your head at me as you read this, acting as though you know exactly how all this stuff works. We all know how it works until we actually have to work it.

By this time, I was getting upset because I didn't have the knowledge that I needed to fulfill my desire to change the flat. So then I started wondering how the tire got flat in the first place. Did it go flat at home? Was she driving on a flat? Did she pick up a nail or screw away from home, bring the car home, and then the tire deflated here at home? How did we get in this situation? All my questioning did was to fuel my frustration. It didn't matter how the tire got flat. The important thing was that I needed to figure out how to lift this vehicle up and put on the spare tire so that we could move on to what we needed to do.

When I couldn't figure it out on my own, guess what I finally did? I pulled the owner's manual out of the glove box and read it. The book told me everything I needed to do. When I followed the instructions in the book, the tire got changed and we got on with our lives. Likewise, if your marriage goes flat, it doesn't matter why it's flat. It doesn't matter whether it started with something that happened at the house, or if one partner stepped out of the relationship and brought some mess back to the house. The important thing is that you figure out how to correct the problem and make the necessary change. You will find the direction you need in the manual God has provided: the Bible. He has answers to your questions as well as direction to help guide your desires in His Word.

You Give Good Love

Then, notice the last thing that the Beloved says to her Lover. Verse 12 closes with, "…there I will give you my love." Now, she wasn't talking about *agape* love! This is not the unconditional, "in spite of" kind of love. We know that is the case because he wouldn't have to be there to receive unconditional love. Regardless of what's going on, the agape kind of love always shows love. God teaches us that we don't wait till somebody gets to a certain place or into a certain situation before we give them agape love. God demonstrated His agape love toward us in that while we were still sinners, Christ died for us (Romans 5:8). He didn't wait till we got better, but while we were still messed-up sinners, Christ died for us. This act demonstrated that His love is unconditional. She's not talking about that kind of love here.

The love she's talking about here is *eros*—it's sensual and sexual. She begins to speak to him seductively, making her Lover some promises that he will not forget. Remember that they are married now; this is her husband she's talking to. This is her spouse, her mate, the person with whom she said, "I do," so it's all right for her to talk to him suggestively, seductively, and sexually. Do you think that's not important? There are people who make millions of dollars doing that very thing on the telephone with total strangers. Some very needy, and sometimes very sick, people pay $5 or so per minute on the phone to hear someone talk seductively and sexually to them. As a married person, you ought to be able to get that at home for free.

The woman in our text begins to make him promises. Sisters, take note. She's telling him what she's going to do when he gets home. This is like calling him on the job and saying, "Hey, baby, it's me. When we get to the countryside tonight, I'm going to give you my love. Don't work late; let's get an early start. Come straight on home, 'cause I've got something, and it's going to be waiting on you." Ladies, it's okay to talk like that. Not only is that kind of suggestiveness okay, but that kind of eagerness on your part can stimulate your marriage. After some people get saved, they get some crazy notion that just because sex feels good, it brings pleasure, and Hollywood has cheapened it, that somehow Christians can't enjoy it, take pleasure in it, or focus their attention on it. Sister, try calling your husband like this; then, watch and see what happens. Now, of course, at first he isn't going to believe it's really you because you've never done anything like this before! Begin to tell him what you're going to do when he gets home. I guarantee you that he won't be able to think about anything else for the rest of the day because it will be the only thing on his mind.

Some brother is probably asking, "Why doesn't that ever happen to me? Why doesn't my wife ever do that?" Remember, first she says, "...*there* I will give you my love." Maybe your wife has not given it to you like that because you aren't *there* yet. "Where is *there*?" you ask. *There* is a place of freedom, an environment where love flourishes. *There* is where the fruit is growing and you find delicacies at your door.

Now, sister, never make a promise you can't keep. Don't call your husband up at work to let him know what you are going to do, and then when he gets home, tell him you were just playing. Even though you were just trying to be cute on the phone, he spent all day thinking about nothing else. He's on the assembly line forgetting what he's supposed to do, or he's in a meeting and has no idea what's being said because he is daydreaming about what you've told him. You can't do that to your man and then not have anything waiting for him. You can't say, "Well, I'm not in the mood now. You don't know how my day has gone...." Some woman will do something foolish like that and then wonder why he's so frustrated for the next two weeks. Don't promise it if you can't carry it out.

Maximum Intensity and Minimum Inhibitions

Our sister in this text is not just making promises. She's letting him know that there is going to be maximum intensity with minimum inhibitions. You see, she says, "The mandrakes send out their fragrance...at our door is every delicacy...." She's saying, "...*every* delicacy. We're going to do a bunch of stuff. We're not holding back tonight. We're going to try every delicacy that we want."

Also, she's telling him that these delicacies are "at *our* door. You aren't going to have to go to anywhere else to find them. You don't have to run to some sister down the street because you aren't getting any delicacies at home. You don't need to try to hook up with a sister on the job because your needs aren't met here at home. I've got all kinds of delicacies for you right here."

These new delicacies the woman is talking about could include a lot of things. For some it could mean having sex at different times that you've not tried before. Some people think that they can only have sex at a certain time of day, like bedtime. No, we can do it at different times. In Song of Solomon 1:13, we read: "A bundle of myrrh is my well-beloved unto me; he shall lie all night betwixt my breasts" (KJV). They made love all night. In chapter 2, verses 16 and 17, it tells us again that they were together all night as he *browsed among the lilies*; remember, he was enjoying her garden. In chapter 7, verse 12, it says they did it early in the morning: "Let us go early to the vineyards...there I will give you my love." You can do it early in the morning, at noon, or late in the midnight hour. You can go home on a lunch break to have a quickie and then get back to the job. You can do it at different times! You're married! There is freedom! You have no restraints and no restrictions!

"New delicacies" could also include making love in new places. Some people think that the only place you can have sex is in bed. Some Christians think that because the Bible talks about "the bed" being undefiled in marriage, it literally means only the bed, but that's not what the verse is saying. The bed is a reference to sexual activity because that's where it commonly takes place, but in marriage, sex is undefiled—anywhere you have it! Just look at the places that the couple in Song of Solomon made love. They did it in the king's chamber, at home, in the hills, at her mother's house, in the mountains, in the countryside, and even under an apple tree. Now, don't send the police to me if you go out and do it in the wrong place, but you *can* try some new places.

It could be that "new delicacies" don't include just new times and new places; she may be talking about new positions, too. You don't always have to do it the same way; you might find that you like some of the new delicacies if you try them. There are a lot of great books that are written by godly authors for Christians which go into detail on this subject. It is okay for Christians to talk about sex and learn how to make their sex lives better. It is okay to get new ideas and try new things!

It's ironic that, on one hand, some people are out paying for sex while others are sneaking around trying to get it from the wrong people—those who don't belong to them—and still others are even trying to get it vicariously by watching someone else do it in movies or on television. Yet, on the other hand, the ones who are married and can do it freely as often as they want and with God's blessing are often the same ones who are doing it mechanically, in the same bed, in the same position, every first Tuesday at 9:15 p.m., whether they feel like it or not. It ranks right up there with the rest of the weekly schedule: "Thursday night, we put out the trash; Friday night, we pay bills; Saturday, we go grocery shopping…."

Why are you not receiving one of God's most precious gifts to you while you are here on earth? Having sex is not only for making babies. It also is for drawing a couple together as one in an intimate bond, for physical and emotional release, for recreation, and for having a good time. You don't have to be bound by inhibitions, false teaching, impure thoughts someone planted in your head long ago, fear, ignorance, routine, or misunderstanding. When the Son makes us free, we are free indeed!

If you are still reluctant to try something new, think about this: the Bible teaches about new things all the time. We read that God is doing a *new thing*. The Bible talks about a *new birth*. It says that we will have a *new name*. It speaks about a *new heaven* and a *new earth*. It tells us that the *mercies of God* are *new* every morning. God is into newness. He blesses us in new ways, such as opening new doors, giving us new jobs, and delivering us from bondage. God gives us new things. It's okay to move on to something new!

"Okay," you say, "I understand 'delicacies' mean different sexual activities, but what on earth do *mandrakes* have to do with anything? What does she mean when she says 'the mandrakes send out their fragrance'?" Mandrakes were considered a love plant, perhaps serving as an aphrodisiac that stimulated a person's sexual desires. But in chapter 30 of Genesis, Rachel, who was barren, asked her sister for mandrakes because they were also associated with conception; they were believed to be an aid for a woman to become pregnant. This Shulammite woman was wanting to enjoy the evening with her husband, but she was also thinking about the future. The fact that the mandrakes came to her mind indicated perhaps that she was happily believing that they might even be blessed with a child—another indication that their love was strong, growing, and fruitful.

In the closing verses of chapter seven, the woman says the delicacies are "new and old, that I have stored up for you, my lover." This isn't the first time they've made love. She knows the "old" delicacies, the things they've done together that they've both enjoyed, but she also has some "new" activities, or delights, awaiting him. You can bet that caught his attention and kept playing with his mind during the day as he wondered what it was she had waiting for him.

Notice carefully the phrase in verse 13: "I have stored up for you, my lover." This indicates that the woman had thought about these activities while she was single and waiting for the right man to come along: a *good* man with whom she could go to the next level. She wasn't unfeeling or without sexual desire; she had sexual thoughts during the time that she was waiting. But instead of having premarital sex just because she had an appetite for it, she "stored up" all of these delicacies for her husband. She didn't settle for lust instead of love. She knew how to maintain self-control and wait for real love to come along. As she waited, she stored up all of those thoughts and ideas, so that one day she could delight her very own husband by exploring "new delicacies" with *him*. I know this is the twenty-first century, and some people find the idea of waiting till marriage to have sex outdated, but there's something very special about being with someone who has waited all her life [or his life] just to be with you. When you think about it, that's what God's Word teaches us to do, so why shouldn't that be special? The story in the Bible of the prodigal son illustrates a contrast; it is a good example of someone who wouldn't wait to do things his father's way. He couldn't wait to obtain what his father had for him but insisted on getting his inheritance early. He took it, enjoyed it, squandered it, and then lost it. If we do things our Father's way, our enjoyment will be without regret and will last a lifetime.

There was a woman in the small town of Goshen, Indiana, who had twelve monkeys living in her house. She had kept them for nine years, but the health department suddenly confronted her and told her that she couldn't own monkeys in a residential area. She responded, "But I've had these monkeys for nine years. Why are they a problem now?"

The officials said, "We understand how you feel, but your neighbors keep calling us, so we have to do something." She learned that the neighbors were afraid she might bring down the property value because prospective buyers wouldn't want to live next to monkeys, and some were afraid that if one of the monkeys got away, it might hurt one of the children in some way. The woman tried to get the area rezoned so that she could hold onto her monkeys, but that attempt failed. The health department told her, however, that there was a more rural subdivision about twenty or thirty miles out of town where she could live with her monkeys. Wanting to keep her monkeys, she felt there was no other choice, so she decided to move on.

This story intrigued me because it reminded me of what is happening too often in our relationships—there's too much monkey business going on. The value of our relationships has gone down, and too many of our children have been hurt. It's time for the monkeys to move on. God has given us so much freedom in marriage, and we just need to learn how to enjoy it. If we recognized how sweet the marriage relationship can be and of what great value it is, perhaps more people would begin looking for the kind of love God desires for us to experience instead of lustful relationships outside of marriage. Desire is fine, but we need to follow God's Book to learn how to enjoy sex the way our Father intended for it to be enjoyed.

Chapter 16

I Love You Just the Way You Are

¹ If only you were to me like a brother,
who was nursed at my mother's breasts!
Then, if I found you outside,
I would kiss you,
and no one would despise me.
² I would lead you
and bring you to my mother's house —
she who has taught me.
I would give you spiced wine to drink,
the nectar of my pomegranates.
³ His left arm is under my head
and his right arm embraces me.
⁴ Daughters of Jerusalem, I charge you:
Do not arouse or awaken love
until it so desires.
⁵ Who is this coming up from the desert
leaning on her lover?
Under the apple tree I roused you;
there your mother conceived you,
there she who was in labor gave you birth.
⁶ Place me like a seal over your heart,
like a seal on your arm;
for love is as strong as death,
its jealousy unyielding as the grave.
It burns like blazing fire,
like a mighty flame.
⁷ Many waters cannot quench love;
rivers cannot wash it away.
If one were to give

all the wealth of his house for love,
it would be utterly scorned.
(Song of Solomon 8:1-7, NIV)

Billy Joel wrote a song—and you may have heard Barry White sing it—entitled, "I Love You Just the Way You Are." It says, "Don't go changing trying to please me…. I love you just the way you are." In the song, he tells his love not to try to change anything about herself…not her hair, her clothes, the way she talks…not anything. He says there is nothing she could do that would make him love her any more. He repeats, "I love you just the way you are." Now that sounds so beautiful and romantic, and it expresses the ideal situation in which we are accepted and loved for who we are, just the way we are. But if the truth be told, we live in the real world, not an ideal one, and only about five years after Joel wrote that song for his first wife, he divorced her. The fact is that very few of us love and appreciate our spouses just the way they are. Too many of us want, and try, to change people into something they are not. Sometimes, if they can't or won't change, we punish them by withholding our full love and commitment.

I'm bringing that up because in Song of Solomon 8:1, it *appears* as though this Shulammite woman is trying to change her man into someone other than who he is. She starts off by saying, "If only you were to me like a brother…." It seems that instead of loving him exactly as he is, she's wishing that he were like one of her brothers.

In actuality, however, there is a different reason why she wishes that he were like one of her brothers. According to social custom in biblical times, men would not even talk to women in public, let alone kiss them or touch them in an affectionate way. That would never happen. That's why Jesus' disciples couldn't understand how He could talk to a woman at a well. Here, this woman is saying that if her Lover had been her brother, she would have been free to kiss him publicly, and no one would have thought anything of it.

Don't Go Changing!

If, however, this woman had wanted to change her man to be like someone else, we really shouldn't get too upset with her because that's how so many of us are. We spend our time trying to make our spouses into someone other than the person God made them to be. Even though the Scriptures tell us that we are fearfully and wonderfully made in the image of God, we come along, trying to change someone...or someone comes along, trying to change us.

Now suppose this woman was telling her man that she would kiss him freely if only he was like someone else. What's going to happen? What some women don't understand is that there is a type of man who will act out of character by putting on an act in order to get a kiss, but after he gets it, he goes right back to being who he really is.

There is probably a woman reading this book who does not understand this. She loves God, has accepted Christ as her personal Lord and Savior, is filled with God's Holy Spirit, and tries to live a life that reflects her relationship with God. But this woman really wants a good Christian man in her life, and she is tired of waiting on God. She reasons to herself: "God is taking too long to bring along a Christian brother, so I'm going to get a worldly man, lead him to Christ, and help change him so that he has Christian character. But I'm going to make sure he understands from the beginning that we are just friends, and that I'm not going to get physical with him or consider marrying him until I see that he's a Christian." So, what's her man going to do? He's going to get a new King James Bible, put a "What Would Jesus Do?" bracelet on his wrist, hang a platinum cross around his neck, show up at church, sit with her on the second pew, and stay there until they finally connect. Eager to be in an intimate relationship, she sees this "change" in him, begins to allow him to be affectionate toward her, and soon they marry. Then the church never sees that brother again because he goes back to being the person he really is.

I'm just trying to let you know that you can't change people. People can change, but *you* can't change them and *I* can't change them. Only God can change a human heart. Second Corinthians 5:17

tells us that if anyone is *in Christ*, that person is a new creation. The possibility for change is there, but if a brother hasn't changed in seven chapters, it's not likely that he will change in chapter 8, either. He's going to continue to be the person that he is, and that's what you need to understand. Marrying someone will not change that person. In fact, a marriage license will not make any difference at all.

You may say, "Well, I just believe that he will be more responsible once we get married." If he's irresponsible before you get married, he's going to be irresponsible after you get married, too. The only thing that you're going to get when you marry is more of what you're getting before marriage…or worse. If he or she is trying to impress you before marriage, what you see then is the *best* you will ever see. If a person begins acting like a Christian or a good person just to draw you into marriage, the acting will stop after you say "I do." It will never be any better than before you get married, but it could become quite worse. If someone is a genuine Spirit-filled Christian who loves God and you and is committed to His work and you, then you will get more of that love and commitment when you get married. Before you say "I do," you have to be sure that you can live with this person—with the talk, the lifestyle, and the issues, because that's what you get.

A couple of years ago, I bought a car for J. Allen, my oldest son, to drive. Because he had just gotten his license and I didn't want him to tear up my car, I bought one especially for him to drive—a 1985 Buick Skylark. It has quite a few miles on it, but it runs pretty well. Now, it isn't a glamorous car, but it gets him safely from Point A to Point B. When I found this car, a sign on the window said, "As is, no warranty." I knew the dealer was telling me, "When you get this home, don't expect it to be any different from what you see right here. When you get it home, if you find something under that hood that you don't like, don't bring it back to me. There is no warranty on this. It is 'as is.'" That's what I'm trying to tell you about relationships. Don't think that when you get them home in marriage that it's going to be any different. They come "as is," with no warranty.

Mutual Submission

Note in verse 2 that the Shulammite woman says, "I would lead you, and bring you to my mother's house—she who has taught me." This sounds as though she would like to be in control of her husband: she wants to lead him. Not only does she want to determine the direction that he goes, but she would also like to take him to her mother's house where he can come under the influence of the one who taught her. All of this is interesting to me. It sounds as if she wants a man she can control. In biblical days, the society was male-dominated. Women looked to men for leadership—but not this sister. She wanted to be the leader.

The word "submit" is one that the Bible uses when referring to marriage. Ephesians 5:22 is a verse that most men know by heart. Right along with "Jesus wept," we know, "Wives, submit to your husbands, as to the Lord." "Submit" is not a bad word or cussword, but when people today hear it, a lot of images pop into their heads. One day, I was watching a discussion on a TV talk show about marriage and family that featured both Christians and non-Christians. In the course of conversation, someone mentioned the word "submit," and one woman on the show became upset, declaring very emphatically, "I'm just not going to worship my husband!" The word "submit" does not mean "worship," and neither does it mean "obey." If it meant "obey," God would have just said obey. Ephesians 6:1 says, "Children, obey your parents," but wives are not children. What the word means is simply to recognize authority. God has ordained that the husband be the head of the family so that there will be order in the home. It has been said that, "two heads are better than one," but not if they are trying to go different directions.

Two people can only dance together if one of them leads and the other is willing to follow. If both are trying to lead, it becomes merely a spectacle, not a dance. There is no beauty, no harmony, and no grace in two people stepping on each other's toes and pushing and pulling at each other because both are trying to lead. It's just as chaotic, awkward, and pathetic to see two people vying for leadership in the home. There is no beauty, harmony, or grace in that home.

That being said, it is amazing how many people, in getting to Ephesians 5:22, skip right over the verse immediately before it. *Before* the Bible tells wives to submit to their husbands, it says in verse 21: "Submit to one another out of reverence for Christ." In marriage, as well as in the body of Christ in general, we are commanded to be submitted one to another. Not only is the wife supposed to submit to her husband, but the husband has to submit to his wife as well. There is mutual submission. In our marriage, for instance, there are times when my wife Sharon needs to submit to me, but there are other times when I need to submit to her. There are some areas in which Sharon is equipped with more knowledge and more ability than I have. Her gifts and talents supersede mine in particular areas. That being the case, it would be a waste of her gifts and a total lack of respect for her as a person if I ignored what God has implanted within her by insisting that she follow me as I struggle and limp along, leading us nowhere. Why wouldn't I want to submit to her and let her take us higher in some area than I could ever take us?

When I used to teach the "Before You Say 'I Do'" course at our church, one question would always come up with each new group when we discussed the issue of submission. It never failed. Someone would always ask, "Who should keep the checkbook in the marriage?" I would throw the question back to them: "Who do you think ought to keep it?" Someone usually said, "I think the man should run it. The man is the head of the house, so he should be the one managing the money, keeping the checkbook, and keeping things in order." I always responded, "So, do you believe that the question of who should lead in managing the family finances is based solely on gender?" After giving them a second to think about it, I told them that I thought it should be based on intellect and ability. In other words, which one of you can count the best? Doesn't that make sense? Shouldn't the person who can pay bills on time and balance the checkbook take the lead in this area? If you marry a certified public accountant, and you can't add 2 + 2, guess who ought to be keeping the checkbook? Marriage is about mutual submission. I'm not against women leading men in this way. The problem with the woman in our text is the type of leadership she wanted to exert.

Within this context, she is saying that if she could change him, then she would lead him. She doesn't want to lead him to a neutral place where they come together to learn from each other and work together to develop their own approach to their marriage. She wants to take him down to her mother's house, specifically emphasizing "...she who has taught me." She appears to be saying, "I want you to hear from my mother. My mother can instruct you, just as she did me. I know the way things should be because of what my mother taught me. You need to learn this, too."

Outside Influences

Do you know what messes up so many marriages? Often, it's not the husband or the wife, but an outside influence that can have a negative impact on a marriage and even destroy it. The woman in our text is influenced by outside forces. She has said to her lover, "If you were like a brother to me, then I could be affectionate to you publicly, and then not have to worry about what people are saying." In essence, she is telling him, "The way I'm treating you is based on what others think about me. If I showed affection to you, then my peers wouldn't approve, and I'd get too much pressure from them. I'm more concerned about what they think about me than what I'm doing to you or how you might be feeling." That's what's wrong with some of you right now. You and your spouse would just be fine if other folks would just stay out of your business.

But, you keep bringing other people into your business. For instance, brothers, you are hanging out with some of the fellas watching a game, shooting some pool, or just hangin' together— no big deal. You check your watch and realize that it's later than you thought and you had really expected to be home before now. So you pull out your cell phone and start to make a call to your wife. Some of the other brothers start saying things like, "Aw, you checking in, huh? You know she's running you; you know that you're whipped, right? How come you can't just do what you want to do?" So you give in to the pressure of others, rather than being accountable, responsible, and respectful to the woman that you married. What you should say to them is this: "Yeah, I'm getting ready to call my queen, because she needs to know where her king is. If I treat her like a queen, then I'm going to be the king of my castle."

Sisters have to put up with pressure, too. Some friend says, "Girl, I wouldn't put up with that if I were you. If I were in your place, let me tell you what *I* would do...." We all get pressure from outside influences, and if we don't handle it right, it can have a negative impact on our marriage.

Now in our text, the woman wants to take her man to her mother's house, which would indicate a problem at the outset. Why should she want her mother involved in the relationship with her man? She mentions that her mother taught her. Does she want further instruction from her mother? The King James Version says it like this in verse 2: "I would lead thee, and bring thee into my mother's house, who would instruct me...." Do you see something strange with the order of that sentence? She is saying first that she will lead him, but *then* she will get instruction from her mother. First she leads, *then* she gets instruction? Why is she trying to lead someone without instruction? Don't you need to get the instruction *before* you start heading in a certain direction?

If a doctor is getting ready to perform an operation on you, wouldn't you want that person to get instructions *before* starting the procedure? Would you be comfortable with someone who doesn't know what he's doing, standing over you with a scalpel in hand, placing a call on his cell phone to a more experienced surgeon and asking, "Now what should I do?" No, you've got to get the order right. *First,* you get the instruction; *then,* you may be able to lead someone else. Why would she take him to her mother's house anyhow? Doesn't Genesis 2 talk about two people leaving father and mother and clinging only to each other, becoming one? Where does Mother fit into that? There are only two in marriage, not three.

Have you noticed that during our reading of eight chapters in the Song of Solomon, every now and then the woman's mother pops up, but she never talks about her father? It appears that there had not been a man in her mother's life, at least up to this point. We don't know what happened to him, or if he was ever around at all. But if the woman's mother doesn't have a man, how is she going to instruct her daughter on how to relate to a man? You have to be careful whom you go to for help. Some woman may be quick to tell you, "Girl, I wouldn't do that," or "He's got you doing this? Naw, you just tell him...." Before taking the advice of another woman, you need to check and see what she's got going with her man. Is hers the kind of relationship that you want to have with your husband? Look at what she's got first before you swallow everything she's got to say. Now, listen well. I am not saying that godly women who aren't married or those who don't have a man in their lives can't teach you anything. They can, and many do, offer wise and valuable counsel from the Word of God. What I am saying is simply to be careful where you go to get your help.

Now let's suppose that this Shulammite woman's mother and father actually had a long and happy marriage. Let's say that they were married for forty years and are only apart now because he went on to be with the Lord. The Shulammite woman may remember her happy childhood, knowing that her parents loved her and loved each other, too. She may have grown up thinking that she always wanted to have a marriage just like theirs. Now she has her man and wants to take him to her mother's house so that her mother can help them learn how to relate to each other. She wants to be just like her mother and relate to her husband in just the same way. She's thinking, "Momma was married for forty years, so she must know something about how to keep a marriage together. I want to learn how to treat my husband the way Momma treated Daddy."

It's great to learn from a woman who had a good marriage. If she was married for forty years, she obviously does know something about relationships. But wait a minute, sisters. Even if you go to your mother to get wise advice, you have to remember that your mother is married to your father and not your husband. Your husband is not your father. What your mother did with your father may have worked for her man, but it doesn't mean it's going to work for your man. Your man is not your daddy! You need to find out what works for *your* man, what meets *his* needs, and how you can best relate to *him*.

You have to remember that when you're getting help from other people, you are picking up principles, not practices. First, you have to understand and learn the principles, then you flesh them out with actual practices. The principles are going to stay the same, but how we express them may change. The principles include the following: 1) wife, respect your husband; and 2) husband, love your wife the way Christ loved the church. How you practice those principles may be different from the way someone else practices them.

For instance, let's say your parents have been married for forty years, and your mother says, "Baby, I respect my husband. You need to respect your husband." That's the principle. "Well, Momma, how do you respect him?" Your mother says, "Your daddy doesn't like to talk, so I don't talk to him. That has worked for us for forty years. He doesn't like to be bothered, so I respect him and give him his space. I don't say anything to him, and he doesn't say anything to me. We've been together for forty years." That's the practice. So suppose you go home and substitute the practice for the principle. You stop talking to your husband, but *your* husband loves to talk. He's very personable and loves to interact and communicate. Now he's frustrated and perturbed, trying to figure out why you won't talk to him. You need to follow the principle, but at the same time, talk to God and your spouse to determine how best to implement that principle in practice. What meets the need for one man or woman becomes a nuisance or obstacle for another person.

The only frame of reference that the Shulammite woman seemed to have was what she learned in her mother's house. It seems that the only male-female relationship that she has been able to observe up close is the relationship between her mother and her brothers. She has to be careful because if she has learned how to treat a man by watching the way her mother treated her brothers, she will treat her husband like her son. If she never saw her mother and father inter-acting, talking together as two adults, working out their differences, showing affection to each other, and caring for one another's needs, she may subconsciously learn that the way a woman relates to a man is the same way she saw her mother relate to her brothers. Do you think that's part of the problem in some of our marriages—that husbands and wives are treating their spouses like children? "Sit here, eat this, go there, wear this, put this on, and be home by such and such." Doesn't that sound as if you are talking to a child? If you are treating your adult spouse like a child, you're going to have some psychological issues to deal with, but you may not care if your main goal is to control him or her.

Reward – Punishment

It sounds as though the Shulammite woman is suggesting to her man that if he were different (more like her brother), she would show him great affection. She is using what I call the reward–punishment system. She says in verse 1, "If only you were like a brother to me, I would kiss you," and in verse 2: "I would give you spiced wine to drink, the nectar of my pomegranates." I would kiss you? I would let you drink my spiced wine? I would give you the nectar of my pomegranates? These are simply images that she is using to refer to her sexuality. She's talking here about offering him sexual favors.

Look at the wording: "I *would* kiss you. I *would* let you drink of my spiced wine. I *would* let you taste of the nectar of my pomegranate." If you are in a relationship that's full of *would's* and *should's*, it isn't meeting anybody's needs. If someone says, "I would kiss you," that means he or she is not kissing you. "I would let you drink of my spice wine" means that you are probably thirsty. "I would let you taste of the nectar of my pomegranates" means that you aren't getting any oral delights. "I *would* do something" is the way someone talks when using a reward–punishment system. "*If* you let me control you, *if* you let me change you, *if* you let me lead you, *then* I will let you drink of my spiced wine and the nectar of my pomegranates. But, if you *don't* do what I say, I'm going to withhold my spiced wine from you." It's a reward–punishment system. If you do what I ask you to do, I'm going to reward you by releasing my spiced wine. If you don't do it, I'm going to withhold my pomegranates from you.

A wife today who is practicing that system might say to her husband, "You know what? You did really good. You've been nice to me. You've talked to me, so we've communicated well. You helped me to pick up my car this week. You took the kids and gave me a night out. I'm going to give you some." Then next week comes around, and she says, "I told you to wash that car and cut that grass. That garage still hasn't been painted. I'm not giving you anything."

It's a reward–punishment system. You have to be careful with that because the Bible says in 1 Corinthians 7:4 that your body doesn't belong just to you anyway. In marriage, the wife's body belongs to her husband, and the husband's body belongs to his wife. The Bible says very explicitly that you should not deprive each other. If you don't meet each other's sexual needs, you leave room for the enemy to come in.

Now there will be some woman somewhere who is saying, "I understand what you're saying, but it just doesn't make sense to me. Giving or withholding sex is the only way I can get my husband to do anything." You need to look at this from a different perspective. The reward–punishment system is foolishness for you and frustration for him. Think about what you are saying and doing. You tell your husband, "All right, you haven't been acting right. You haven't been doing right. I'm not going to let you drink my spiced wine for thirty days." You're going to let him go without spiced wine for thirty days? You're going to make him go thirty days without anything to drink? You're going to withhold the only thing that quenches his sexual thirst for thirty days, and somehow you think that this is going to turn out to your advantage?

Let me explain it this way. I have a lot of awards and rewards of various types. They're all over the walls and on tables in my main office, in my second office, and at home. In essence, they say, "We want to express our appreciation to you for what you have done...." They include framed pictures, certificates, trophies, plaques, and all kinds of mementos. These awards have come from television stations, radio stations, newspapers, schools, colleges and universities, conferences, other churches, and conventions. I've gotten them from old people, young people, Black people, White people, the east coast, the west coast, the north, and the south. I'm not saying all of that to boast; I'm just trying to make the point that everybody gives rewards.

So, you place your man in a period of punishment for the next thirty days. He didn't behave as you wanted him to, so you are not giving up any rewards. You need to know that you are not the only person offering rewards: he can find rewards from all kinds of people in all kinds of ways.

You say, "But he can't do that. He's a Christian. He can't drink any other woman's spiced wine, only mine. God said so." That is true, but in 1 Corinthians 7:5, God also tells you not to deprive your spouse of your body. The only exception to that is if both of you agree that you need to spend a period of time in prayer, seeking God so earnestly that just as you fast by not eating, you are going to go without sex for a brief period of time as you focus all your attention on God. But then the verse warns, "Then come together again so that Satan will not tempt you because of your lack of self-control." If you are doing something outside the will of God that makes your husband vulnerable to temptation and allows so much room for the enemy to come in, you will have to share in the responsibility if something happens that is not according to your scheme.

The Right Response

So, how does a man handle this kind of behavior from his woman? Here in the text is a woman telling her man that she wishes he were like her brother and wants to take him to her mother to get some instruction. Just think about what this man could have said. He could have replied, "What do you mean, like your brother? Your brother is no good. He's the same one who burned you back in chapter 1 by exposing you to the elements and messed you up. He made you work on his stuff, but wouldn't help you. You know your brother is no good, yet you still want to take me to your mother's house? She's the one who taught your brother to be like he is. Is that what you want me to learn from her? What does she know anyhow? Your mother doesn't even have a man because she hasn't been able to keep one...."

There are a lot of things her Lover could have said, but instead, do you know what he does? Look at verse 3. He puts his left arm under her head and then takes his right arm and embraces her. Think about it. Even though she's going on with her foolish talk, he begins to caress her, hold her, and help her relax and rest. Even though she isn't meeting his needs at that moment, he starts meeting hers. He's affectionate, caring, and loving toward her.

Sometimes you've got to begin sowing seeds, even when you don't feel like it. Eventually, as Galatians 6:9 tells us, if you don't grow weary in well-doing, you will reap what you sow. No matter what your woman is doing or saying, you don't want to sow seeds of anger, bitterness, and resentment because you don't want to reap a life filled with all sorts of negative things. If you meet her needs, eventually she's going to turn around. You don't overcome evil with evil, but as Romans 12:21 says, you can overcome evil with good. You've just got to love her, caress her, hold her, minister to her, and meet her needs. Tomorrow, when *you're* the one acting crazy, the seeds you have planted will be growing and you will reap what you sowed today. Instead of the anger and bitterness you deserve, she will be able to hold you, love you, and meet your needs.

Spousal Support

In verse 4 of chapter 8, the woman tells the sisters in the community not to awaken her love. Her man is resting. How could that be? How could he stay with a woman who has just said such frustrating things to him? How could he be resting? Those who know the Lord can rest in Him no matter what is going on outside. If the Lord gives you peace, no one can take it away from you. Your spouse didn't give you that peace, so your spouse can't take it away. No one can take what God has given to you. In the very midst of what you're going through, you need to go ahead and love the other person and maintain your peace.

Then watch what happens in verse 5: "Who is this coming up from the desert (or "wilderness" in the KJV), leaning on her lover?" The woman says, "Under the apple tree I roused you; there your mother conceived you, there she who was in labor gave you birth. Place me like a seal over your heart, like a seal on your arm; for love is as strong as death, its jealousy unyielding as the grave." Just a few verses ago, it seemed that she wanted to change him and control him, but he responded by loving her. As he began to love her by creating a peaceful environment in the home, she began to come out of the wilderness—out of the wild situation she was in. Love has a way of bringing people out of wild situations. Who is this coming out of the wilderness? It's the same woman. Her man has helped her to come out of her wilderness because his love did not fail in the desert situation. She is now coming out of that place, leaning on her lover, so she has spousal support. Her man is the one helping her out of this.

We need to understand that the wilderness meant a place of wandering to the Hebrew people. When they got delivered out of bondage in Egypt and were trying to make it to the Promised Land, they wandered in the wilderness for forty years. Not only were they wandering, but after such a long period of time, they also started wondering if they were ever going to make it out of there, if leaving Egypt had all been in vain, and if they were ever going to make it to the place that God had promised. Even though you may not be wandering physically, some of you are wandering psychologically, emotionally, and even spiritually. You have no direction in your life, no real destination where you feel you ought to be, and no understanding of the plan or purpose God has for your life. You're wandering and wondering, but the good news of the text is that God is able to bring you out. No matter how messed up your situation is, no matter what you're strung out on, no matter what you're addicted to, no matter how low-down you are, and no matter how far into the wilderness you've wandered, you serve a God that is able to bring you out.

Life from the Labor of Love

So, how does one come out of the wilderness? Let's look at how the Shulammite woman comes out. She comes out in three ways: with life, lifted, and leaning.

First, she comes out with life. How does she get life? The text says her mother gave it to her. Her mother labored in love and gave her life. If you're going to come out of the wild situation you're in, the first thing you need is life. How do you get life? John 3:36 says, "Whoever believes in the Son has eternal life, but whoever rejects the Son will not see life...." Also, the familiar John 3:16 (KJV) says, "For God so loved the world he gave his only begotten Son, that whosoever believeth in him should not perish, but have everlasting life." In John 10:10, Jesus said, "I have come that they might have life, and that they might have it more abundantly." When you enter into a relationship with Jesus Christ, then you have life.

Christ will give you life, but that life by itself is not enough to get you out of the wilderness. That's why her man said, according to the King James Version, "I raised thee up under the apple tree," or "I lifted you up." Notice, too, that it was under the apple tree. Remember back in chapter 2, verse 3, the woman describes her lover "as an apple tree among the trees of the wood," and says, "with great delight I sat in his shadow…." As she sat in the shadow of the apple tree, his love lifted her and awakened within her a love that she had never known before; it took her from being an abused and neglected woman to being someone who was loved and cared for. In 2:4, she said, "…his intention toward me was love." There is an old hymn entitled, "Love Lifted Me." Love—both God's love and the love of a husband or wife—has the amazing power to lift people.

Do you know why he was able to help her come out of the wilderness? It's because back in chapter 3, he himself was in the wilderness, and sixty mighty men of God brought him out. Others helped to bring him out, so he knew how to help someone else to come out. His Beloved came out leaning on him.

God brings all of His children out of the wilderness, but He doesn't bring us all out in the same way. Some of us come out limping, some of us come out leaning, and some of us come out lying on a stretcher, but God brings us all out. Once we come out of the wilderness, we have to do as this man did by going back in to help bring someone else out. We have to let those who are wandering and wondering know that God can bring them out. We have to get beyond trying to convince people that we never did anything wrong and have always been holy and righteous. We've got to let people know the truth. We have to say, "I was in the wilderness, too, just like you are, but someone showed me a way out. I can show you, too. Come on; I'll help you."

I was in the wilderness for a long time myself. I was messed up, but God was able to pull me out. That's because someone was willing to come in and get me where I was and take me out to where He was. Isn't that what Christ did for all of us? Didn't He come to where we were, so that we can go to where He is? That's what we need to do for others, too. We needed someone to lean on and help us come out of our wilderness; now we can be there to help others find a way out and support them if they need someone to lean on.

Just think how much of a difference we could make in our world if we stopped trying to change people and concentrated instead on introducing them to the One who can truly change their lives. Just think what a difference we could make in our communities if we stopped finding fault with others and started trying to help them out of their wilderness experiences. Just think what a difference we could make in our marriages and in our homes if we stopped trying to change and control our spouses, instead concentrating on simply loving them as they are and meeting their needs. We need to quit trying to do what only the Holy Spirit can do in someone's life.

Love Lifted Me

The book of Genesis tells us how God stooped down and scooped up dust, shaped it into a man after His own image, breathed into him the breath of life, and made him into a living soul. Only He who made man in the first place can remake a man. In the New Testament, there was a woman caught in the act of adultery. The religious leaders brought her to Jesus and asked if He agreed with the Law of Moses that she should be stoned. Jesus stooped down and wrote something in the dirt.

God created a life from the dust of the earth. Jesus wrote in the dirt of the earth when He was in the process of saving a life. God is willing to get His hands dirty for our sake. As the old saints said it back in the day, "The Lord sits high but looks low." We are never so low-down that God can't reach us. Remember, Jesus came down to where we are so that we can go up to where He is. As that old song says, "I was sinking deep in sin…but…love lifted me, love lifted me; when nothing else could help, love lifted me."

Chapter 17

How to Treat a Sister

⁸ We have a young sister,
and her breasts are not yet grown.
What shall we do for our sister
for the day she is spoken for?
⁹ If she is a wall,
we will build towers of silver on her.
If she is a door,
we will enclose her with panels of cedar.
¹⁰ I am a wall,
and my breasts are like towers.
Thus I have become in his eyes
like one bringing contentment.
¹¹ Solomon had a vineyard in Baal Hamon;
he let out his vineyard to tenants.
Each was to bring for its fruit
a thousand shekels [g] of silver.
¹² But my own vineyard is mine to give;
the thousand shekels are for you, O
Solomon, and two hundred are for those
who tend its fruit.
¹³ You who dwell in the gardens
with friends in attendance,
let me hear your voice!
¹⁴ Come away, my lover,
and be like a gazelle
or like a young stag
on the spice-laden mountains.

(Song of Solomon 8:8-14, NIV)

We come now to the final chapter of the Song of Solomon, and we can sum it all up as a lesson in understanding how to treat a sister. Chapter 8, verse 8, says, "We have a young sister, and her breasts are not yet grown. What shall we do for our sister ....?" Remember Pastor Freddie Haynes' admonition for sisters to stop letting brothers treat them like pieces of meat they order at a fast food drive-thru? Now, of course, Pastor Haynes is right; nobody should ever treat you like that. But I wanted to bring up that illustration again because it stands in direct contrast to what is going on in this text. In verse 8, these brothers are speaking of the breasts of their younger sister, but they're not trying to treat her like some *thing*, or simply talking about her body parts as they would pieces of chicken. The writer is speaking poetically about this young sister; the brothers are not really talking about her breast size. In fact, in verse 10, the woman herself says that her breasts are like towers. The brothers are actually referring to her immaturity—the fact that she's undeveloped and lacking in experience.

The Daughters of God

The brothers are concerned about how they will handle it when their sister is spoken for, along with the way they are going to treat her when she is committed to marry someone. One thing I really appreciate about them is the fact that they recognize she is a sister. They recognize the relationship they have with her, and that will determine how they treat her. If they thought of her as anything other than a sister, then they would treat her in ways other than as a sister.

Brothers, if we're serious about treating women in a way that will bring honor and glory to God and bless our relationships, we must first understand that women are daughters of God. Since they are God's daughters and we brothers claim to be God's sons, that makes us brothers and sisters. We should, therefore, be in a relationship with them as brother and sister.

That's very, very important, because what you think about a person comes out in the way you relate to that person. As I've mentioned before, you can try to cover up your feelings or act as if they aren't there, but whatever you think about them comes out towards them. Some men dehumanize women because it helps them to rationalize their maltreatment of them. If we see women as having souls, as human beings, and as daughters of God, then we have to respect them in a certain way. On the other hand, if a man can dehumanize a woman, objectify her, and make her seem less than human in his eyes, then he feels he can treat her any way he wants, and it doesn't bother his conscience because he doesn't think of her as human.

That's why terms such as "sex object," as in "she is a beautiful sex object," robs a woman of her humanity and rationalizes her mistreatment. That's why some very popular songwriters now refer to women with the "b-word." If a man recognizes a woman as a female dog, then he doesn't have to treat her as God's daughter. The way we behave toward a person is determined by our image of that person. That's the reason why people of African descent were deemed to be three-fifths human in the early days of our nation's history. By determining that they were not fully human, those of that mindset did not have to treat them as human beings. Instead, they were looked upon both as animals and as property. Because they were not seen as human, created in the image of God, it was considered acceptable to buy and sell them, beat and torture them, separate them from their families, and both use and abuse them. Again, how we think about a race of people determines how we treat them.

So, brothers, if we're serious about treating sisters in a way that brings honor and glory to God, first we've got to recognize that they are God's daughters and our sisters. That is very, very important. Now some brother may think, "I can't think of them as being daughters of God. Look at the way they act, the way they talk, the way they live, and the way they dress. They can't be daughters of God." We have to be careful about prejudging people, however. God didn't call us to use some kind of code to decide who's in the family of God, and who isn't. Our family relationship is determined by something our Father did, not by our own choices.

Let me illustrate. I have one biological sister, Tonette. Tonette and I get along very, very well, and we're blessings to each other. I appreciate her, I approve of her, I accept her, and I love her, but that's not why she's my sister. Tonette lives a good life. She's a

Spirit-filled Christian who tries to live a life that honors God, but that's not what makes her my sister. What makes her my sister and part of my family is something our father did a long time ago. My father did not come to me to ask if I approved of her being in the family. It was his actions alone that made her my sister.

It's the same way in the spiritual realm. God doesn't need your approval to invite someone to come into His family. Even though you may not accept or applaud those He invites in, if God says they're in, they are in. It's based on the fact that God so loved the world, He gave his only begotten Son that whosoever believes in Him becomes a part of the family of God.

Levels of Maturity

This text teaches us that even though everybody is in the same family, not everybody is on the same level. In verse 8, there is mention of a young girl who is undeveloped: "her breasts are not yet grown," or as the King James Version says, "She has no breasts." This is a *young* girl. But in verse 10, the woman says, "My breasts are like towers." Remember, these Scriptures are not actually talking about breast sizes; they are alluding to immaturity and maturity. Verse 8 refers to a woman who is immature, but verse 10 mentions one who is mature. But whether they're immature or mature, they are still in the same family.

We're not all on the same level, but we're all in the same family. One person may have just become a Christian on Sunday, and that person is what the Bible describes as a babe in Christ. I've been saved for more than thirty years, and I may be a little further along spiritually than the babe in Christ, but I have no more value in the family than he or she does. Once you become a Christian, it doesn't matter what level you are on because you are still in the family of God. We've got to stop being so judgmental of one another. A woman who is in Christ is in the family of God, regardless of her level of maturity.

Life of Responsibility

Now with relationship also comes responsibility. This is true of any relationship, whether it is husband-wife, parent-child, employer-employee, among church members, or between coworkers. You cannot have a good relationship when one person is doing everything, but the other person is doing nothing. Anytime that someone tries to renege on the responsibility but still gain the rewards, it is an indicator that something is wrong with that relationship. So, when you are at the point of making a commitment and say, "This is my woman, my sister, or the person God has chosen for me," what you are saying then is, "I recognize that with this relationship comes responsibility, and I am willing to accept that responsibility."

I think I've been in too many locker-room conversations during which the topic of women comes up (and it usually does). The brothers are constantly telling me what their women are doing for them. One says, "My woman is going to do this"; another says, "My woman did that for me"; and yet another says, "I'm going to get this from my woman." In contrast, look at what the brothers say in verse 8: "What shall we do for our sister?" There are two things I like about the brothers in this verse. First, they are acknowledging the woman as their sister. Even when she isn't with them, they aren't acting as though they have no sister; they make it clear that she is a part of them. Second, they aren't thinking about what they can get *from* their sister, but what they can do *for* her. When I enter into a relationship I'm not trying to get rewards without responsibility. If I want the rewards from the relationship, I must be responsible in that relationship.

Have you ever met people who tried to get something for nothing? They enter a relationship for what they can get out of it, not what they can put into it. That's why some relationships get so frustrating. It's like the person who wants to go to the bank to make a withdrawal when he's never made a deposit. He wants a reward without the responsibility. It's like the person who wants to be in good physical shape, but won't push away from the table. He wants the rewards of a strong, healthy body, but he won't jog, walk, or lift weights. In short, he won't do anything to make his desire a reality. We have too many people wanting to reap a harvest, but they haven't planted any seeds. We have too many people wanting the windows of heaven to open for them, but they have not brought any tithes into the storehouse. We have too many people who want to call themselves Christians without ever making a commitment to Christ. We have too many people who want to go to heaven, but they spend their time causing all kinds of hell on earth.

I know it happens in other churches as well, but there are people who want the rewards of being a member of our church without ever committing to the church. I call those people permanent visitors because they come to church all the time without ever joining. When I see them, I ask, "Hey, how are you doing?" They reply, "We're fine, Pastor. We just love this ministry and what y'all are doing." "Oh, you're visiting with us?" I ask. "Yeah, we're visiting." "Well, how long have you been visiting?" "We've been visiting for three years." I feel like saying to them, "Oh no, you're not a visitor! You've been around here long enough that you need to make a contribution to this ministry. You need to do something. Start giving your share into the offering plate. Start giving your time to one of the ministries of the church. If you want the relationship, you need to accept the responsibility."

Now on a personal level, if somebody has been living in your home for three years, that person isn't visiting anymore. He needs to do *something* to make a contribution to the household, whether it's getting a job, paying rent, cleaning up around the house, and/or taking out some trash. We've got to get away from having relationships without responsibility. There are even people who are single but want the rewards of marriage as well. They want to live together, share expenses, have sex, and enjoy companionship. They want everything that married people get without getting married. In other words, they want the rewards without the responsibility.

Going back to verse 8, the brothers are asking themselves what they are going to do to help their sister. They are saying, "Since we're responsible for our sister, we want to make sure she isn't rushing into something she's not quite ready for." They know she's not mature enough right now, but they are discussing what they will do for her when she *is* spoken for—after she does make that commitment. They want her to know that they are making arrangements for her future, but they don't want her to rush into anything prematurely. I wish I could get through to young people the importance of not rushing into relationships, the bed, and marriage. I wish I could get them to understand the importance of maturing before making a decision about marriage.

I believe part of the reason why over fifty percent of our marriages end in divorce and usually within the first four years is because so many of us get married while we're still immature. We're still developing and growing. Our stuff is still small, but we're trying to act big. Even though we really are immature, we think we are mature, but we're not quite ready yet. We just need to learn how to be patient and wait. If you are sixteen or seventeen years old, marriage should be the last thing on your mind. Your mind needs to be focused on developing into the person that God wants you to be, and then at the right time God will hook you up.

You may say, "But I've already found the person I want to spend the rest of my life with." That may be true; I'm not saying you don't have the right person. What I'm questioning is the timing. Is this the right time for you? A young man may want to prove his manhood by getting the woman of his dreams. He's afraid that some other man will come along and entice her away from him, so he wants to rush into marriage. Brother, are you in a position to take care of the woman that God gave to you? If you're still running by your mother's house to get money to pay your car insurance and daddy's giving you money every week to help make ends meet, you don't need to get married. You aren't big enough yet; instead, you need to take time to mature. It doesn't mean that God doesn't have marriage in store for you; it just means that you are not ready yet.

Some young women can't even wait for the right time to have a baby. They aren't married, but they see other people all around them having babies. They think about how cute the babies are, how grown-up their friends seem now that they are mothers, and how good it would feel to have a little baby to love them. Are those the right reasons for bringing a child into the world? Does the fact that other people are doing it mean that it is the right thing for you to do right now? I'm not suggesting that you shouldn't have a baby, but is it the right time for you? We've got to learn how to do things in God's timing.

The Timing of God

I had to learn that in my own marriage, but I had to learn about waiting for God's timing in my ministry as well. The Lord called me to preach when I was a seventeen-year-old senior at Arlington High School in Indianapolis. The anointing of God was on my life to preach at that young age, but I didn't get called to pastor the Eastern Star Church until I was twenty-five years old. Even though God had long ago determined that I would one day serve as the pastor at Eastern Star Church, it wasn't time for me to do that when I was seventeen. God knew I wasn't ready for it then. Yes, I was a Christian; I had the call of God to preach; I wanted to preach; I was already living in Indianapolis; and my home was just down the street from the church. It seemed that everything was in place, but God knew I wasn't mature enough to handle it yet. At seventeen, I would have been more of a detriment to the church than an asset. I would have hurt the church, rather than helping it. God wasn't going to give me that ministry until I was ready to handle it.

So, God continued to work on me. I had to go to school and get exposed to life. I had to get some experience by pastoring another church. I had to go through some ups and downs and experience a lot of growth before I could be ready to step into the role of the pastor at Eastern Star Church. At the same time God was working on me, He was working on the church as well. They had gone through two or three pastors and experienced some ups and downs, ins and outs, and rights and wrongs. I was waiting on the Lord to fulfill His purpose for me, and they were waiting on the Lord to bring along the right pastor. So, we both waited as God worked on them and worked on me. At the right time, He brought us together.

Right now, God is working on you, but He's also working on that person He wants you to be with. He's doing things in your life and that other person's life. When it's time for you to be together, God will make it happen.

I love that those brothers in verse 8 were treating their sister properly. They could see who she was right now—a young sister, a little sister—but they also could see what she was going to become. Even though she wasn't ready yet, they knew that someday she would be spoken for. Sister, when you start talking with a man about marriage, someone you are considering spending the rest of your life with, you need to make sure that he is able to see not only who you are right now, but also recognizes that you are not who you will be later on. God isn't through working with you yet. You are a work in progress because God is still developing you. You need a brother who will give you the space and the room to grow so that you can become what God wants you to be.

If you get the wrong brother, he won't want you to grow or change. When you try to improve your mind through education, he'll wonder what's wrong with you. When you try to follow closely after God to develop your spiritual life, he will accuse you of being fanatical: "Why do you want to go to Sunday School?" "You don't need to go to revival; we went to church on Sunday." "Why are you spending so much time praying and reading the Bible? You don't need to do all of that to be a Christian." Make sure your man understands and supports your desire to keep God first in your life. Make sure that he will encourage you in your spiritual growth and not feel jealous of the love you have for God.

Some of you sisters may think that brothers like that don't exist, but I promise you that they do. They can't *see* the future, but they have a vision for the future. Not only can they look at you and appreciate you for who you are right now, but they can also see a woman who will continue to grow and mature into a fuller expression of the person God intends for you to be. To this end, they will help you keep your eyes focused on what is ahead. The enemy tries to get you to just look at where you've been—to focus on your past so that you'll miss out on your future. The enemy tries to get you to look at your past mistakes, your past failures, and the times when you let God down. You used to smoke, drink, and go clubbing. You have regrets about your past lifestyle now. You wish you had never slept with that man, gotten a divorce, given birth to a baby out of wedlock, or allowed a man to mistreat you as that one brother did.

The enemy keeps you focused on the past. Do you know why he does that? It's because he knows that he can't mess with your future. God has so many good things lined up for you in your future, and he realizes that he can't touch that. But if he can get you to spend your time feeling bad about all that's happened in the past, including all of your failures and sins and regrets, you won't be able to receive what God has for you in the present or rejoice about what he has prepared for you in the future. A good brother will help you to keep your past behind you and your eyes focused on God, who has both your present and your future in His hands.

A Wall of Purity and a Door of Promiscuity

Notice how well-prepared the brothers are in our text. On that day when she is spoken for, they say, "If she is a wall, we will build towers of silver on her. If she is a door, we will enclose her with panels of cedar." These brothers are thinking about the future. They don't know what lies ahead, so they are making contingency plans. They have a Plan A and a Plan B. If the sister is a wall that is fortified and strong, they will build for her a palace of silver. If she is a door with folks coming and going, they will build for her a panel of cedar wood. But notice, too, that the plan they implement is based on the sister's actions. If she is a wall, chaste and pure, and does not let men come and go as they please, the brothers will build towers and a palace of silver. But if she is a door where any man can come and go, then they will build a panel of cedar wood.

Now, sisters, watch this. Both the cedar wood and the silver are luxury items that are expensive. A brother will spend money on you either way. If you are a wall of purity, he'll spend money. If you are a door of promiscuity, he will definitely spend some money. Either way, he uses creativity, ingenuity, energy, and money because he's going to build something with you. But what he builds depends on you; how you act will determine how he acts. Some sisters think they need to be a door of promiscuity to get a brother to notice them. They feel that they have to take their clothes off and act like a prostitute in order to get a brother to notice them. What they don't realize is that the brothers have already noticed them.

Whether it's a brother in the club or a brother in the church depends on where you are spending your time. You can be sure, though, that a brother has noticed you. He's watched how you walk, how you talk, what you wear, how you treat other people, and even the choices that you've made. You may say, "No, if a brother has noticed me, why hasn't he said anything to me?" In part, he's watching to see if you are a wall or a door. He's trying to see if you are pure or promiscuous. He may be willing to make an investment, but where he puts his energy and money will be determined by how you act.

Are you a door or a wall? Think about it. The door symbolizes promiscuity where anybody can come and go. Have you've noticed how many doors in this day and age are so easy to open as you walk up to them? It requires no effort and no energy; you don't have to say anything or do anything. You don't have to have a number, a code, a key, or anything because they are automatic doors. That's how some women are. They are so easy that you don't even have to get their number. Just walk up to them, and they open up.

Not only are there automatic doors, but there are also revolving doors. Revolving doors are only installed if a building is expecting more than one person to come through. No company would put in a revolving door if they are expecting only one customer to come and go. The revolving door is made for heavy traffic. Some sisters are like that.

Brothers, take note. You need to be careful about walking up to automatic doors and revolving doors. You have to keep in mind that a whole lot of folks have walked in before you, and some are going to come in after you.

Some women, however, are more like walls. A wall means security and protection. Not just anybody and everybody can come in. A wall is strong and has fortitude; it symbolizes purity. A brother won't treat a wall like a door. How you treat yourself is how a brother will treat you. He waits to see what you are before he approaches you. So, if you treat yourself with respect, he shows respect to you. If you act like a lady, he treats you like a lady. If you behave as a Christian woman, he treats you as a Christian woman. He responds to your behavior. That's why the woman in the text says she is a wall.

Let me throw this in, too, sisters, because you have to be careful about internalizing what a brother thinks of you. I told you that people have a way of dehumanizing you so that they can treat you any way they want to. What happens is that too many people internalize what other people say about them. If someone calls them the "b-word," they start thinking that they are the "b-word." If someone says they are nothing, they start thinking they are nothing. Yet, this woman is not letting others define who she is; instead, she makes it clear that she is a wall. She doesn't care what others think about her because she knows who she is.

Serenity in His Eyes

But now a word of encouragement for any sister who has been a door in the past, or even a doormat. You don't have to continue to be that way in the future. The right contractor can change you from being a door to a wall. You can make up your mind that you are tired of folks coming and going in your life, having no respect for you as a person. You can determine that you are a wall. You do not have to be tied to any man, but instead you can stand as a wall by yourself. The woman in the text says, "I am a wall and my breasts are like towers." She is no longer an immature girl who is waiting for a man to determine who she is.

Then she says of her Lover, "I was in his eyes as one that found favor" (KJV), or, as another translation puts it, "...in his eyes as one who brings peace" (NRSV), or "...in his eyes like one bringing contentment" (NIV). Notice, too, that this contentment, this favor, or this peace is in his eyes—not in her eyes—and not in *their* eyes. This sister doesn't care about other brothers. She knows she can't please every man and doesn't even want to try. She is determined to please only one man: her husband. There is a serenity in what the woman sees in the eyes of her man. The woman says she's a wall, which stands for strength. Then she says her breasts are like towers, which stands for maturity. Then she says she finds peace in the man's eyes. The formula for serenity is strong personality + maturity = serenity.

It's different for the woman who is promiscuous. In contrast to strength, maturity and serenity, she finds promiscuity, immaturity, and chaos. But if that is what you are experiencing as a door, don't sell yourself short. If you are married, you can bring contentment to your husband and serenity to your relationship.

Remember, too, that there is nothing wrong with a desire to please your husband. Think about the difference in the way some women treat their supervisors at work in contrast to the way they treat their husbands at home. What blows my mind is that a woman may dress a certain way, behave a certain way, and speak a certain way when talking to her supervisor. But she's a very different person when greeting her husband in the home. She may be more interested in pleasing folks outside of her house than the one man in her house.

Pleasing God

As we draw to a close, I have a word for the single people reading this book. If you do not have a spouse, there's only one Person you should be trying to please, and that Person isn't the man or woman you are trying to get: it's Jesus Christ. Something is wrong when you become obsessed with pleasing someone who may or may not be the person you will spend the rest of your life with. Concentrate instead on pleasing God.

Do you know what pleases God? Look at 1 Corinthians 1:21: "God was pleased through the foolishness of what was preached to save those who believe." *That's* what pleases God—the proclamation of His Son, Jesus Christ the Savior. If you want to please God, stop talking about meaningless things and start talking about what Jesus Christ has done in your life. Start talking about the relationship you have with Him.

Do you know what else pleases God? Colossians 1:19 says, "For God was pleased to have all His fullness dwell in him," that is, in Jesus. If you want to please God, allow His Holy Spirit to fill you. Stop trying to let other people fill you; instead, allow the Holy Spirit to come into your life.

In addition, Hebrews 13:15 and 16 says, "Through Jesus, therefore, let us continually offer to God a sacrifice of praise—the fruit of lips that confess his name. And do not forget to do good and to share with others, for with such sacrifices God is pleased." Through the sacrifice of praise and doing good to others, we please God. You please Him when you proclaim Him! You please Him when you are content with Him! You please Him when you praise Him! God is worthy of our praise. We need to make up our minds to praise Him in order to please Him and not be concerned with pleasing others or ourselves.

In 2002, at the Six Flags in Denver, a man died when he fell out of a roller coaster. When I heard about this incident, I paid close attention because my sons and I often ride roller coasters. I wouldn't want to do anything that would put my family in danger, so I followed up on that story to find out what happened that caused the man to fall out of the roller coaster. The investigators finally determined that there was nothing wrong with the roller coaster. It was operating just as it was supposed to. The man fell out and died because he removed his seat restraints.

The restraints in the roller coaster are designed to ensure the safety of the riders. When a person gets in, the restraint fits down over the shoulders and lap of the individual to make sure the person is secure. This is necessary because a roller coaster doesn't just travel smoothly along a straight track. No, it goes up high and then drops down low; it twists and it turns and goes every which way. The restraints aren't intended to keep the person from enjoying the ride; instead, they are in place to keep the person safe so that he or she doesn't fall out and get killed. But this man did away with the restraints, so he died.

This is the way it is for us regarding sex. God gave us sex to enjoy. He wants us to experience the intimacy and pleasure of sex, but He also gave us some restraints. These restraints aren't intended to be a burden to us, keep us from having fun, or prevent us from enjoying ourselves. Instead, God knows that without the restraints, we are putting ourselves in danger and risk killing ourselves. The restraints are as much a gift to us as the sex. God doesn't want us to hurt ourselves, and He doesn't want us to hurt others. He wants us to enjoy ourselves fully and to do so with no regrets.

My prayer for you as we bring our discussion of *Song of Solomon* to a close is that you will first draw close to God, get to know Him, and develop a strong and committed relationship in which He will always be your First Love. I pray that you will learn to know yourself as God has created you, to see yourself as He sees you, and to know how much He loves you. Then I pray that God will lead you into friendships and relationships that will bring honor to Him and great joy to you. If God has already led you into marriage, or does so in the future, I pray that you will know the sweetness and power of love, even as God intended for you to give and receive.